Remembering the Lower East Side

THE MODERN JEWISH EXPERIENCE

Paula Hyman and Deborah Dash Moore, editors

Remembering the Lower East Side

American Jewish Reflections

EDITED BY
Hasia R. Diner,
Jeffrey Shandler, and
Beth S. Wenger

INDIANA
UNIVERSITY
PRESS
Bloomington and Indianapolis

THE AUTHORS AND THE PUBLISHER WISH
TO ACKNOWLEDGE THE GENEROUS
SUPPORT OF THE LUCIUS N. LITTAUER FOUNDATION.

This book is a publication of
Indiana University Press
601 North Morton Street
Bloomington, IN 47404-3797 USA

http://www.indiana.edu/~iupress

Telephone orders 800-842-6796
Fax orders 812-855-7931
Orders by e-mail iuporder@indiana.edu

© 2000 by Indiana University Press

The paper used in this publication meets the minimum requirements of
American National Standard for Information Sciences—Permanence of
Paper for Printed Library Materials, ANSI Z39.48-1984.

Manufactured in the United States of America

Library of Congress Cataloging-in-Publication Data

Remembering the Lower East Side: American Jewish reflections/edited by
Hasia R. Diner, Jeffrey Shandler, and Beth S. Wenger.
    p. cm.—(Modern Jewish experience)
    Includes index.
    ISBN 0-253-33788-7 (cloth:alk. paper)
    1. Jews—New York (State)—New York—Social conditions. 2. Lower
East Side (New York, N.Y.)—Social conditions. 3. New York (N.Y.)—
Social conditions. 4. New York (N.Y.)—Ethnic relations. I. Diner, Hasia R.
II. Shandler, Jeffrey. III. Wenger, Beth S., date IV. Modern Jewish
experience (Bloomington, Ind.)
F128.9.J5 R36 2000
974.7'1004924—dc21
                                                        00-031042

1 2 3 4 5 05 04 03 02 01 00

Contents

Part 1. The Dynamics of Remembrance

Contents

Part 2. Contemporary Recollections

Acknowledgments

This anthology is the product of a collaborative effort. On a rainy weekend in the spring of 1998, thirty-five scholars gathered at New York University to explore the dynamics of Lower East Side memory and to consider the changing ways that this unique neighborhood has been embraced by American Jews over the course of a century. The insights shared during the conference and the active participation of the large audience that attended convinced us of the timeliness and importance of bringing together these innovative perspectives on the Lower East Side.

We owe a great debt to the Skirball Department of Hebrew and Judaic Studies at New York University, which sponsored the conference, and to the Louis H. Solomon Department of Hebrew Culture Fund for generous financial support. Professor Robert Chazan, the S. H. and Helen R. Scheuer Professor of Modern Jewish History at New York University, enthusiastically supported our plans for the conference from the start. We are especially grateful to Professor Lawrence Schiffman, the Ethel and Irwin A. Edelman Professor of Hebrew and Judaic Studies and chair of the Skirball Department, for his unwavering commitment to the project. Special thanks also go to Diane Leon-Ferdico, the conference coordinator and Skirball department administrator, and to Janet Novey, the department secretary, for their attention to detail and planning.

We offer our most profound thanks to the contributors to this anthology, who dedicated their scholarship and expertise to this volume.

Acknowledgments

Their willingness to meet deadlines and their commitment to bringing this project to fruition has made this anthology possible.

We also want to express our deep appreciation to the other scholars who presented papers and actively participated in the conference. Tresa Grauer, Andrew Heinze, Jenna Weissman Joselit, Ellen Kellman, Barbara Kirshenblatt-Gimblett, Max Page, Esther Romeyn, Allon Schoener, Peter Schweitzer, Lauren Strauss, and Ellen Wiley Todd graciously shared their work and helped to make the conference a success. We are also grateful to the scholars who offered to chair conference sessions. Arthur Goren, Jeffrey Gurock, Alan Kraut, Daniel Soyer, Jack Tchen, and Steve Zeitlin guided lively discussions and lent their insights to the conversation. We were fortunate to have had film director Joan Micklin Silver join us to provide a stimulating presentation about her work on the Lower East Side.

Our editor at Indiana University Press, Janet Rabinowitch, helped us transform a conference into a book. We thank her for her belief in this project, for her editorial skills, and for shepherding this book through publication. We particularly appreciate the generous grant from the Lucius N. Littauer Foundation that provided funds for the illustrations in this volume, and we are grateful for the help of the Foundation's program director, Pamela Brumberg.

It has been a privilege for us to work with such a diverse group of scholars, artists, and community leaders and to collect their creative work into one volume. As we stand one hundred years from the era of mass Jewish immigration, we are pleased to present these new explorations into the meanings of the Lower East Side.

HASIA R. DINER
JEFFREY SHANDLER
BETH S. WENGER

Remembering the Lower East Side

Introduction: Remembering the Lower East Side

Hasia R. Diner,
Jeffrey Shandler,
and Beth S. Wenger

—A Conversation

In May 1998 we convened a two-day conference at New York University on the Lower East Side as a site of American Jewish remembrance. Over the course of the year following the conference we continued to discuss the subject among ourselves via the Internet while preparing this volume to go to press. We offer a sampling of our virtual conversation as an introduction to this volume.

Jeffrey: It might be best to begin by thinking about the role that timing plays in the changing meanings of the Lower East Side. Certainly, the Lower East Side has a considerable history of being recognized and scrutinized as the largest and most vibrant immigrant Jewish neighborhood, a history dating back to the period of mass immigration itself. At the last turn of the century, the Lower East Side was already a locus of Jewish representation, singled out as "the ghetto" by observers, who

1

Haria R. Diner, Jeffrey Shandler, and Beth S. Wenger

saw the area inhabited by Jewish newcomers who spoke, worked, and lived unlike previous groups of Jews who had come to America. From the start, this place—albeit defined by different names and different geographical boundaries—was distinguished as a Jewish "proving ground" in America.

In recent years, we have seen increased interest in the neighborhood as a locus of American Jewish heritage, evinced by new publications, performances, works of art, and especially tourist productions. In fact, our 1998 conference on remembering the Lower East Side can be seen as another manifestation of this phenomenon—especially given the fact that it attracted, in addition to scholars, quite a few members of the general public, for whom discussing the Lower East Side was less an academic enterprise than a personally engaged, emotionally charged experience. So why is all this happening now? How does this relate to the dynamic of American Jewish history since the period of mass immigration at the turn of the last century? How does the act of remembering the Lower East Side relate to its actual history and to that of New York more generally? How does it relate to contemporary issues of heritage and public expressions of ethnicity in American culture?

Beth: I agree that there has been a new surge of interest in the Lower East Side in the 1990s, an interest fueled by a third and fourth generation of Jews seeking a collective past, and by contemporary expressions of ethnicity and culture. However, rather than framing the timing question as a 1990s re-creation, I am more inclined to see the Lower East Side as a site continually in the forefront of American Jewish consciousness, as a place and an idea that has been reinvented in different ways to suit the cultural needs of various generations. As I have written elsewhere, American Jews began reinventing the neighborhood almost at the moment that it ceased to be the center of Jewish population. In the 1920s and 1930s, as immigrant Jews began to move to more spacious and desirable neighborhoods, they created a new, often nostalgic, relationship with the Lower East Side. The neighborhood helped to frame their collective experiences as American Jews, helped them to make sense of change, and to create a narrative history and a physical context for locating Jewish communal origins. (Indeed, what is particularly fascinating about the Lower East Side is the way that it became a touchstone of Jewish identity and history, even for Jews not of East European origin or descent and for those who had never lived there or had ancestors who lived there.) By the 1960s, a new generation of Jews once again turned to the Lower East Side as a site for meaning, in an era marked by a revived interest in ethnicity across the country and at a time when middle-class American Jews had grown more distant from their immigrant past. The Lower East Side as a neighborhood and a site of memory was never lost, waiting in the wings to be resurrected, but ran more continuously as a thread through American Jewish culture.

Hasia: My sense is that most of the texts written at the time of immigration and settlement were actually less place-oriented and place-specific. In writing and other kinds of observation, immigrant Jews located their actions in "the ghetto" or on particular streets, specific sections, but they neither used the "Lower East Side" designation, nor did those words have capital letters. It had not become reified into a proper noun. As such, I do not think that they had a conception of a singular, inte-grated, spatially undifferentiated neighborhood. There is little evidence to suggest that women and men living in the neigh-borhood during its height as an immigrant center defined themselves as "Lower East Siders." Since World War II, begin-ning slowly and building intensively through the 1960s, the Lower East Side was not only transformed into a proper noun, with capital letters, but it came to be the locus of Jewish memory in a very focused way. Place emerged as a crucial element in Jewish narratives, as Jews explored who they were, or more importantly, who they had been and had become, and located those transformations in a single place, *the* Lower East Side. In the culture spawned by the 1960s, the Lower East Side seemed to be a perfect American Jewish "old home," full of class-conscious workers, poor people who flexed their collective political and cultural muscle, East European Jews who rejected the hegemony of the "bad guys," in this case, the German Jews, but also American bourgeois culture in general. This was the place where immigrant Jews could be authentic and real, uncompromising, before they moved out and began to cave in to middle-class respectability. In the cultural moment of the 1960s, when ethnic groups wanted to present themselves as the custodians of (a largely imagined) authentic culture, unsullied or uncorrupted by outside influences, the Lower East Side provided that site for American Jews.

Finally, by the 1990s, the Lower East Side took on a pedagogic role for American Jews. In a community concerned about intermarriage, assimilation, and homogenization, the Lower East Side emerged as a kind of gigantic, urban teaching device. Hebrew school groups, synagogue tours, bar/bat mitzvah classes from all over the United States come to learn something on the Lower East Side. Jewish educators, broadly defined, have lifted the Lower East Side out of its history as a warren of streets into an exemplar of undiluted Jewish life.

Jeffrey: There seems to be a generational ebb and flow of interest in the Lower East Side as a Jewish landmark. Is this because the 1930s and '60s were watershed decades for American Jews, with regard to demographics, economics, and culture? Is this also true for the 1990s?

Beth: We do seem to be leaning toward a generational paradigm based loosely on this model: The immigrant generation gave the neighborhood its initial reputation as the center of Jewish experience; then, in the 1920s and '30s, immigrants and their children who no longer lived in the neighborhood re-created the Lower East Side on their own, often nostalgic, terms; that reinvention continued and took on new characteristics amid the "new ethnicity" of the 1960s; finally, contemporary Jews revived the Lower East Side yet again as part of the multicultural landscape of America in the 1990s. I do think there is some merit in this paradigm, particularly if we view the Lower East Side as a canvas on which successive generations designed their "founding myth" to fit their own social and cultural concerns.

However, we ought to be careful to remember that the Lower East Side was never monolithic at any historical moment. In every generation, the Lower East Side had multiple meanings, and different groups imagined and used the neighborhood in a variety of ways. Although some portraits of the Lower East Side clearly dominated at certain times, we might think of the Lower East Side as a constant battleground for giving meaning to Jewish experience. Within each generation, simultaneous versions of the neighborhood existed: there was a left-wing East Side, replete with labor organizing and strikes; a religious East Side that housed hundreds of congregations; a Yiddish East Side, home of the leading Yiddish writers and artists and of a flourishing cafe society; a commercial East Side, where shoppers flocked for bargains; an ethnic East Side that provided traditional Jewish foods and music; and the list goes on. As we consider the dynamics of Lower East Side memory, we should also consider the selectivity of things remembered and give voice to the competing constructions of the Lower East Side.

Hasia: We might also explore the connection between the relics of the past and the kinds of re-creations that have surfaced, particularly in recent years: How much of what has been left over in some rough way has come to represent the most permanent and salient markers of the Lower East Side? Scholars and other creators of memory texts cannot and do not draw upon "everything" about the Lower East Side, but, like all of memory, Lower East Side memory acts as a kind of filter or sifter. What has gotten caught in the pot of memory? Who have emerged as the figures of memory, its heroes and villains, its stock characters who serve as exemplars of certain Lower East Side and Jewish themes? We, American Jews at the turn of the millennium, have peopled the urban space of the Lower East Side with certain iconic figures, some real, some composite. Why those? It is striking, for example, that we remember the many Lower East Side laborers, but very few of the entrepreneurs who turned a profit in the neighborhood. Lower East Side memory culture abounds with the poor, but not with those who succeeded economically. Furthermore, we tend to think of people living on the Lower East Side as occupying a world framed by a bounded neighborhood. But, in fact, these were women and men who ranged, quite easily, all over the city for work and leisure.

Jeffrey: I agree; the complex give-and-take among competing notions of what is selected for remembrance on the Lower East Side can sometimes prove to be a telling case study in cultural politics. At the same time, some elements seem to have enduring appeal. We might consider, for instance, how the tenement serves as an icon of the Lower East Side immigrant experience, in examples ranging from its appearance on the cover art of almost every book about the neighborhood to the creation of the Tenement Museum. And yet, of course, so much of immigrant life took place outside of tenements—not only at work or on the street, but also in schools, cafes, libraries, lecture halls, synagogues, parks, and at outdoor events, such as rallies, demonstrations, and parades. What are the implications of privileging one kind of edifice or site, such as the tenement, over others?

Hasia: Even as the tenement signifies the poor living conditions of the Lower East Side, it also exemplifies the vibrant qualities of urban life. Perhaps one of the fascinations that historians and others, products of quieter and more suburban spaces, have with the Lower East Side has come from the fusion of public and private, the disappearance of any kind of boundary between inside and outside. This was, after all, a place where things were bought and sold on the streets, where people slept on the roofs of their buildings, on the fire escapes, and where—at least as described in the memoir literature—parents and children, husbands and wives, neighbors, and strangers interacted volubly with each other in public.

Beth: The interactions of the Lower East Side raise another crucial issue about Lower East Side memory. The neighborhood was home to several ethnic groups during the immigrant period, and to this day it remains one of the most multi-ethnic districts in the city. Indeed, both the Tenement Museum and some walking tours of the Lower East Side frame it as a multicultural site. Remembered in this way, the Lower East Side tells a universal story about America as a nation of immigrants, underscoring the themes of ethnic diversity and emphasizing the possibilities offered to immigrants in a democratic society. Yet, at the same time, American Jews have claimed the Lower East Side as their site of memory to a greater extent than any other ethnic group, embracing it as the Plymouth Rock of American Jewish history.

Jeffrey: In some ways, the Lower East Side of today resembles other iconic sites that Jews have called "home": the Land of Israel during the period before the modern State of Israel was established; Eastern Europe after World War II. In all three of these places there is a "Jewish absence" of some kind, and it is this, I think—rather than simply a Jewish *presence*, past or present—that inspires visitors, actual or vicarious, to re-animate the environment with their visions of a vibrant past.

At the same time, the value American Jews place on the Lower East Side is closely tied to the specific character of the neighborhood—not only what of the past is lost or has endured, but also what is new. At the turn of the millennium the Lower East Side has witnessed an expansion of the Asian residence at its southern end and the gentrification of what is now known as the East Village at its northern end. High-rise housing projects in the southeastern corner of the Lower East Side are also seeing a new influx of Jewish residents, mostly young Orthodox families from the city's outer boroughs, who are attracted as much by the area's history as by the relatively affordable housing. Other sections of the Lower East Side have also become a very "hip" place for recreation, embraced by gen-Xers who go to the bars, boutiques, and performance spaces that have recently opened there. A growing number of Jewish performers are drawn to the Lower East Side because they find there a coincidence of Jewish heritage and hipness. In a city that has become cleaner and nicer, the Lower East Side is a place that still feels a bit on the "edge," while also being relatively safe and accessible (unlike Brownsville, the "Lower East Side" of Brooklyn). For me, this new cultural edginess is epitomized by going to Lansky's Lounge, located behind Ratner's Dairy Restaurant, which visitors must enter through a back alley, as if they were sneaking into a Prohibition-era speakeasy.

Beth: While some New Yorkers have created a new, cutting-edge culture on the Lower East Side, most American Jews still come to the neighborhood to imagine the old, immigrant world. The district has become, as Hasia mentioned before, "a gigantic, urban teaching device" that attracts tourists from across the nation and even worldwide. In this sense, the Lower East Side has taken on a meaning that transcends New York and even transcends history. The neighborhood has arguably become the most popular site of Jewish memory, where Jews from different generations and different hometowns search for a glimpse of their collective past and hope to discover something "authentically" Jewish—however constructed, nostalgic, and imagined that vision of the Lower East Side might be.

Jeffrey: This is precisely the reason why it is now a strategic moment to assess the meaning of the Lower East Side, tracing the arc of memory from the immigrant generation's heyday to its passing. Today, the immigrant generation, the first East European Jewish settlers of the Lower East Side, are all but gone. Their children are now senior citizens. The third generation, the last with any living connection to immigrant culture, is an aging population. We are now seeing fourth and fifth generations come of age, who have virtually no first-hand attachments to the Lower East Side. For these generations of American Jews, the Lower East Side is as much a part of the Jewish "old world" as is Eastern Europe. In fact, the State of Israel may feel more familiar to them as an "ancestral homeland," as so many American Jews have traveled there, studied modern Hebrew, and met Israelis. But if direct, familial connections are disappearing, newly invented ones are perhaps that much freer to flourish.

Hasia: I agree—at the opening of the twenty-first century, the Lower East Side remains a canvas on which American Jews will continue to fashion images of the past and project visions for the future.

A Note on the Essays in This Volume

The essays collected in this anthology grew out of the first scholarly conference devoted to exploring the Lower East Side as a site of American Jewish memory. The essays are divided into two groups, the first of which looks at the Lower East Side in its heyday as the hub of immigrant Jewish culture and at the immediate aftermath of that era. Moving beyond the already well-documented history of the neighborhood, these essays explore the contests over representation that took place among the people who lived there and those who wrote about it in later years. The authors of these articles investigate the multiple facets of life on the Lower East Side and consider the emerging repertoire of memory that began to take shape around the neighborhood. Moses Rischin writes about the naming of the Lower East Side, while Deborah Dash Moore and David Lobenstein survey its photographic legacy, which made the neighborhood's streets and the Jews who lived on them among the most photographed in history. Paula Hyman focuses on the contested meaning of the Triangle Shirtwaist Fire, the great conflagration of 1911, which gave this neighborhood its most famous martyrs. Riv-Ellen Prell probes the erasure of memory, as she asks why the "ghetto girl"—a commonly recognized figure in early twentieth-century immigrant Jewish discourse—disappeared from later depictions of the Lower East Side. David Kaufman and Stephan Brumberg address two kinds of sacred spots in the history of the Lower East Side and examine their shifting meaning. Kaufman treats the history of Lower East Side synagogues and their multiple uses over time, while Brumberg considers the role of perhaps the most cherished Lower East Side institution, the public school. Suzanne Wasserman, exploring the Lower East Side as a tourist site, demonstrates that Jews outside the neighborhood have long engaged with the area and used it to fulfill their own cultural needs. Taken together, these essays offer a variety of perspectives on the competing visions of the Lower East Side. They also search among those images produced in the immigrant era for the seeds of its memory culture, which developed long after the men and women who lived there either passed away or moved to different neighborhoods with more of the amenities of middle-class life.

The second group of essays in this volume examines the upsurge of interest in the Lower East Side in recent years as a site of Jewish heritage and cultural innovation. Jack Kugelmass's analysis of the creation of the Lower East Side Tenement Museum, Eve Jochnowitz's unpacking of one of the neighborhood's most famous "destination restaurants," and Seth Kamil's reflections on Big Onion Walking Tours of the neighborhood demonstrate the extent to which tourist productions now define encounters with the Lower East Side. These are complemented by Joseph Dorman's thoughts on invoking the legacy of the Lower East Side in a documentary film about New York intellectuals and Aviva Weintraub's exploration of a "site-specific" work of performance art, staged in a former Lower East Side synagogue, both of which consider how the neighborhood's power as a locus of heritage is realized in performance. A final essay by Mario Maffi, an American studies scholar in Italy, suggests how the Lower East Side has achieved iconic status beyond the Jewish and the American worlds. These six essays offer wide-ranging insights into how a place that has come to embody American Jewish heritage serves as a point of reference in charting the course of public memory, as we contemplate the distance between past and present.

Part 1.

The Dynamics of Remembrance

Toward the Onomastics of the Great New York Ghetto: How the Lower East Side Got Its Name

Moses Rischin

To its most recent historians, it seems axiomatic that for the last half century the Lower East Side "has become the most popular locus of American Jewish memory," as Beth Wenger has intimated, and, in some measure, as Jenna Joselit has reminded us, our vision of the Lower East Side has been "a deliberate, willed act of creation," as in greater or lesser degree, are so many of our memories, at least in their details.[1] Without pretending to address the mythopoesis of place directly, let me proceed to outline, describe, and analyze the steps that led to the emergence of the proverbial Lower East Side before it became proverbial and a cynosure of the collective American Jewish memory. Then let me suggest the need to appreciate a heretofore little, if at all, perceived defining historic moment in that development when its predecessor, the Great New York Ghetto, was vested with a freshly perceived modern élan, voice, and cultural dynamic that was to give new energy to immigrant Jewish life for decades to come.

Since its heyday in the first decade of the twentieth century when its 542,000 inhabitants constituted the densest and most visibly volatile critical mass of immigrants in the nation's history, the Lower East Side has come to cleave to the Jewish and larger American imagination. With the end of World War I, the stark decline in Jewish immigration pending its virtual cessation; the backlash against all things foreign and not so incidentally, Jewish; the murderous East European pogroms; the ongoing threats to displaced loved ones almost everywhere; and a historic sea change, all combined to generate a profound need for an "emotional point of reference," as Deborah Moore has put it, one close at hand, that propelled first- and second-generation American Jews to hearken back to the Lower East Side for succor and service and the sheer sensation of Jewish connectedness.

Even as so many Jews uneasily sought to put its telltale marks behind them, to shake off every trace of foreignness and to distance themselves from its ever more seedy precincts, many more eagerly laid claim to that venerable, avidly American and avidly Jewish halfway house that tenuously linked them to the hundreds of ever more remote shtetls of their birth and the larger immigrant and post-immigrant Americas of their dispersion. Purely and simply, it was for most Jews the only American address of all their sharing, however fleetingly. There, by virtue of all of their individual acts of migration, the many had elected, in their fashion, to become one. So epochal a rite of passage needs no explication. At that moment in its history, fact not figment, reality not fantasy, was conspiring to vest the Lower East Side with an ever resurging metropolitan élan. Still radiating outward to the whole Jewish universe and beyond, it bespoke the creation in just a few explosive decades of a world-centered American Jewish hub in a country and a city like no other. In that "womb," as Kate Simon once called the Lower East Side,[2] more Jews had sojourned and entered upon a new life than at any other time or place in all of Jewish history, exceeding by far the momentous mass migration of so many hundreds of thousands to the new State of Israel between 1948 and 1951, as well as the Israel-bound latter-day mass migration in the 1990s, totaling more than 800,000, from the former Soviet Union, which quadrupled the number of Russians coming to Israel after 1970, when emigration from the Soviet Union was first permitted.

With the onset of the Great Depression, the time for the Lower East Side's sanctification had come. With the Federal Writers Project taking charge, a formidable cut-rate WPA dig into all aspects of the New York cosmopolis was assured. The full-blown stocktaking that followed, energized by an unprecedentedly inclusive American sensitivity to ethnic democracy, made certain that generous attention would be given to the story of the Jews of New York and of the Lower East Side. By the 1960s, eighty years and more after the onset of the great Jewish migration, the Lower East Side, with a Jewish remnant of but 20,000, at last was ripe for canonization and full-bodied historical analysis and retrospection, as it has continued to be ever since for fresh-eyed walkers in the city and zealous interrogators of the historical record.

Presumably, as one of the canonizers, this historian has been expected to reflect on that canon. For one who is completing a biography of Abraham Cahan, the symbolic and existential centrality of the Lower East Side in the American no less than in the American Jewish consciousness has been inescapable. Both in its acceptance and in its rejection, the ceaseless dialectic of that special place has embedded itself into all discourse. This has been most pronounced when it comes to addressing and re-addressing the themes of community and of identity, of place and of person in the modern world. As a student of immigration as well as of Jewish immigration, this historian has been keenly aware, no less than was Cotton Mather, the third-generation historian of New England "From Its First Planting in the Year 1620, Unto the Year of Our Lord 1698," that he too was writing about immigrants "flying from the depravation of Europe to the American strand."[3] For America's Jews, the Lower East Side's granite stone and asphalt, rather than Plymouth Rock, have constituted that "American strand" from which so much has followed.

But when precisely did that latter day "American strand" acquire its name, if not quite the Yiddish precursor and equivalent for *Loisida,* as it has been called by Latinos in recent decades? Assuredly, neither Plymouth Rock nor the Lower East Side were so named by the aborigines.[4]

The designation *the Lower East Side* raises questions of origins, provenance, nomenclature, taxonomy, and usage that, to my knowledge, have neither been addressed directly by historians, including this one, nor by the diverse aficionados of New York's proverbially diverse ethno-geography. One thing is certain: The dyadic division of Lower Manhattan into East Side and West Side by the begetters of Broadway projected a matrix but made no provision for defining its lower and upper divisions. When precisely the attribute *Lower* was affixed formally to the East Side of Lower Manhattan, priming that greater neighborhood for all-American coronation by the Federal Writers in the midst of the Great Depression as "a familiar chapter in the epic of America," remains moot. Yet by 1938, nationally and locally, the poorest Jewish neighborhood in the city formally had been elevated to mythopoetic stature. "Crowded, noisy, squalid in many of its aspects, no other section of the city is more typical of New York," wrote the Federal Writers. Second only to Harlem in the number of families granted federal aid, the Lower East Side was portrayed as a stellar player in the emergence of American democracy and as a virtual twentieth-century exemplar of the nation's multi-ethnic "New World Symphony," even as it was exalted in a litany of clichés. "The district is best known as a slum, as a community of immigrants, and as a ghetto; yet not all of the district is blighted, not all of its people are of foreign stock, and not all are Jewish. From its dark tenements, generations of American workers of many different national origins and an amazing number of public figures have emerged; politicians, artists, gangsters, composers, prize fighters, labor leaders."[5] And so it went. Quintessentially American, quintessentially New York, quintessentially cosmopolitan, Jewish and pluralistic, the Lower East Side packed a gratifyingly big message.

Yet before the turn of the century, the term *Lower East Side* was rarely, if ever, used to describe either the Jewish or the larger immigrant quarters, which had yet to be geographically or otherwise legitimated as such. Both the Lower East Side in name and the Lower East Side as the vortex of Jewish immigrant New York still awaited investiture. Only after 1900 when a new generation of tenement house reformers began to describe the 10th ward of Manhattan as "the greater lower East Side bailiwick of Russian and other eastern European Jews" and "the Lower East Side of New York" as "the most densely populated spot in the world" did the area assume its present name.[6]

Before then, the indefatigable Jacob Riis, the noted housing reformer and the nation's pioneer muckraker, invariably had been credited with the discovery of New York's lost subcontinent of the Lower East Side. But nowhere, whether in his landmark article in *Scribner's* Christmas issue of 1889 entitled "How the Other Half Lives," in his classic of the same name, or in his tireless succession of publications on tenement-house New York, did Riis ever specifically refer to the Lower East Side. Two reasons may explain this omission: The unfathomable city fathers simply were slow to identify and legitimate that geographic entity and Riis himself reflexively conflated the menacing immigrant-tenement other half with New York's geographic other half, the still indeterminate total East Side. Even Riis's often cited tribute to New York's Joseph's coat of immigrant "colonies"—"A map of the city colored to designate nationalities, would show more stripes than on the skin of a zebra and more colors than any rainbow"—was so sweeping, garish, condescending, and sensational in its brush strokes as to subvert his attempt at a grand cosmopolitan gesture. Not surprisingly, "Klein-deutschland," or Little Germany, still in its heyday and in many respects the direct forerunner of the Jewish Lower East Side, went unremarked. Inadvertently throughout the nineties, Riis continued to blazon forth reports into the public consciousness not only of a poor, ignorant, dirty, and sweated district, but also of a singularly unrepentant "Jewtown," coupled unwittingly to its adjacent, heathen "Chinatown" which he absolutely abhorred. Even as he grew more solicitous and even admiring of the Jewish immigrant world, Riis could not shake off his addiction to the conversionist hymnals of the Bowery home mission evangelicals that in great part imbued his own commitment to reform and to aiding "the other half."[7]

But before Riis's "Jewtown" was to fade away and the Lower East Side to replace it, a profoundly transformative event took place. Within just a few years, the Jewish quarter was to be mythopoeticized and was to assume what Roland Barthes has called "the proper name," in this case the *New York Ghetto*, a designation that would transcend conventional topographic boundaries, for it was "at once a 'milieu' . . . into which one must plunge, steeping in all the reveries it bears," as Barthes discerningly has construed the function of "the proper name" or "the Name," in his words again "a proper object . . . a voluminous sign . . . always pregnant with a dense texture of meaning."[8] That name resonated with a stubborn polyphonic new-found obstinately Jewish and immanently American authenticity, juxtaposing Old World and New, Talmudism and the Brooklyn Bridge, literature and life, and worthy of the epic of Jewish ingathering. No longer borne down by a name thrust upon it by strangers of slothful habit of mind or mouth or one demographically enjoined by new public directives generated by the all-consuming pressures of urban geography, "the New York Ghetto" resounded to the mesmerizing dissonances of its own civilizational crises.

For nearly a decade, a new public perception of the Jewish immigrant milieu soared into view. Whether called "the Great New York Ghetto," "the American Ghetto," or some variant, it reverberated with the vigorous imperatives of a new cosmopolitan American and Jewish spirit. Importantly, the term *New York Ghetto* first burst prominently into print not in a sociological study, tenement house report, sermon, or newspaper column, but in the subtitle notably of the original American Jewish novel, *Yekl: A Tale of the New York Ghetto* (1896), where Abraham Cahan artfully depicted the radical changes wrought by the modern world on ordinary lives shaped by traditional Jewish ways. In that great American quarter and world Jewish depot, the titanic battle in full tilt of books and of centuries but, above all, of everyday circumstances, first was celebrated and projected into public consciousness most genuinely and forcefully by Cahan.[9]

Surely Cahan was not the first American to use the term *ghetto*. Yet

17

in the late 1880s when he casually introduced the word into his column in Charles A. Dana's hip *New York Sun*, it apparently was still unknown to educated Americans. Only in 1892 when the newly founded Jewish Publication Society released Israel Zangwill's *Children of the Ghetto*, a novel of contemporary London's Whitechapel in disarray, did the term begin to acquire public currency. Causing a stormy episode in Anglo-American Jewish circles, that unflinching volume was to be catapulted into quasi-bestsellerdom and its testy young English author into international renown. Although silent about this event in his memoirs, Cahan certainly must have taken more than passing notice of Zangwill, for 1892 was the year when Cahan first made note of his "ambition" to be "connected with American literature."

As editor of New York's influential Yiddish socialist weekly, popular public lecturer and labor leader, and noted American delegate to the second and third congresses of the Second Socialist International in Brussels and Zurich in the early 1890s, Cahan had visited Zangwill's London Ghetto on four occasions in three successive years. Ever in quest of a new American language, an ideational framework, and the appropriate literary form to wed his readers' needs to his own, Cahan certainly would have restively examined Macmillan's elegant one-volume 1895 trade edition of Zangwill's novel, if he had not already done so in an earlier printing. With a three-page glossary, "reluctantly added," confessed Zangwill, listing all the transliterated, italicized Yiddish words and phrases, excepting "those words which occur but once and are then explained in the text," their English equivalents, and a key to their original language source (whether in Hebrew, German, Greek, Russian, or "corrupt") Zangwill's book would energize Cahan no end. Even if the Russian realist in him was repelled by Zangwill's romantic Dickensian prose, Cahan, the prospective American man of letters, ever alert for soundings to test his own voice, must have been lifted to a heightened sense of his own literary potentiality on reading the opening lines of Zangwill's "Proem": "Not here in our London Ghetto the gates and gabardines of the olden Ghetto of the Eternal City," wrote Zangwill. "The . . . Ghetto . . . upon which our pictures will be cast is of voluntary formation." Cahan's eye must have rested even longer on the novel's final scenes, written in half-obliging response by Zangwill to the suggestion made by the chairman of the publication committee of the Jewish Publication Society in Philadelphia, Mayer Sulzberger, that "your hero or heroine might emigrate to . . . 'the land of the free and the home of the brave,'" and on Zangwill's salute to America, where he submitted, "Judaism is grander, larger, nobler" and provocatively, if somewhat ominously, "will make its last struggle to survive."[10]

The implicit call by the English author to a prospective kindred voice across the Atlantic seemed intended for the likes of Abraham Cahan, who, in fact, was soon to be applauded and recognized by Zangwill as his American counterpart. And that was quick in coming, for the supreme accolade accorded *Yekl*, that first big tale of "the New York Ghetto," transformed a prospective book notice into a major cultural, no less than a literary event. In a front-page feature review in the Sunday literary section of the *New York World* of July 26, 1896, the nation's and the globe's foremost mass-circulation newspaper with unsurpassed sales of 600,000 copies daily, William Dean Howells not only acclaimed Cahan "the new star of realism" and "a writer of foreign birth" who "sees things with American eyes" along with Stephen Crane but perspicaciously went on to speculate on the future of spoken English as obliquely broached by Cahan. "We shall have a New York jargon, which shall be to English what the native Yiddish of his characters is to Hebrew," prognosticated the acknowledged dean of American letters, "and it will be interlarded with Russian, Polish, and German words, as their present jargon is with English vocables and American slang."[11]

The first instant celebrity of "the New York Ghetto" of his own naming, Cahan was to be quickly recognized as the leading spokesman of New York's and the nation's Russian Jews. In a robust two-page apostrophe interjected into his novel's narrative, which bordered on an Emersonian declaration of an American Jewish immigrant cultural coming of age, Cahan made vividly luminous his vision of this ineffable historic moment in America's Jewish re-genesis.

"The New York Ghetto," affirmed Cahan, was not only "the Ghetto of the American metropolis [but] the metropolis of the Ghettos of the world . . . one of the most densely populated spots on the face of the earth—a seething human sea fed by streams, streamlets, and rills of immigration flowing from all the Yiddish-speaking centers of Europe. . . ." And with near-Whitmanesque cadence, prodigiousness, and élan, Cahan proceeded to sing out all the varieties, conditions, and places of origin of the newcomers—the expellees, the runaways and the refugees, the shut-outs and the shut-ins, the degraded and the outcast, the rabbis, the merchants, and the artisans, who "all come in search of fortune." And, continued Cahan in the same dithyrambic voice, there is not "a tenement house but harbours in its bosom specimens of all the whimsical metamorphoses wrought upon the children of Israel of the great modern exodus by the vicissitudes of life in this their Promised Land of today. . . . [These multitudes of] all sorts of antecedents, tastes, habits, inclinations, and speaking all sorts of subdialects of the same jargon, thrown pellmell into one social caldron, [comprise] a human hodge-podge with its component parts changed but not yet fused into one homogeneous whole."[12]

The following year, Adolph Ochs's new *New York Times*, in seeming response to Cahan's rhapsodic pronouncement, graciously bid welcome to "a Jewish ghetto . . . the largest in the New World . . . right here in New York." Its inhabitants, "unique among the races of the globe [and] so human, intensely so, [if] . . . somewhat strange to us," were, concluded the *Times*, "worth the study of the careful student of humanity."[13]

Surely Cahan, above all, was that "careful student of humanity." Unanimously elected editor of the new Socialist Yiddish daily, the *Vorwärts*, just seven months earlier, he had peremptorily resigned on being denied the free hand that he required. When the admiring Lincoln Steffens straightaway invited him to join the staff of the *New York Commercial Advertiser*, New York's most ancient and dullest daily, Cahan abruptly was plunged into the watershed years of his American education. Under Steffens's inspired editorship, the new *Advertiser*, like no other newspaper in New York or anywhere else for that matter, was cultivating an energetically inclusive all-metropolitan social sensibility joined to high journalism, quiet art, and serious literature. Sustained by a singular staff spirit, the *Advertiser* immediately afforded Cahan a unique niche as senior oracle, literary guide, and ambassador extraordinaire to the counterculture of the "New York Ghetto" to which his colleagues Hutchins and Norman Hapgood were singularly attuned and in which Steffens, himself a self-styled *Yiddisher-Goy*, found a distinctive foil, along with the other immigrant quarters, for his running critique of correct New York.[14]

In his recognized new role as literary eminence and first voice of the New York Ghetto, Cahan proceeded to write a landmark article for the *Atlantic Monthly* in response to the threat of pending restrictive immigration legislation. His "The Russian Jew in America" (1898) also proved to be the first authoritative retrospective of the Russian immigration, from its beginnings in 1882, "opening an important chapter in the history of the Jewish race," where its most gifted advocate eloquently re·ited the virtues of his fellow Jews, especially of those living in Manhattan, "the largest center of Hebrew population in the world." After quoting extensively from the latest reports by Jacob Riis and other expert "Christian Americans," testifying to the sterling qualities of the immigrants, he then proceeded to write a virtual panegyric detailing the remarkable cultural attainments of the "great New York Ghetto," most notably of its "religion full of poetry and of the sources of good citizenship," its many houses of prayer in all their multiplexity, its unsurpassed Yiddish literary culture, its patriotism during the Spanish-American War, its passion for English, its little known "educated Russian-speaking minority forming a colony within a Yiddish-speaking colony," and the resultant addition of "the Russian tongue . . . to the list of languages spoken by an appreciable portion of the polyglot immigrant population."[15]

By the turn of the century, in an ever more cosmopolitan Greater New York, Cahan's creation, "the New York Ghetto," was being burnished into a new Jewish text as a succession of literary and public events made evident. His own two volumes of New York ghetto tales led the way, quickly going into British and Russian editions, as well as appearing in translation in the thick Russian journals in St. Petersburg. *Songs from the Ghetto* (1898) by Morris Rosenfeld, the uncrowned ghetto laureate, was both transliterated from the Yiddish and rendered into American prose by Harvard's Leo Wiener, himself the author of the pioneer *History of Yiddish Literature in the Nineteenth Century* (1899). In *The New Metropolis* (1899), a volume celebrating the new Greater New York, its editor, H. Idell Zeisloft even composed a paean to the American ghetto—"Out from the ghetto will go the lessons of Judaism: Brotherly love—universal peace." In the 1901 mayoralty race, an eight-page reform election campaign daily, titled *Kol fun der geto* (*Voice of the Ghetto*), was distributed free in thousands of copies for eleven successive days by an uptown backer of the victorious Fusion Party. Hutchins Hapgood's classic *The Spirit of the Ghetto* (1902), which Cahan had nurtured so devotedly, projected a vibrantly complex Ghetto world that fortified and embellished Cahan's claims for the Ghetto as did no other printed work.[16]

Finally, the publication in 1905 of the collectively composed volume, *The Russian Jew in the United States*, marked the culmination of what was in effect Cahan's New York Ghetto era. In many respects a compendious sequel to his *Atlantic Monthly* piece of 1898 that the editor, Charles Bernheimer, featured in abridged, unrevised form, the volume, like the original Cahan article, was a measured brief in support of Jewish immigration. With some three dozen special articles by almost as many contributors, the book also was intended to commemorate the protean first chapter in the history of the first generation of Russian Jewish immigrants to America that Cahan had inaugurated. Throughout the book, which focuses primarily on New York and its Philadelphia and Chicago counterparts, repeated references to the "ghetto," the "New York Ghetto," "the Great Ghetto," and "the Great New York Ghetto," make it evident that Cahan's Ghetto had caught on, though not always in the spirit that he intended. In his opening lines, the book's editor seized upon the ghetto theme and acclaimed Zangwill's *The Children of the Ghetto* "a masterpiece," which portrayed, as did no other work, "Jewish characters [in] their lifelikeness with all its intensity." No less pointedly, in closing, the editor felt the need to cite Cahan's moving article in the *American Monthly Review of Reviews* on the tragic fate of the obsolete Chief Rabbi of New York, Jacob Joseph, a "man of the third century," whose death, like his life, in the New York Ghetto of the nineteenth century had been turned into a grim harlequinade.[17]

At last, in the first years of the twentieth century, just as "the New York Ghetto" appeared to have gained wide sanction, the name *the Lower East Side* came into its own. Precisely in what year or month or on what day or hour or by what fiat this occurred, remains obscure, at least to this historian. Surely, the consolidation of Greater New York, its prodigious population growth, and its many systemic changes prompted the city fathers to adopt a new calculus of urban geography, as is evident in the first map, titled "New York Lower East Side," to come to my attention (fig. 1.1). On this disappointingly nondescript, poorly printed, little more than curiously wayward street guide, borrowed doubtless from the city files or the Real Estate Record, the Lower East Side falls ten blocks short of 14th Street, its later northern limits, and is bounded by Broadway, the East River, and the Battery, where it seemingly encompasses the whole eastern half of Lower Manhattan, with Wall Street thrown in for good measure. More to the point, in the book's index the map of the Lower East Side and those for its Philadelphia and Chicago analogues are the sole listings to be found under the head "Ghetto," signifying that geography and Jewish identity were to be seen as one.[18]

The enhanced recognition of the consonance between geography and identity in these years, between the freshly legitimated Lower East Side of place and the ever more discernible Great New York Ghetto of the spirit, could not have come at a more auspicious time. However unceremoniously and incalculably, it signaled the emergent maturity of the first-generation sons and daughters of the great Jewish migra-

Fig. 1.1 This map, one of the first to identify the Lower East Side as a distinct neighborhood of Manhattan, appeared in S. Bernheimer's *The Russian Jew in the United States* (Philadelphia: John C. Winston, 1905).

NEW YORK
LOWER EAST SIDE

tion. As the Lower East Side entered upon its heyday, the emboldened scale of New York, of Jewish immigrant life, and of the generations that followed gave the spirit of that place national and global dimensions. Its most prominent spokesman and man of letters, Abraham Cahan, editor of the *Forward* and increasingly, in the course of his long life, of the whole Yiddish press, would show himself to be not only the putative "careful student of humanity" whom Adolph Ochs's *New York Times* had beckoned to study the Great New York Ghetto in 1897, but the lifelong nurturer of a cosmopolitan Jewish social and cultural sensibility steeped in the spirit of "the metropolis of the Ghettos of the world." As the first to discover and affirm its possibilities, to cultivate its capacities, and to promote and explicate its potentialities, Abraham Cahan was destined to personify the soul of a whole epoch.

A century after the discovery of the Great New York Ghetto, the visible Jewish Lower East Side has virtually vanished from public sight. Except for vestigial tradespeople, remaining at large are a few solitary monuments, rescued from the wrecker's ball and hallowed most especially by the Lower East Side Tenement Museum and by walking tour guides to memorialize an historic Jewish locale. By contrast, its invisible other half appears to be approaching another form of de-actualization, namely, by *mythopoesis*. Exemplified thus far by Charles Liebman's snapshot perception of the history of the Lower East Side as the symbol of the "sacred history" of all of America's Jews and the pass-key to their *genesis americanus*, that trope of the sacrosanct has been notably pursued with high historical seriousness by Hasia Diner. After carefully detailing the historical events and trends that culminated by the 1970s in the sacralization of the Lower East Side, Diner concludes that not only does that place loom as the special "holy space," informing legend and icon for all of America's Jews, but that it has become a paradigm as well for the grand narrative adopted by America's Jewish community historians, affording them a niche comparable to the place of the New England legend in the grand narrative of American history.[19]

Unlike the almost tangible imagery of the Lower East Side, the buoyant cosmopolitan vision of the Great New York Ghetto that emerged at the turn of the twentieth century has eluded genuine scrutiny and even curiosity. Significantly and symptomatically, in 1906, one year after the publication of *The Russian Jew in the United States*, a pallid edition of that landmark work appeared under the imprint of The Liberal Immigration League, reflecting its response to the failed first Russian Revolution, the horrendous pogroms that followed, and the mounting fear of ever more massive Jewish immigration. Not only was the title changed to *The Immigrant Jew in America*, but the names of the editor, the mostly Jewish, thirty-odd contributors, the reading list, and the index all were scratched. Cahan's article was retitled "The Jew in the United States," in conformance with the book's new title, and the salient references to Zangwill and Cahan as the representative voices of an expansive Anglo-American Jewish sensibility were also dropped.[20]

Under the circumstances, the term *ghetto* would, like the designation *Russian*, appear ever more alien compared to the increasingly America-tinged Lower East Side. For long thereafter and into our own time, the ghetto association would seem parochial, even un-American and unseemly to many Americans. Coupled with the refractory racial dilemmas of a segregated urban society, the "ghetto problem" would be given an increasingly recalcitrant cast. After World War II, knowledge of the Nazi ghettos rendered the usage demonic.

Within the next half century, the planet's American, Jewish, and global axes were to shift full circle. The vision of the Great New York Ghetto, which the canonizers of the Lower East Side in no way effectively addressed, at last appears primed for examination. In so altered a universe of discourse, learned younger historians have an enviable opportunity to build and rebuild on the foundations staked out by their predecessors, no less than on the best contemporary scholarship in a dozen collateral disciplines. Equipped with freshly honed linguistic, cultural, and intellectual skills, refined and developed in a singularly propitious climate for the pursuit of Jewish historical studies, they also have ready access to a range and plenitude of national, state, local, Jewish, and international research institutions and resources never quite imagined heretofore. Their errand, one of many worthy ones, may well be to extend the boundaries of the study of that first "metropolis of the ghettos of the world" to encompass the New York world metropolis and beyond at its heights, its depths, and above all, at its vital center into the twenty-first century.[21]

NOTES

1. Beth S. Wenger, "Memory as Identity: The Invention of the Lower East Side," *American Jewish History* 85 (March 1997): 4 and passim; Jenna W. Joselit, "Telling Tales: Or, How a Slum Became a Shrine," *Jewish Social Studies* 2 (Winter 1995): 54ff.

2. Daniel Soyer, *Jewish Immigrant Associations and American Identity in New York 1880–1939* (Cambridge, Mass.: Harvard University Press, 1997), pp. 161ff.; Deborah Dash Moore, *At Home in America: Second Generation New York Jews* (New York: Columbia University Press, 1981), p. 66; Kate Simon, *New York Places and Pleasures* (New York: Meridian Books, 1959), p. 56.

3. Ruth Wisse, "Language as Fate: Reflections on Jewish Literature in America,"

Studies in Contemporary Jewry 12 (1996): 144, 147; see Moses Rischin, ed., *Immigration and the American Tradition* (Indianapolis: Bobbs-Merrill, 1976), pp. xxiii, 9ff.

4. See Graham Hodges, "The Lower East Side," and Kenneth A. Scherzer, "Neighborhoods," in Kenneth T. Jackson, ed., *The Encyclopedia of New York City* (New Haven, Conn.: Yale University Press, 1995), pp. 696–697, 804–805. See also Mario Maffi, *Gateway to the Promised Land: Ethnic Cultures in New York's Lower East Side* (New York: New York University Press, 1995), pp. 29–34.

5. Federal Writers Project, *New York City Guide* (New York: Random House, 1939), p. 108; Beth Wenger, *New York Jews and the Great Depression* (New Haven, Conn.: Yale University Press, 1996), p. 84; Federal Writers' Project, *New York Panorama* (New York: Random House, 1938), pp. 81ff.

6. Roy Lubove, *The Progressives and the Slums* (Pittsburgh: University of Pittsburgh Press, 1962), p. 262; Robert W. DeForest and Lawrence Veiller, *The Tenement House Problem* (New York: Macmillan, 1903), frontispiece; see, e.g., columns in the New York newspapers as printed in Allon Schoener, ed., *Portal to America, 1870–1925* (New York: Holt, Rinehart and Winston, 1967), pp. 105, 120, 127, and 132.

7. See Jacob Riis, *How the Other Half Lives*, ed. Sam B. Warner, Jr. (Cambridge, Mass.: Harvard University Press, 1970), pp. viii, 20, 70–89; Bayrd Still, *Mirror for Gotham* (New York: New York University Press, 1956), p. 211; David C. Hammack, *Power and Society: Greater New York at the Turn of the Century* (New York: Russell Sage Foundation, 1982), p. 94 for ethnographic map in 1890; and Stanley Nadel, *Little Germany: Ethnicity, Religion, and Class in New York City, 1845–80* (Urbana: University of Illinois Press, 1990), pp. 1–11, 29–46; Roy Lubove, *The Progressives and the Slums*, pp. 55–56; Louise A. Mayo, *The Ambivalent Image: Nineteenth-Century America's Perception of the Jews* (Rutherford, N.J.: Fairleigh Dickinson Press, 1988), pp. 166–168.

8. Roland Barthes, "Proust and Names," in *New Critical Essays*, trans. Richard Howard (New York: Hill and Wang, 1980), p. 59.

9. Jules Chametzky, *From the Ghetto: The Fiction of Abraham Cahan* (Amherst: University of Massachusetts Press, 1977), pp. 57ff.

10. See Abraham Cahan, *Bleter fun mayn lebn*, vol. 2 (New York: Forward Association, 1926), p. 327; Jonathan Sarna, *JPS: The Americanization of Jewish Culture* (Philadelphia: Jewish Publication Society, 1989), pp. 39–42, 307; Israel Zangwill, *Children of the Ghetto* (New York: Macmillan, 1895), pp. v, ix, 551–553, 516–517. Also see Elsie Bonita Adams, *Israel Zangwill* (New York: Twayne, 1971), pp. 19, 52–63; and Bryan Cheyette, "Englishness and Extraterritoriality: British-Jewish Writing and Diaspora Culture," *Studies in Contemporary Jewry* 12 (1996): 22–24.

11. Edwin H. Cady, ed., *W. D. Howells as Critic* (London: Routledge, 1973), pp. 256–262.

12. Abraham Cahan, *Yekl: A Tale of the New York Ghetto* (New York: D. Appleton and Co., 1896), pp. 28–30.

13. *New York Times*, 14 November 1897, in Schoener, *Portal to America*, pp. 55–56.

14. See Moses Rischin, ed., *Grandma Never Lived in America: The New Journalism of Abraham Cahan* (Bloomington: Indiana University Press, 1985), especially pp. xvii–xliv.

15. Abraham Cahan, "The Russian Jew in America," *Atlantic Monthly* 82 (July 1898): 128ff.

16. M. Rischin, *The Promised City* (Cambridge, Mass.: Harvard University Press, 1962), pp. 228, 236, 239; H. Hapgood, *The Spirit of the Ghetto* (Cambridge, Mass.: Harvard University Press, 1967), p. xxxi.

17. Charles S. Bernheimer, ed., *The Russian Jew in the United States* (Philadelphia: J. C. Winston, 1905), pp. 5, 32ff., 413. See Abraham Cahan, "The Late Rabbi Joseph, Hebrew Patriarch of New York," *The American Monthly Review of Reviews* 26 (September 1902), 311–314; Abraham Cahan, "A Back Number," *New York Commercial Advertiser,* January 24, 1901, in Rischin, *Grandma,* pp. 72–73; and Menahem Blondheim, "Divine Comedy: The Jewish Orthodox Sermon in America, 1881–1939," in Werner Sollors, ed., *Multilingual America: Transnationalism, Ethnicity, and the Languages of American Literature* (New York: New York University Press, 1998), pp. 191–214.

18. Bernheimer, *The Russian Jew,* pp. 42, 422; see Deborah Dash Moore, "The Construction of Community: Jewish Migration and Ethnicity in the United States," in Moses Rischin, ed., *The Jews of North America* (Detroit: Wayne State University Press, 1987), pp. 105ff.

19. Charles S. Liebman, "The Religious Life of American Jewry," in Marshall Sklare, ed., *Understanding American Jewry* (New Brunswick, N.J.: Transaction Publishers, 1982), p. 109; see Hasia Diner, *Making Space Sacred: The Lower East Side in American Jewish Memory* (Princeton, N.J.: Princeton University Press, 2000).

20. See Edmund J. James, ed., *The Immigrant Jew in America* (New York: B. F. Buck and Co., 1906).

21. See Moses Rischin, "The Megashtetl/Cosmopolis: New York Jewish History Comes of Age," *Studies in Contemporary Jewry* 15 (1999): 177ff.; Cahan, *Yekl,* p. 28.

Photographing the Lower East Side: A Century's Work

Deborah Dash Moore
and David Lobenstine

We *see* the Lower East Side. The neighborhood's absorbing legacy lives in our senses, and we conjure its history through tastes, smells, sounds, and sights. It is nearly impossible to think about the Lower East Side without envisioning its streets, filled with people. Whether you grew up there or have never walked the Lower East Side, the neighborhood pulses with rich and vibrant associations. But why is it that so many of us, outsiders and insiders alike, "remember" the Lower East Side? The answer is that the experience of the Lower East Side is as much created as it is lived, and, therefore, we cannot imagine the Lower East Side apart from a century of photography that has frozen its images in our minds. As a result, a study of how the Lower East Side has been photographed, then and now, provides insights into both the histories of the neighborhood and the visions of the people who created those histories. Such an exploration illuminates, too, the power of images to take hold of our memory.

Our conclusions derive from a body of roughly two hundred and fifty images, compiled from published books, private collections, and museum and library archives. We include photographers both famous and unknown, across a gamut of aesthetic sensibilities and social and political motivations. It is only fitting that so diverse a cast has shaped the visual legacy of so diverse a place.

A variety of new immigrant groups settled the Lower East Side—Germans, Italians, Poles, Russians—but Jews came to dominate the neighborhood over a century ago and created its poverty-stricken, culturally vibrant milieu. The last half-century has witnessed this Jewish pre-eminence recede before a new constellation of foreign cultures. And as the neighborhood experienced its many changes, people continued to take photographs. What we found was this: Before the Great Depression of the 1930s, pictures of the Lower East Side are characterized by physical and/or emotional distance from the subject, along with the photographer's desire to load the image with evidence of foreignness and economic distress. Through the 1930s and '40s, the photograph moves closer to its subject, evincing greater concern with an internal life than with external evidence of the neighborhood's condition. After World War II, irony inserts itself into photographs as older images are reconfigured into historical documents of a past era. Some of the more recent photographs memorialize the neighborhood's Jewish legacy, while others attempt to ignore this past. However, all contemporary photographers of the Lower East Side must contend not only with its vividly inscribed past, but also with the rapid cultural transformations of its present.

Representations of the Lower East Side fall within a broader framework of images of New York City. In general, photographs of the city fit into two categories. The first conveys its vastness and is evident in Samuel Gottscho's sweeping panoramas, Berenice Abbott's grand skyscrapers, or Andreas Feininger's swarming Coney Island beaches. The second category focuses on smaller scenes and individual people, and can be seen in the postures of Helen Levitt's playing children or Weegee's blackened, sweaty exposures of the gritty city's victims and its celebrants. The majority of New York City's images belong to the first group; photographers continually are drawn to the vast gestures of the urban landscape. Photographs of the Lower East Side, however, exhibit the opposite tendency. There is little grand architecture here, and the largeness of the city is often subsumed beneath the forceful presence of destitution, people, and culture.

The early photographs—those taken from 1890 through the 1920s—

are carefully framed in their cultural or class context. These photographs seek to capture the striking physical world of the Lower East Side, including its poverty and alien cultures, for presentation to an outside audience. The enormous overcrowding (by 1890, to quote Moses Rischin's classic account, "the Lower East Side bristled with Jews") and a population density that rivaled Bombay attracted the curious and the outraged, those seeking the exotic and those championing social reform.[1] Photographers wanted both.

Allon Schoener writes of this period: "Life was a panorama of hardship, misery, poverty, crowding, filth, uncertainty, alienation, joy, love, and devotion." It seems that everything could be found in the Lower East Side, except, perhaps, wealth. We use such a sweeping vocabulary to describe the neighborhood because its confluence of languages, ethnicities, religions, and traditions is nearly unparalleled. But our vocabulary also comes from the attention that the Lower East Side has attracted; its history remains alive because of feverish documentation. The life of the Lower East Side and its representations are inseparable, as the latter both defines and constricts the former. Schoener continues, "much of this was documented fully by journalists, photographers, and social workers. The American press saw immigrants as a curiosity," and reporters "assiduously examined every detail of Lower East Side life from food to the wigs worn by women. Accounts of their visits to the Lower East Side created an immediacy that can be equaled only by the photographs of Byron, Hine, Riis, and numerous other documentary photographers, who created a vivid pictorial legacy of the difficult environment in which immigrant Jews found themselves upon landing in America."[2] But this photographic "immediacy" is complex; the "vivid pictorial legacy" is chosen and shaped by these photographers, for reasons admirable and ignorant, initiating a tradition of representation as potent as the neighborhood itself.

In early photographs we view an undeniable attraction to the dirt and poverty and foreign cultures of the area, but very little attention to Schoener's notion of "joy, love, and devotion." These photographers see selectively *because* they are outsiders. They document a combination of what immediately confronts them—the shock of poverty and difference—and what conforms to their vision of how the area *should* look. Byron photographs women shopping along Hester Street in 1898, and we can feel the foreignness immediately: the pushcarts that hang off the curb, the busyness of people buying and selling we're not sure what, the incongruity of the American flag hanging in the background (fig. 2.1). Photographs like Byron's teach lessons, bringing us into familiarity with the newcomers' world. The Lower East Side must have

Fig. 2.1 Joseph Byron, "Hester Street, Jewish Quarter,"
1898. By permission of the Museum of the City of
New York, The Byron Collection, 93.1.1.15380.

seemed a magnet of difference, a foreign place calling to be presented
to the America just beyond its borders.

A century later, Byron's image remains central to our concept of
how the Lower East Side appeared. Always crowded, always dirty, always different. Although we may regard his "Hester Street" as a stereotype, a reductive image, it nevertheless spurs nostalgia. Byron con-
firmed a vision of the Lower East Side, a vision that no doubt existed
before him, but one that he crystallized in the consciousness of New
York. So powerful was his vision that photographers have imitated it
for one hundred years. Even artists who seek to repudiate Byron's stereotype, as we will see eight decades later in Bill Aron's work, return to
it nevertheless.

Photographs like Byron's remain significant because they helped

Deborah Dash Moore and David Lobenstine

create the neighborhood, both visually and physically. As these pho-tographers opened up the Lower East Side, they inevitably confronted its barely veiled problems. Indeed, the first people to photograph the neighborhood seriously, namely Jacob Riis, Lewis Hine, and, to a lesser extent, Joseph Byron and his son Percy, were concerned with the depth of its poverty and the seeming chaos of its cultures. While Riis and Joseph Byron were immigrants, their experiences differed from those of Jews who settled the Lower East Side. Identified as Americans, these photographers saw the neighborhood as outsiders, and documented its life from their distant, but poignant, perspective. A journalist, Riis turned to photography reluctantly, to convey a drama absent from his prose, and used it to further his program of urban reform.[3] Hine consid-ered his own photographs a form of social work, designed to help the people whose burdens he captured. And although Joseph and Percy Byron specialized in high society and magazine photographs, their firm sought to document the city's life in all its rich diversity.

Jacob Riis's photographs stimulated a new awareness of the plight of the poor. Riis's legacy as a muckraker is well known: His writing and lectures, amplified by his photographs, provoked sweeping reforms in housing, labor, and education. But it is significant to see how the ingre-dients of his pictures effected such change.

To present the severity of this world to an outside audience, Riis returns continually to its small streets and crowded tenements. In a photograph of Baxter Street Alley, dated circa 1898, we are confronted with garbage and grime (fig. 2.2). A man stands with his back to us. The foreground is a mess of shapes. Those in the middle ground—whole families, it seems, crouched amidst indecipherable bundles—are shifting, blurry ghosts of people. They are representatives of the ten-ants of squalor. They do not yet have faces.

Another example is Riis's "Bottle Alley, Mulberry Bend," also taken circa 1898 (fig. 2.3). We see an old stone floor spilled with trash, abutted by worn stairs that run along the backs of dilapidated tene-ments. All is limp and in demise, from the haggard clotheslines to the rickety wooden stair beams. In this wasteland, Riis gives us a man lean-ing on a windowsill and a girl standing in a doorway, both alone, both tiny, peering into the emptiness. There is an awful proximity between them and hopelessness. The people are muted in the photographs of Baxter Street Alley and Bottle Alley; they are the same size as the trash among them. In this world where poverty is a constant companion, Riis's composition and accumulation of details clothe the bleakness in a physical body.

Alexander Alland, another photographer of New York City, calls

Fig. 2.2 Jacob A. Riis, "Baxter Street Alley," c. 1898. By permission of the Museum of the City of New York, The Jacob A. Riis Collection, #272.

Fig. 2.3 Jacob A. Riis, "Bottle Alley, Mulberry Bend," c. 1898. By permission of the Museum of the City of New York, The Jacob A. Riis Collection, #348.

33

Riis's photographs "sordid documents" that "aroused the public indignation that led to many reforms."[4] Alland's classification, reflecting the perspective of an established documentary tradition, helps us understand these early photographs. These "documents" press upon us, as outsiders, the *facts* of this immigrant world. And they are "sordid": literally coated with the dank life of the neighborhood. Riis worked as a police reporter, and his photograph of Bottle Alley was actually used as evidence at a murder trial. In *The Battle with the Slum*, he writes, "The X marks the place where the murderer stood when he shot his victim on the stairs."[5] His photographs were proof not only of murders but also of the daily difficulties confronting these small people. (In an unsettling connection, the straps of the girl's dress also form an X across her chest.) Riis says in his autobiography that his writing "did not make much of an impression—these things rarely do, put in mere words—until my negatives, still dripping from the dark-room, came to reinforce them. From them there is no appeal."[6] The images of early photographers seemed incontestable. Packages of material life transported beyond the Lower East Side, they testified to the glum facts of a mass condition.

Indeed, many of these images are inspired by shock, and aim to communicate that shock. We cannot recall how unimaginable some of the situations portrayed must have been to outsiders. Still in its youth, the camera at the turn of the century was largely a tool of the middle and upper classes, and the audience for these photographs would have had little awareness of the daily realities of the Lower East Side. Many of the photographs are structured for this audience: They are brief but graphic lessons in the nature of poverty, in the ways and hows of immigrant life.

Lewis Hine also crafted his photographs as instructive tools. The intricacy of their details and composition can overwhelm. Hine's "Bedroom of an Italian Family," taken in 1910, shows a mass of decrepit objects (fig. 2.4). The various forms are difficult to delineate in the bleakness of the room. We see how compact the family's life is, and how dingy. The figures are crumpled among their possessions, staring without expression, the blank look of need.

A woman and two children sit in the back of a tenement room, as far from the camera as possible. In the narrowness of the room, we see them from a great distance. An irreconcilable gap looms between the viewer and the subject. As with Riis's photograph of Bottle Alley, we are peering into a foreign world from our privileged position outside it.

Although this is an Italian family, it could easily be a Jewish one. Though Riis, Hine, and Byron often record their subjects' ethnicity,

Fig. 2.4 Lewis W. Hine, "Bedroom of an Italian Family," 1910. By permission of the Lewis W. Hine Collection, Milstein Division of United States History, Local History & Genealogy, The New York Public Library, Astor, Lenox and Tilden Foundations.

the notation is usually little more than a title. The force of these photographs, as the photographers saw them, lay in exposing strangeness and poverty, and not in distinguishing between Russians and Poles, or Jews and Italians. With rare exceptions, turn-of-the-century photography creates a generic ethnic mass, rendering specific groups similar in their common plight, and in comparison to the vast difference between them and their audience.

Immigrants were further grouped together in their efforts to assimilate, another purposefully documented aspect of Lower East Side life. Take, for example, an anonymous photograph of Italian men learning English at the James Center, a neighborhood settlement house, circa 1900 (fig. 2.5). The picture is taken from the back of the room, looking down the rows of perfectly aligned men. In the front stands a teacher, his posture dignified, pointing to the blackboard. We see the backs of the students' heads, all similarly groomed atop similar suits, their hats and overcoats arranged on a shelf in the left corner, with the words "SELF CONTROL," "OBEDIENCE," and "KINDNESS" printed above the blackboard. The female equivalent shows a room of Italian women learning to sew, also in the James Center (fig. 2.6). They are diligently working, one woman in the foreground pinning a dress and sporting a huge smile. Their bodies are clear and individually articu-

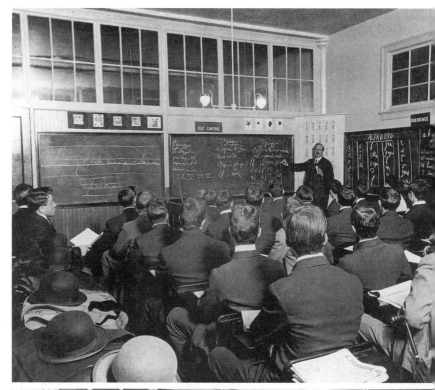

Deborah Dash Moore and David Lobenstine

Fig. 2.5 Unknown photographer, Italian men learning English, c. 1900. By permission of the Children's Aid Society.

Fig. 2.6 Unknown photographer, Italian women learning to sew, c. 1900. By permission of the Children's Aid Society.

lated as they move into their new lives. Compared with the blurred flurry of Byron's Hester Street, these perfectly still images display inherent order. They read like a guidebook on the proper path to assimilation. The subjects, far removed from the tangled masses of the street, comfort us in their quiet commonality that they are indeed becoming Americans.

While some pictures shock and others reassure, both types share an intentional structure. Just as the nineteenth-century photographer Matthew Brady is rumored to have posed dead bodies on his Civil War battlefields, in order to capture what a "proper" battlefield looked like, so do Lower East Side photographs reflect a sense of what a "ghetto" *should* look like. Here we find an interesting tension, because these images, at once innovative and genuinely revealing, also conform to American expectations of immigrant life. Byron's many images of Hester Street, for example, were used to illustrate H. Idell Zeisloft's *The New Metropolis*, published in 1899.[7] But a single photo proved incapable of portraying just how crowded the Jewish neighborhood was, or seemed to be. To solve this problem, a composite was made of several photographs; the result is a space that teems with people, with no room to turn, no place for pushcarts or carriages, a street literally impossible to inhabit (fig. 2.7). Yet we accept such images easily, even eagerly, as they confirm our stereotypical perceptions of a densely packed immigrant neighborhood, a real Jewish "ghetto."

Riis's "Baby in Slum Tenement, Dark Stairs—Its Playground," taken circa 1890, shows a small child standing on the landing of a staircase (fig. 2.8). The emotional force of the picture derives from the child's isolation and the fact that the image of the child, particularly his face, is blurry. He cannot be seen as an individual. The subject of the photograph is abstracted, made a symbol of his kind of life, a desolate urban existence devoid of nurturing love. Tenements cannot produce individuals with distinct personalities, Riis seems to be telling us. This image is frequently reproduced, for its artistry and its implications, as it is both a beautiful and profoundly dogmatic photograph.

Distance, physical and/or emotional, defines many of these early photographs. They seek to squeeze the harried world of the immigrant

Fig. 2.7 Joseph and Percy Byron, "Hester Street: The pushcart market on Friday morning at the height of the Sabbath trade," c. 1899. By permission of the Museum of the City of New York, The Byron Collection.

Fig. 2.8 Jacob A. Riis, "Baby in Slum Tenement, Dark Stairs—Its Playground," c. 1890. By permission of the Museum of the City of New York, The Jacob A. Riis Collection, 90.13.1.122.

into each image. As almost metaphoric representatives, they are packed heavy with facts and evidence, giving us indicators of an economic condition. But we must appreciate these images, for not only do they demonstrate the tension between expectation and reality in the turn-of-the-century Lower East Side, they also reveal the disarming power of symbol and allegory, and the complexity of the immigrants' individual lives that remain unknown beyond the frame.

To demonstrate how the sensibility of early Lower East Side photography changes, we can compare Byron's image of Hester Street (see fig. 2.1), taken in 1898, to A. Eriss's "Music for the Masses," taken around 1939 for the Citizen's Housing Council (fig. 2.9). Like Byron, Eriss also gravitates to the street culture of the Lower East Side, but the composition of his photograph lends it a very different conclusion. Rather than taken from an elevated position looking down on the scene, it is shot from street level. We feel the masses of people and the hustle of movement, but the picture focuses on a single teenage boy playing the violin, and on another boy who holds a felt hat for money. In comparison, Byron's depiction of the street seems like a catalogue of strangeness, lacking the individuality that Eriss invests in his image.

The change in perspective is not unique to Eriss. Rebecca Lepkoff's "On Cherry Street," taken in the 1940s, reveals some of the apparent similarities and inherent differences between this generation of photographers and their turn-of-the-century forebears (fig. 2.10). "On Cherry Street" and Hine's "Bedroom of an Italian Family" (see fig. 2.4) share several characteristics. In both, people are seen at a distance, the frame reveals a poor world, and the view is packed with details. These two images, however, differ fundamentally.

In Lepkoff's photograph we casually witness mundane, almost insignificant, relationships: people talking on the sidewalk, watching each other, kids playing on the stoop. Hine, in contrast, strives to ex-

Fig. 2.9 A. Eriss, "Music for the Masses," c. 1939. By
permission of the Museum of the City of New York,
39.265.18.

Fig. 2.10 Rebecca Lepkoff, "On Cherry Street,"
1940s. By permission of Rebecca Lepkoff.

pose his poorest subjects to us: He bares their desolation for our scrutiny, and the results are clinically observed bodies. Lepkoff gives us no more than a glimpse: She stands contentedly on the periphery and refuses to force her camera into these lives. The result, ironically, is that she produces a view of great intimacy. While Hine forces the audience into an understanding of poverty, Lepkoff's image does not assume its importance as a social statement. The economics behind Lepkoff's "On Cherry Street" are subsumed beneath the routine moments of its residents. Both Hine and Lepkoff reveal a fascination with detail, but the former's is instructive, and the latter's is appreciative.

Both photographs contain a flurry of objects. But Hine's photograph suggests that those items threaten to overwhelm the lives of his subjects, making their dreams of a decent life, of proper housing and education, impossible. By the 1940s, however, despite the continued deplorable living conditions (the Lower East Side had some of the city's cheapest housing), photographers moved toward a modernist preoccupation with curve and light and shape. Thus, in Lepkoff's photograph we sense an appreciation for tawdry objects without an underlying call to action. A broken window is captured alongside the worn precision of bricks, and the sway of drying laundry receives the same treatment as the rubble of an empty courtyard.

Beginning with the photographs of the 1930s, we observe less distance from the subject, along with a desire to document the full circumference of the neighborhood's life—including its ordinariness— rather than solely its differences. These photographers, however, were strongly influenced by a documentary tradition begun by Riis and Hine. Roy Stryker, head of the Farm Security Administration documentary team of the 1930s and '40s, described the aim of photography as to "speak, as eloquently as possible, of the things to be said in the language of pictures," and to know "enough about the subject-matter to find its significance in itself and in relation to its surroundings, its time, and its function."[8] Stryker's words bridge the old and new approaches, as well as their inherent differences. Hine and Lepkoff, Byron and Riis all use photography to confront their era's social realities through their respective aesthetic lenses. But Lepkoff and her contemporaries find the significance of the subject *in the subject itself;* their images do not represent or symbolize, but seek to value ordinary lives.

This shift in perspective came over time, as by the 1930s the Lower East Side had lost much of its strangeness. Not only had Jews migrated to neighborhoods in Brooklyn and the Bronx where they replicated many of the signature elements of the Lower East Side—especially its pushcart markets and crowded shopping streets—but a new generation

Fig. 2.11 Roy Perry, "Learning to Be an American Citizen," 1938–1940. By permission of the Museum of the City of New York, 80.102.18.

of native New Yorkers had come of age, the children of immigrants. Beth Wenger writes that unlike studies from the turn of the century, "the documentaries of the interwar years focused less on exposing the desperate conditions in the neighborhood and more on deciphering the meaning and recording the vestiges of a 'disappearing' Jewish culture."[9]

For many of these young photographers, the Lower East Side was less an emblem of difference than a place of personal import. Some had even grown up in the neighborhood. Photographers felt able to get closer, to look into it more deeply. Roy Perry learned photography in the context of the city's streets, in its public high schools and colleges. Born on the Lower East Side, Perry returned to the neighborhood after graduation to observe the changes that had occurred. Although he no longer lived there, Perry did not distance himself from the lives of his former neighbors. Like Eriss, Perry worked for social service agencies, documenting their work to assist fundraising efforts. And his photographs depended upon timing, because he did not ask anyone to pose for him.

Perry's closeness to this life is reflected in the intimacy of his photographs. A beautiful example is his image of a Jewish woman in her seventies being taught to write English, taken between 1938 and 1940 (fig. 2.11). The title, "Learning to Be an American Citizen," places it in

the classic assimilation genre, preceded by the images of men learning English and women learning to sew (see figs. 2.5 and 2.6). But the compositions of the pictures distinguish Perry's from the others, as his epitomizes the collapse in distance that occurs in the 1930s. We sit at the desk next to the elderly woman and her teacher, an intimate witness to their efforts. There is little room here for metaphor—no American flag or symbolic content—and we are left only with the texture of a notebook, the patterns of their clothing, their wrinkled faces and intent eyes. This is a world that Perry seems to know and appreciate, and a world that trusts him enough to reveal its vulnerability. A son of Jewish immigrants, Perry might have been photographing the earnest efforts of a family member—an aunt or grandmother, or even his mother.

The generous replication of people's everyday lives seen in Perry's approach appears on the street as well, in such images as Arthur Leipzig's "Pitt Street Pool," from 1947–48 (fig. 2.12). Used to illustrate the jacket of his book, *Growing Up in New York,* this photograph gives us a poignantly ordinary moment.[10] A jumbled row of boys, waiting to get into the municipal pool on Pitt Street, watch as a police officer escorts away a boy who has tried to cut the line. The photograph is eye-catching because Leipzig has vividly rendered a momentary drama of childhood. The bodies and expressions of the boys are absorbing because they are unexceptional. Leipzig is concerned with aesthetics, not ideology, with the ordinary rather than the extraordinary. The rhythmic interplay of the boys' white t-shirts suggests the improvisations of jazz. His is a small world rendered precisely, a revelation of the remarkable encased in tiny snatches of unremarkable time.

As they moved closer to the lives of their subjects, documentary photographers also began to attend to issues of gender. With the notable exception of Jessie Tarbox Beals and Alice Austen, New York photography at the turn-of-the-century was a male occupation. The 1930s and '40s witnessed a dramatic increase in visions of the city offered by women. Lee Sievan's "Mulberry Bend—Gentlemen of Leisure," taken in the 1940s, is an example of an image that both engages cultural presumptions and searches for compelling aesthetic form (fig. 2.13). Sievan's composition and tone is beautiful: The men form a pyra-

Fig. 2.12 Arthur Leipzig, "Pitt Street Pool," 1947–1948.
By permission of Arthur Leipzig.

Fig. 2.13 Lee Sievan, "Mulberry Bend—
Gentlemen of Leisure," 1940s. By
permission of Howard Sieven.

mid along the steps, their clothes dark and sun-baked against the bright stone. The influence of modern aesthetics is evident. But "Gentlemen of Leisure" is also distressing. The men are out of work; a boss stands on the right, signing up day laborers. Sievan confronts a male world that watches her as fiercely as she watches it. The photographer is no longer in absolute control, as Hine and Riis seem to be when shooting their wide-eyed and helpless subjects. Willing to risk confrontation, Sievan welcomes the increasing speed and portability of the camera that urges the photographer toward new possibilities.

The possibility for an image to have both cultural undertones and a deeply felt life is one of the continuing achievements of Lower East Side photography. This is the gift of photographs from the 1930s and '40s: They resonate because they are of ordinary moments—daily bits of life—made extraordinary by the circumstances surrounding their lives—poverty, assimilation, joys and anxieties. These photographs fuse two distinct modes of representation, the evidential and the internal. Both share an inherent necessity. The perspective of these photographers, like the preoccupations of turn-of-the-century photography, reflects the artists and their concerns. The turn toward a documentary style is prompted by an ideological commitment to the masses—"the people"—which endows their subjects with such radiant possibilities.

After World War II, the documentary tradition takes different paths, veering off into irony and history. Vivian Cherry's photographic series "Game of Guns" covers children's play that was heavily influenced by the recent war. In a photograph taken in 1948 of a boy shooting his toy gun from behind cellar steps, we glimpse the intensity of the child's world against its adult backdrop (fig. 2.14). The boy is oblivious to the movie poster announcing *Crossfire,* the first postwar film to explore antisemitism in the American military, but *we* are not. In fact, our understanding of the photo depends on our ability to read, to see different meanings of "crossfire" in the image. Frank Paulin's arresting photograph of children's play in 1956, "Lower East Side Playground," introduces us to a dramatically different neighborhood, one filled with public housing projects rather than aging tenements (fig. 2.15). The face of working-class life has changed. The boy stands amid bushes; there are young, slender trees in the background. The contrast of the almost bucolic setting confronted by a child in a gas mask produces an image of the Lower East Side that is difficult to assimilate. We scarcely recognize this picture, so sharply does it diverge from established expectations and a half-century canon of representations. But Paulin's subject matter also diverges from the Lower East Side canon, as he comments less on the neighborhood and its social problems than on reverberations of the Cold War in American society.

Fig. 2.14 Vivian Cherry, "Crossfire,"
1948. By permission of Vivian Cherry.

Fig. 2.15 Frank Paulin, "Lower East Side Playground," 1956. By permission of Frank Paulin.

Deborah Dash Moore and David Lobenstine

This era also transforms turn-of-the-century photographs of the Lower East Side into accurate documents of a distant era. As bulldozers leveled tenements to create housing projects, historians sought to understand immigration and the neighborhood's role as the place where Jews began their American odyssey. Moses Rischin's *The Promised City: New York's Jews, 1870–1914* (1962), Allon Schoener's *Portal to America: The Lower East Side, 1870–1925* (1967), and the republication in paperback of Jacob A. Riis's *How the Other Half Lives: Studies among the Tenements of New York* (1970) recast the Lower East Side as the cradle of urban reform. The process changed how viewers saw old photographs, privileging those images that invited empathy rather than outrage or pity.

When the editors of Riis's paperback edition looked for a cover photograph, they turned not to Riis's own images but to a warm, appealing shot of children playing house on a fire escape (fig. 2.16). Taken by an anonymous Tenement House Commission photographer on Allen Street on August 4, 1916, the photograph draws the viewer close to the children. Beneath the blankets behind the boys can be seen two girls. Although their clothes are ragged, one boy smiles at the photographer. The long stretch of elevated tracks situates the tenement as it directs the eye into the frame. This is hardly a photograph Riis would have taken; there is nothing wrong here. The image provokes sentimentality, nostalgia even, not a sense of injustice.

The transformation of old photographs into historical documents appears vividly in Rischin's choice of Byron's composite image of Hester Street (see fig. 2.7) to accompany *The Promised City*. Rischin picked the photo because it illustrated a book of the era—*The New Metropolis*, published in 1899—and thus represented how contemporaries saw the Lower East Side. Once placed in a history book, however, the composite photograph acquires new authority. No longer is it an illustration confirming Americans' turn-of-the-century expectations of immigrant foreignness. Looking at the crowded street, we accept it as an accurate document of the period. We ignore the impossibility of the buying and selling in the middle of the street; we overlook the varying scales of the figures. The image confirms fevered shopping for the Sabbath. It reminds us of the pious traditions of immigrant ancestors and symbolizes the "ghetto."

The documentary tradition revived in the 1970s, when photographers again flocked to the Lower East Side. Obviously, the Lower East Side that these photographers encountered and continue to meet differs substantially from that of Riis or even of Roy Perry. The Chinese

Fig. 2.16 Unknown photographer, "Allen Street, Third Story Front, Group of Children on Fire Escape," 1916. By permission of the Museum of the City of New York, Gift of Tenement House Department, 31.93.14.

had become the dominant ethnic group, and the Jewish presence was only a whisper of what it had been at the turn of the century. One of the few consistencies is that the curious continue to come.

Contemporary photographers must respond not only to this changing environment but also to earlier representations of the area. These two forces shape the artists' images into a dramatic recasting of a new neighborhood, a place wildly different, but steeped in its own tradition. Here there is no history without the jarring present.

The result is a new form. In the 1970s and 1980s, more photography books were published on contemporary Jewish communities than in any previous era.[11] We have based our findings for the recent era on three of these books: *The Lower East Side: A Guide to Its Jewish Past with 99 New Photographs*, by Ronald Sanders (1979); Bill Aron's collection *From the Corners of the Earth: Contemporary Photographs of the Jewish World* (1985); and *The Lower East Side: A Contemporary Portrait in Photographs*, edited by Esther Brumberg and Sy Rubin (1984). This self-conscious documentation by Jewish photographers, writers, and editors of a particular culture and area did not exist in the first half of the twentieth century. It is evidence of a reliance on the Lower East Side both as it can and can no longer be seen. These collections articulate the Lower East Side not as a morass of poverty and foreignness, but as a repository of Jewish culture, a place to find one's history.

Jacob Riis and his generation photographed the Lower East Side to *uncover* a foreign world. Bill Aron and other contemporary photographers return to *recover* a tradition and culture. Aviva Weintraub writes that "many of these photographers defined their work as salvage, to capture and preserve 'disappearing communities' on film."[12] Ironically, the new photographers also find a foreign world that they must choose how to portray.

Sanders's book is an extreme example of recovery. The book begins with a series of turn-of-the-century photographs crammed with street life, rife with pushcarts. This is the genre initiated by Byron's "Hester Street"; Sanders's inclusion of these images is further evidence that this view has become the canonical image of the Lower East Side, the view we have long since come to expect. Even through the 1920s, when legislation restricted immigration and mobility emptied the Lower East Side, a variety of photographers followed Byron's lead, making the Lower East Side conform to imagined and remembered expectations of a neighborhood more crowded and more unmanageable than it actually was. The belief designed reality. Our desire to see the neighborhood as it should look increases as the world we want to recall disappears. Pushcarts were removed from the streets by city authorities during the Depression, and nostalgia moved in to fill their physical absence. It seems that we cannot see the Lower East Side in our time without returning to its visual origins.

In Sanders's book, we are given contemporary photographs only after a demonstration of what was. But as we move to the present in the photographs of Edmund Gillon, the flurry and vitality of the old culture disappears. Instead, Gillon posits a Jewish past almost solely in the *architecture* of the Lower East Side; in the majority of photographs, people are incidental. It is through these buildings and their associations that we can gloss what once was. One such photo portrays a series of storefronts, seen from beyond parked cars and across a broad street (fig. 2.17). The caption reads, "The old Forward Building, 175 East Broadway, is marked today by a sign in Chinese. While the *Jewish Daily Forward* operated in the structure, it was one of the most important focuses of the Jewish community."[13] Along the row of non-Jewish shops—the India Discount Center, K & K Import, Sari Sari, etc.—we can barely make out which building is the significant one. The past has been covered by the clutter of cultural change. These photographs can only present the façade, leaving us with the task of imagining a flourishing culture. On the facing page, Gillon shows us the entrance to the Forward Building [not pictured here]. We see the Chinese sign alluded to previously, small and at the bottom of the frame. Posing next to it, curiously, stand an older Jewish couple. They are short, dressed in black. The pair echoes the sign, their bodies making a similar square, as if both are landmarks, the one of an older culture in transit, the other new and firmly attached to a transformed architecture.

Gillon's photographs are also interesting for what they *don't* comment on. One view along Orchard Street shows commerce as a backdrop to several African American men walking shirtless down the street (fig. 2.18). The caption says only, "The merchandise displayed in cardboard boxes is characteristic."[14] The image cannot decide on its subject. A tension emerges between the commerce that Gillon wants to portray, with its Jewish tradition, and these other people who inevitably move into the frame, drawn in part by the cheap goods for sale and in part because they now live in the neighborhood (unlike many of the Jewish merchants).

On the whole, these photographs evoke little emotion. Their desire to see through the image into what *was* emphasizes the streets and buildings as artifacts of Jewish culture, rather than seeing a present, lived environment. This series seeks to reveal the past of a shrinking culture, nearly invisible to the uninitiated. Gillon neither combines aesthetics with social import, as the Depression-era photographers did,

Deborah Dash Moore and David Lobenstine

Fig. 2.17 Edmund Gillon, Along the street of the old Forward Building, c. 1979. By permission of Edmund Gillon.

Fig. 2.18 Edmund Gillon, Scene on Orchard Street, c. 1979. By permission of Edmund Gillon.

nor does he shock us with foreignness; rather, his photographs illustrate, grudgingly, the altered face of the Lower East Side, in order to invoke the vestiges of tradition.

The opening section of Bill Aron's *From the Corners of the Earth* is entitled "The Lower East Side Revisited: 1974–1984." Like Sanders and Gillon, Aron comes, as he writes, "to capture and preserve" the community of the "old Jews."[15] It is not surprising, then, that Aron begins his Lower East Side section with an image of Orchard Street from 1977 (fig. 2.19). The caption reads: "Orchard Street is just as it was fifty years ago, only the signs are now in English instead of Yiddish."[16] Aron emphasizes continuity amidst a changing world. Alongside Byron's "Hester Street" (see fig. 2.1), we can see that Aron's "Orchard Street" pays homage to the canonical image of the Jewish Lower East Side as a site of crowds and commerce. Here is the view we return to, the sweep of people, of culture, of difference. In contrast, though, Aron calls his scene "a festival of bargains."[17] The photograph no longer documents poverty; rather, it celebrates the exchange of money and goods. Ironically, it was just such small-scale business that carried immigrant Jews out of poverty and the Lower East Side.

Aron combines the perspectives of turn-of-the-century photographers and Depression-era photographers, as his images move easily from the distanced to the intensely personal. One such photograph is "Hair Tonic," his 1976 street portrait of a Hasidic boy (fig. 2.20). The image seems to be traditional, particularly as Hasidim often have a timeless quality, removed from the present moment by their striking dress. In reality, however, this image has no photographic antecedents. Children, while photographed relentlessly in the first half of the century, were usually divorced from a specific religious context. This boy inaugurates a new tradition, hinting at the complexity of both contemporary orthodoxy and Jewish self-portraiture. It harks back to Roman Vishniac's photos of Polish Jews on the eve of World War II.

How far we have come from the brutally simple metaphor of Riis's

Fig. 2.19 Bill Aron, "Orchard Street," 1977.
By permission of Bill Aron.

"Baby in Slum Tenement" (see fig. 2.8). The young Hasid looks straight into the camera, arms spread, revealing himself, but simultaneously his hat covers his mouth, disguising his full face from the picture. He is an individual—for Aron endows the standard black dress with a texture and richness, capturing him precisely—and he is also a sociological statement, a representative of his religious group. The sign in the background, "Nature Tonic for Men," hints at allegory, at the daily collision, sometimes amusing, sometimes devastating, between Hasidim and their secular urban environment.

Most of Aron's pictures take orthodox Jews as their subject. This choice emphasizes his thematic relationship with Hine and Riis. For while Leipzig and the other documentary photographers of the 1930s and '40s purposely sought out the ordinary—these Jews weren't distinguished from their Italian neighbors—Hine, Riis, and Aron seek the emblematic. They are attracted to extremes. In the beginning of the century, these were the foreign, swarming poor. Today, Jewish difference is embodied most obviously in the deeply religious.

Religious culture is simultaneously thriving and collapsing in Aron's representation. His famous 1977 photograph, "The Oldest Synagogue in New York," of the Anshe Chesed synagogue, now Anshe Slonim, captures the glory and the ruins (fig. 2.21). We see the floor of the synagogue strewn with discarded wood from broken pews, and above, sunlight streams through the windows, evoking the building's former grandeur. Interestingly, the photo exerts a power similar to Riis's and Hine's revelations of poverty. Aron's images helped to fuel the impetus for recent synagogue restoration, just as his predecessors provoked advancements in city housing and education. The key difference, though, is that the latter's revelation of poverty relies on the shock of seeing an unknown world, while Aron's picture seeks to goad Jewish communal memories, to spur Jews into a recovery of their past. Aron's photograph also reverberates with other images of destroyed synagogues, perhaps most powerfully those burned in Germany during the Nazi pogrom of Kristallnacht in November 1938.

Fig. 2.20 Bill Aron, "Hair Tonic," 1976.
By permission of Bill Aron.

Fig. 2.21 Bill Aron, "Anshe Chesed
Synagogue," 1977. By permission of Bill
Aron.

Aron writes that "the principal strength of photography [is] as a sociological method, for the photograph can give the viewer an emotional connection with—as well as an intellectual understanding of—the scene depicted."[18] Here we return to the convictions of Riis and Hine, to teach the viewer about a culture. Photography's gift, Aron suggests, is its ability to prove the existence of its subject. The Hasidic boy is an individual, but he also implicates the presence of a larger Jewish community, and the image asks us to acknowledge that community, just as the devastated synagogue invites collective responsibility for its neglect.

Aron diverges from earlier tradition, however, for he is an insider, and intends his photographs for the Jewish community; by contrast, Hine and Riis took their pictures for an audience a world apart from their subject. Why are Aron's pictures for Jews, too? Because they do not shock, or insist, but are a self-conscious effort to document the presence of Aron's own culture in its everyday moment. Several documentary traditions converge in Aron's representations of the Lower East Side, those drawn from the American past as well as those stemming from Jewish ethnographic photography of prewar Europe.

One significant photographer whose work did not make it into the more contemporary books about the Lower East Side is Seymour Edelstein, who in the late 1980s took a series of portraits of Jews at work. The subject is not uncommon: Lewis Hine photographed a vast array of workers, from cotton pickers in the South to the builders of the Empire State Building; and in 1940, the documentary photographer Alexander Alland shot the employees of a Chinese newspaper, among others. Edelstein refocuses this tradition specifically onto the work of Jews, and by reflection, onto himself. Weintraub writes of the "mirror-like quality of photographic images," which "allow the photographers as well as the photographed to reflect upon and thereby alter and expand their own sense of self."[19] Edelstein's photographs strive to evoke normality; in the tradition of Lepkoff and Perry, they are quiet and compassionate exposures of daily life. With each image, Edelstein notes solely the name of his subject and the picture's location, testifying to the quiet continuity of Judaism, both in the Lower East Side and throughout the city. This series does not suggest that Judaism is disappearing—there is no urgency in the images—but rather, that Judaism maintains itself, unremarkably, perhaps just as these photographs help to maintain the photographer's own sense of self.

One such image is a portrait of a *sofer*, or scribe, Rabbi Eisenbach, bent over an unfurled Torah scroll, taken on March 9, 1988, at 49 Essex Street (fig. 2.22). It bears an immediate resemblance to Roy Perry's image of the elderly woman being taught to write English (see fig. 2.11).

Fig. 2.22 Seymour Edelstein, "Rabbi Eisenbach," 1988. By permission of Jean Edelstein.

Deborah Dash Moore and David Lobenstine

We see only the arms and head of the scribe. He wears gloves smudged with ink; white strands of hair stick out from the back of his skullcap. His work is painstaking and slow, not unlike the photographer's. Edelstein's project fits somewhere between documentary photography and the sociological approach of Bill Aron. He attends to matters of shape and physical detail, but his work is not colored by ideological notions of the heroic masses. Simultaneously, his series explores Jewishness, but is not concerned with recovering a lost tradition. From butchers to candle makers, Edelstein journeys through a Jewishness that seemingly always was and always will be, unfazed by fears of disappearance and declension.

The third book of images, Esther Brumberg and Sy Rubin's *The Lower East Side: A Contemporary Portrait in Photographs* (1984), references and then supersedes both current concerns over the state of Judaism as well as the century's traditions. With the photographs all taken between 1973 and 1984, the book weaves "a poignant tapestry of what is here and now on the Lower East Side, but with strong echoes of the past," according to Michael Frey, Executive Director of the Henry Street Settlement, which exhibited the images and sponsored the book's publication.[20] The editors embrace Frey's sentiment: "It is as if the 1930s and 40s meet the 1980s here—jostling, competing, co-existing. Worlds collide, blend, ignore each other, clash."[21] The editors want to see a world chaotic and rich but ultimately harmonious, for this is the only way we can still find the traditions of the past in the world around us, beneath the messy accumulation of cultural shifts. But the book's ninety-six photographs do not display such an all-embracing picture.

The book begins, like Sanders's collection, with bare streets, devoid of people, the desolation and poverty implied. But unlike Gillon's photographs, the narrative of Brumberg and Rubin's collection quickly abandons the idea of searching for the Jewish Lower East Side in its architecture. The essay is soon overwhelmed by people, and the visual traditions of the Lower East Side inevitably peek through the collection.

One such example is Rebecca Lepkoff's photograph of an intergenerational group, taken in 1983 (fig. 2.23). We can see its particularities best through a contrast with Andreas Feininger's image of two women shopping on Orchard Street, dating from the 1940s (fig. 2.24). The latter is purposefully composed, governed by an aesthetic of the curve that runs through the women's figures. The two women are dressed to go shopping—their hats fashionable and their stocking

Fig. 2.23 Rebecca Lepkoff, "Women Together," 1983. By permission of Rebecca Lepkoff.

Deborah Dash Moore and David Lobenstine

Fig. 2.24 Andreas Feininger, "Orchard
Street," 1940s. By permission of the
Museum of the City of New York,
55.31.159.

seams straight—taking part in the ritual of display. The storeowner, meanwhile, watches them, not sexually, but to see what they are buying. It is a modernist photograph that focuses upon the shapes of commerce and gender. Lepkoff's photograph, in contrast, is decidedly non-modernist. The composition is not as sharp and intentional as Feininger's; the women spread in clumps along the sidewalk, without the visual organization of Feininger's curve. Lepkoff's is a female vision of her community, as suggested by its title, "Women Together." She is concerned with the personal relationships between these generations of women, rather than commercial ones.

"Women Together" also harks back to Byron's "Hester Street," another photograph in which the shoppers are predominantly women. Between these two images we can see the vast change in the visual perspective of the Lower East Side. While both Byron and Lepkoff document ordinary aspects of street culture, the tone of each is contrary. Seeing strangeness, Byron packs his image with details, and as a result remains distant from the individual lives; by contrast, in confronting a scene almost mundane in her world, Lepkoff seeks solely to document the interplay between the women, and moves among them in taking the picture. But like Byron, she does implicate these women as representative of a larger community, taking Bill Aron's sociological viewpoint to frame a gendered, rather than religious, culture.

Alongside these evocations of tradition is a distinctive break with it. Geoffrey Biddle's photographic series along Avenues A and B epitomizes a new view of the Lower East Side, as seen in one image of a boy and his family (fig. 2.25). Here borders are inadequate, people are cut off, the compositions are lopsided—life is bleeding past the edges. The boy literally has to bend to fit into the frame. The camera cannot contain the drama, an implicitly non-Jewish one. There are no explicit ethnic markers, and Biddle, unlike Hine (see fig. 2.4), does not care to label the family he photographs. This neighborhood is a place of great contrasts, a site of turmoil and sudden stillness. Tradition seems to dissolve in the face of this seemingly chaotic, overflowing life.

Biddle writes in his introduction to *Alphabet City*, a book which includes the above photograph, that "this book is called *Alphabet City* because it isn't for the people in the pictures. . . . *Alphabet City* is for the people who want to know about the inner city, and even more it is for the people who don't want to know."[22] Biddle's assertion reminds us of Riis and Hine and Byron, the revealers of the Lower East Side a century ago to a reluctant but curious audience of outsiders. He believes that the unknowing audience still exists; that the larger world must confront this inner-city microcosm. Only the subjects and techniques have changed. The teeming drama of the foreign masses has been re-

Fig. 2.25 Geoffrey Biddle, "Avenue A Between
10th and 11th Streets," 1974–1984. By
permission of Geoffrey Biddle.

placed by the domestic drama—more familiar but perhaps no better understood—of the African American and Latino communities. Biddle's
jagged, lopsided, seemingly uncomposed compositions are the suitable
means to convey today's Lower East Side, just as the details of dirt and
difference felt essential at the turn of the century. Perhaps the break
with tradition is never total.

The last images of Brumberg's collection are a series of portraits by
Steve Satterwhite, taken in a storefront studio in 1973. One example is
an image of a man standing behind a woman (fig. 2.26). In this photo-

Fig. 2.26 Steve Satterwhite, "Portraits," 1973. By
permission of Steve Satterwhite.

graph and throughout the series, the people try to compose themselves
but ultimately cannot. They are not proper subjects for the formalities
of portraiture. They are bleary-eyed and crooked, they are black and
Hispanic, and they are poor. Their awkward but beautiful presence also
challenges the tradition of Lower East Side photography. Photographed
in a studio, this couple exists without context. This is the Lower East
Side stripped of our ingrained images, without a Jewish presence or

67

legacy. These portraits suggest people who live outside of the neighborhood's history; they are postmodern heirs to Riis's "Child of the Tenements."

Furthermore, Satterwhite's portraits are not intended for an outside audience. The series aims to give the men and women of the neighborhood, formal portraiture's improper subjects, images of themselves, for themselves. Unlike Hine, Satterwhite does not rend them open for an audience's education; the subjects stand before us with all their quirks, and it is difficult to make them represent anything but themselves. We have here a different kind of social work, not the great societal innovations provoked by Riis and Hine, but a more subtle attempt to empower people to see and claim their own individual identities.

We cannot, however, conclude with this unhinged present. Brumberg and Rubin close their visual essay of the Lower East Side with Aron's picture of Orchard Street (see fig. 2.19). This image was also featured on the poster for the exhibit at the Henry Street Settlement that preceded the book. We return to, and are left with, the canonical view. This choice suggests that all photography of the Lower East Side, regardless of its subject, its divergence from tradition, is in some way contained by the canon. These are the pieces that are stilled within us. These reference points contain the Lower East Side within history and memory.

The turn of the century saw a distance between the photographer and the subject. This gap corresponds with the social chasm between the Lower East Side's foreignness and poverty and the perceptions and audience of Hine, Riis, and Byron. The next hundred years of Lower East Side photography grappled with that distance, and the aesthetics and emotions it contains. First it shrinks and then it expands (uneasily) once again. During the Depression we move toward aesthetic values that valorize working men, women, and children and imagine the lives of individuals etched on their faces. And as we turn into the present, we see an evolution from and rejection of earlier models, both a self-conscious recovery of the past and an effort to authentically document a dramatically different present.

A century of Lower East Side photography lets us witness the gravitational pull of visual history. Taking a photograph is an act shaped by the past—by images embedded in the artist's mind, by beliefs and perceptions of what is and should be in the frame. History gives us our sense of the present and the meanings of place and space. Regardless of the trajectory and intentions of the artist, photographs of the Lower East Side must contend with what has come before. Herein lies the neighborhood's fundamental, iconic power, its ability to draw generations of photographers to its worn streets. To photograph the Lower East Side is to enter a dialogue with great urban images of the past, renowned for their social power and intimacy, for their dogma and aesthetics. The images that we recall—and periodically rediscover—reflect the potent meeting between the impulses of an individual artist and the visual and cultural richness of the neighborhood. They inscribe a past into the memory that animates our present.

NOTES

1. Moses Rischin, *The Promised City: New York's Jews, 1870–1914* (Cambridge, Mass.: Harvard University Press, 1977), p. 79.

2. Allon Schoener, *Portal to America: The Lower East Side, 1870–1925* (New York: Holt, Rinehart and Winston, 1984), pp. 10–11.

3. See Keith Gandal, *The Virtues of the Vicious: Jacob Riis, Stephen Crane, and the Spectacle of the Slum* (New York: Oxford University Press, 1997), for a provocative interpretation of Riis and his photography.

4. Alexander Alland, *Jacob A. Riis: Photographer and Citizen* (New York: Aperture, 1974), p. 12.

5. Jacob A. Riis, *The Battle with the Slum* (New York: Garrett Press, 1970), p. 308.

6. Alland, *Jacob A. Riis*, p. 16.

7. E. Idell Zeisloft, ed., *The New Metropolis* (New York: D. Appleton and Co., c. 1899).

8. Alland, *Jacob A. Riis*, p. 14.

9. Beth S. Wenger, "Memory as Identity: The Invention of the Lower East Side," *American Jewish History* 85, no. 1 (March 1997): 14–15.

10. Arthur Leipzig, *Growing Up in New York: Photographs* (Boston: David R. Godine, 1995).

11. Aviva Weintraub, "Visiting a 'Vanished World': Photography and the Jewish Lower East Side," in *YIVO Annual* 21, ed. Jack Kugelmass (1993): 190.

12. Ibid., p. 190.

13. Ronald Sanders, *The Lower East Side: A Guide to Its Jewish Past with 99 New Photographs* (New York: Dover Publications, 1979), p. 54.

14. Ibid., p. 40.

15. Bill Aron, *From the Corners of the Earth: Contemporary Photographs of the Jewish World* (Philadelphia: The Jewish Publication Society, 1985), p. 10.

16. Ibid., p. 11.

17. Ibid., p. 11.

18. Bill Aron, "A Disappearing Community," in *Images of Information: Still Photography in the Social Sciences*, ed. Jon Wagner (London: Sage Publications, 1979), p. 67.

19. Weintraub, "Visiting a 'Vanished World,'" p. 215.

20. Esther Brumberg and Sy Rubin, *The Lower East Side: A Contemporary Portrait in Photographs* (New York: Persea Books, 1984), p. 8.

21. Ibid., p. 5.

22. Geoffrey Biddle, *Alphabet City* (Berkeley: University of California Press, 1992), pp. iv–v.

Beyond Place and Ethnicity:
The Uses of the Triangle Shirtwaist Fire

Paula E. Hyman

On March 25, 1911, a fire broke out at the Triangle Shirtwaist factory just before closing time on Saturday evening. One hundred forty-six employees, almost all of them young Jewish and Italian immigrant women, lost their lives.[1] Unable to escape through the one unlocked door, the narrow staircase, and the inadequate elevators, many chose to jump to their deaths from the eighth and ninth floors; others succumbed to smoke inhalation and were incinerated in the factory itself. "The morgue is full of our victims," shrieked the headline of the *Forverts* on March 26th; "the whole Jewish quarter is in mourning."[2] All of New York's daily papers were filled in the days following the fire with poignant stories of the young women who became flaming torches as they fell to the sidewalks below the Asch Building. The Triangle Fire shook the residents of the Lower East Side, some of whom lost loved ones in the disaster and most of whom realized that they too were vulnerable as poor immigrant workers.

From the beginning, however, the meaning of the fire was contested and universalized; it was not bound by the victims' ethnic communities or by their gender. The question of who "owns" the history of
the fire has elicited different responses over time. The memory and
continued commemorations of the Triangle Fire have continued precisely because of the universalizing interpretations brought to the fire
by labor activists and historians, fiction and essay writers, poets, and
filmmakers. In the past fifteen years, feminists, scholars and activists
alike, have restored gender as an important feature of the story. Because this horrible event speaks to multiple constituencies, it is remembered as an *American* event when so many other tragedies have been
rather quickly forgotten.

The Triangle Shirtwaist Company was an integral part of the imagined community of the Lower East Side not primarily because of its
geographical location; it stood on the margins of the Lower East Side,
in the Washington Square area, in a building on the corner of Washington Place and Greene streets. It played a major role in the immigrant Jewish consciousness because most of its five hundred workers
lived on the Lower East Side and because it had been, in the year and a
half before the fire, a focal point of the efforts to unionize the ladies'
garment industry, which employed so many immigrant Jewish workers.
Incidentally, the strike did not bring unionization to the Triangle Shirtwaist Company; its workers had to return to the shop without a union
contract (in large part because the system of internal contracting made
the company resistant to unionization).[3]

The fire captured the imagination of the immigrant Jewish community, though with less emphasis on the female gender of the vast
majority of victims than one might expect (and no mention of the Italian workers who perished). When the *Forverts* printed studio photographs of twenty of the victims on March 27th, only four of them were
men, and the paper did not comment on the disproportionate number
of women among the dead.[4] Morris Rosenfeld, the sweatshop poet, published an emotional poem on the first page of the *Forverts* four days
after the fire. Damning the rich and "the system," he memorialized the
dead in specifically Jewish terms: "Now let us light the holy candles /
And mark the sorrow / of Jewish masses in darkness and poverty / This
is our funeral / These our graves / Our children . . . "[5] Similarly, the
paper evoked a Jewish disaster, the Kishinev pogrom, to describe the
scenes of mourning at the morgue, reminiscent of "the Kishinev cemetery after the slaughter."[6] It recounted human interest stories, of girls
who had been planning weddings and had funerals instead, of individual women who had not yet been identified days after their deaths.[7]

The fire also entered popular immigrant Yiddish culture through a song written by J. M. Rumshishky in 1911, "'Mamenyu' or Mourning for the Triangle Fire Victims"; its lyrics, about an orphan boy on the one hand and a mother mourning her dead daughter on the other, surprisingly make no explicit reference to the Triangle Fire itself.[8] A *tkhine*, a Yiddish prayer written for a largely female audience, published in a 1916 collection of such prayers by the Hebrew Publishing Company and republished at least once, was dedicated to those who died in fires and was understood to refer to the Triangle Fire.[9]

However, the public funeral held on April 5th for the (then) eight unidentified victims of the fire revealed the fact that the memorialization was not left to the immigrant Jewish (or immigrant Italian) community alone, even though the leaflets of the labor movement calling on "fellow Workers" to join the funeral procession were written in Yiddish and Italian as well as English.[10] With the passage of time the memory of the fire has been borne primarily by organized workers and recently by working-class feminists as well.

Labor activists and social reformers took charge of bringing the lessons of the fire to the larger civic community. The ILGWU and the Women's Trades Union League (WTUL), the cross-class women's association of wealthy reformers and workers, used the fire to argue for heightened safety regulations and greater concern for the conditions of workers in general. The vigorous presence of the WTUL and of female labor activists, especially Rose Schneiderman, brought gender visually into the communal response, but labor women and their supporters did not focus specifically on women's concerns. Instead, while acknowledging the special vulnerability of women, they stressed the need to protect all workers from the potentially hazardous environment of the shops.[11] Only at one meeting was the issue of gender highlighted. A rally sponsored on March 31st by the Collegiate Equal Suffrage League presented women's suffrage as a necessity for ensuring workers' rights. Women had died because they were not able to act politically. A banner on the platform pronounced, "We demand for all women the right to protect themselves." In her speech, Dr. Anna Shaw, a well-known suffragist, turned to the men in the audience and proclaimed, "If you are incompetent, then in the name of Heaven, stand aside and let us try."[12]

The day after the fire, the WTUL convened the first protest meeting of labor and civic leaders; the meeting resulted in the formation of a committee, headed by Rabbi Stephen Wise, to draft new safety legislation.[13] Members of the Joint Relief Committee and the Red Cross conducted studies, which they subsequently published, on the economic needs of the families of the fire's victims.[14] On April 2nd, the WTUL succeeded in bringing together at the Metropolitan Opera House persons from every neighborhood of New York City, from the Lower East Side to the Upper East Side, as well as clergy of every religious affiliation. Jacob Schiff, then the treasurer of the New York chapter of the Red Cross, presided, and the meeting adopted a resolution calling for the establishment of a Bureau of Fire Prevention and more extensive safety regulations.[15] The New York City Fire Department and the fire extinguishing industry also weighed in, calling for mandatory use of automatic sprinklers. The General Fire Extinguisher Company even issued a special edition of its *Automatic Sprinkler Bulletin*, dedicated to the Triangle Fire and entitled "The Life Hazard of Fireproof Buildings and Its Cure."[16]

Responding to the public concern over the loss of life, New York City newspapers condemned the poor formulation and enforcement of safety regulations for workers far more often than they pointed to the culpability of the owners.[17] They called for legislation mandating the installation of new fire-fighting equipment. The socialist press was less concerned with safety regulations developed within a capitalist system than in labeling the consequences of the fire a crime. After the two owners of the Triangle Shirtwaist factory were found not guilty of manslaughter in a December 1911 trial, the *International Socialist Review* printed an article entitled "God Did It" that reported: "A New York jury composed of capitalistic cockroaches has absolved Harris and Blanck of the murder of 147 [sic] young workers in the Triangle Shirtwaist Factory fire of March 25, 1911."[18]

As Arthur Goren has pointed out, the fact that there were different groups vying for ownership of the public commemoration of the Triangle Fire became evident when funeral plans were made for its unidentified victims. Orthodox Jewish circles challenged the decision of Local 25 of the Waistmakers union, the WTUL, and the Workmen's Circle, a Jewish socialist group, to hold a silent march as part of the public funeral because they feared the politicization of a religious ritual. Political figures also sought to ban a "labor parade." Christian clergy, along with political leaders, opposed burial in a Jewish cemetery. In the end, the march took place with two distinct groups—downtown immigrant Jewish unions and uptown labor, socialist and women's suffrage leaders—converging from two different directions. The victims were buried in an ecumenical ceremony in the non-sectarian Evergreen cemetery in Brooklyn.[19]

It was the labor movement that ultimately assumed ownership of the memory of the fire by adopting the incident as a potent symbol of

Paula E. Hyman

the need for the unionization and political mo-
bilization of workers. It was the labor movement that committed itself to the annual commemoration of the fire, a ritual that continues
to this day.[20] For many labor activists, the fire
was a transforming event that brought home to
them the critical necessity of their work. David
Dubinsky, later president of the ILGWU, attributed his life-long commitment to the labor
movement to the fire, and Fannia Cohn, a
prominent labor activist, wrote that "it was the
Triangle fire that decided my life's course."[21]
Elizabeth Hasanovitz, too, who heard about the
Triangle Fire while still in Russia, describes the
moment of silence in her shop on March 25,
1914, as well as the union-sponsored memorial
that evening as an important lesson in her
political education.[22] As historian Annelise Orleck summed up the impact of the fire on women
labor activists, "The fire and the factory inves-
tigations that followed left an imprint on the
women that recast their political priorities and
cemented their relations with one another."[23]

For the labor movement, the fire was first
and foremost an issue of class, not of ethnicity
or of gender—an issue that exposed the true nature of capitalism. At the April 2 Carnegie Hall
meeting, Rose Schneiderman indicted American society and its laws:

> We have tried you good people of the public—and
> we have found you wanting . . . The strong hand of
> the law beats us back when we rise—back into the
> conditions that make life unbearable . . . I can't talk
> fellowship to you who are gathered here. Too much
> blood has been spilled. I know from experience it is
> up to the working people to save themselves. And the only way is through a
> strong working-class movement.[24]

Some twenty years later, Fannia Cohn referred to the Triangle Fire to
send the same message. In an article that appeared in 1934 in the
ILGWU's paper *Justice*, she wrote,

> The best memorial for our martyrs of the Triangle Fire and the many others
> who sacrifice their health and very lives in their effort to build our Union, is

Fig. 3.1 In the aftermath of the Triangle
Fire, labor activists joined together to
mourn the dead and demand
improvements in working conditions.
Courtesy of Kheel Center, Cornell
University, Ithaca, New York.

a resolve to continue our efforts to have the workers more strongly united in the economic and political fields, coupled with a workers' education movement that would help to create a new environment lending itself to fundamental political, social and economic changes dictated by working class needs.[25]

In their commemorations of the fire, labor leaders continued to invoke the issue of worker safety. At the fiftieth anniversary commemoration in 1961, representatives of the ILGWU, the New York City Fire Department, and New York University (which by then owned the building), as well as Eleanor Roosevelt and Frances Perkins and twelve elderly survivors of the fire, joined to honor the victims. David Dubinsky, president of the ILGWU, addressed the audience of five hundred, calling for Governor Nelson Rockefeller's veto of the Albert-Folmer bill recently passed by the state legislature. That bill, which he called an outrage and which the ILGWU journal *Justice* labeled the "Firetrap Bill," would have delayed for more than a year the implementation of legislation requiring new fire safety measures that had been endorsed by the New York City Fire Commissioner.[26] The ILGWU has also frequently sponsored exhibitions to mark the anniversary of the fire.[27] Finally, the labor movement was responsible for the two plaques that are affixed to the Asch building, now renamed the Brown Building. The first was placed by the ILGWU itself in 1961, the second, by the National Park Service in 1991, launching its Labor History National Historical Landmark theme.[28] In 1994, the New York State Department of Labor distributed a commemorative flyer that attributed its own founding to the Triangle Fire.[29]

With the recognition of the fire as a universal symbol of worker exploitation, the specific ethnic dimensions of the fire have been lost. The ILGWU flyer for a rally to be held on the anniversary of the Triangle Fire in 1994 used the 1911 incident as an opportunity to protest contemporary fires in Asian factories. Reflecting its current constituency, the ILGWU printed its text in English and Spanish.[30] U.S. Secretary of Labor Robert Reich invoked the fire in a similar manner in 1996 when he placed a public service announcement entitled "No Sweat" on the Internet. Referring explicitly to the "needless" deaths of the Triangle Shirtwaist Factory Fire, the announcement focused on laborers in California working in similar conditions and illustrated its call for consumers to boycott sweatshop products. The Internet site showed a picture of an Asian-American woman worker.[31] With the rise of feminism, women's labor and feminist organizations have recently participated actively in the commemoration of the fire. In 1990, for example, N.O.W., the New York City Coalition of Labor Union

Fig. 3.2 This plaque commemorating the Triangle Fire was placed on the Asch Building (now the Brown Building, on New York University's campus) by the International Ladies Garment Workers Union. Below it is another plaque indicating that the building was registered as a National Historic Landmark in 1991. Photograph by Eli Diner.

Women, and the Women's International League for Peace and Freedom were among the organizers of the annual ritual.[32]

As the Triangle Fire became an American, rather than an American *Jewish*, story, it attracted the attention of writers and filmmakers. In the multicultural environment of late-twentieth-century America, the fire points to the common experience of American workers of diverse ethnic origins and religious backgrounds. Chris Llewellyn introduces her book of poems on the fire with an author's note that the Triangle Factory's workers, nearly all of whom were female, were "primarily Russian or Italian, although twelve nationalities were known to be 'on the books.'"[33] For two authors of recent children's books on the fire, the story offers a reassuring message—that even tragedies have a positive impact on American life. Zachary Kent concludes his rather lurid nonfiction account of the fire, illustrated with photographs and stressing the inadequacy of safety regulations at the time, with the statement that "[F]rom the ashes of the tragic Triangle factory fire came help for millions of United States laborers today."[34] Similarly, Holly Littlefield's fictional *Fire at the Triangle Factory* includes an afterword that notes that "it became clear to many people that the laws needed to be changed."[35] At the center of her story she places a specifically American theme, the ability of Americans to transcend differences. The young heroines of the tale are a Jew and a Catholic whose difference is framed more in terms of religion than ethnicity and whose friendship contributes to their survival.

Similar messages pervade the television docudrama "The Triangle Factory Fire Scandal," broadcast in 1979.[36] In the Triangle Shirtwaist Factory of the filmmakers, Jewish and Italian workers are one big, happy family, equally (if erroneously) represented among the labor force. They not only work side by side but they converse and joke, in English, of course, and attend each other's parties. Although all are recent immigrants who share aspirations for success in America, the conflict between the Old World and the New is presented only in a Jewish context, perhaps because the producers as well as the directors of the film seem to have been Jews or perhaps because of the influence of the film *The Jazz Singer*. Sonya, a Jewish worker, who has previously declared, "We can dream, we can be anything we want," later laments, "My father doesn't understand about America." Although several of the main characters die in the fire—one romantically involved couple with the *sh'ma* (the Jewish affirmation of faith) on their lips—the film ends on an upbeat note. Life goes on, notes a heading, and the spiffily dressed survivors jauntily proceed to the Easter parade (which took place only weeks after the fire). Nor did the victims die in vain, for the film concludes by noting that in the wake of the fire the ILGWU gained support and strength, new safety standards were put in place, and a state commission of labor was established.

The Discovery Channel Online has produced a web site entitled "The Great Triangle Fire" which is less fanciful than the television docudrama but which assesses its impact in similar terms. After recounting the story of the horror, the narrative concludes with the "profound impact" of the Triangle Fire on "fire safety and labor laws" and on American politics in general. The author of the text, freelance writer Thomas Bedell, asserts that Frances Perkins, Franklin Roosevelt's secretary of labor, "witnessed the tragedy [and] claimed the seeds of the New Deal sprouted from the Triangle Fire's ashes." In a section called "Tragedy Repeats Itself," the site also includes descriptions of factory fires of the late twentieth century.[37]

Fire at the Triangle Factory

by Holly Littlefield
illustrations by Mary O'Keefe Young

Beyond Place and Ethnicity

I learned just how much the fire has been universalized and incorporated into American legend when a Yale undergraduate working in the library told me that his high school marching band, in Annapolis, Maryland, had named itself the Tilden Triangle Fire Band. Why? To contrast a political tragedy—Tilden's failure to attain the presidency in 1876 despite winning the popular vote—with a real, personal tragedy, the fire. The teenagers had the good sense to see the two tragedies in different terms.

Recent poetry evoked by the Triangle Fire also builds on the universal elements of the event. Robert Pinsky, America's poet laureate, incorporates the Triangle Fire, "the infamous blaze," into his poem "Shirt," a meditation on the many words necessary to describe a shirt and its making(s). Although the fire is the centerpiece of the poem, its victims lack all ethnicity. Only contemporary workers figure as ethnic beings in the poem—Korean and Malaysian sweatshop workers in the first stanza and "a Black/Lady in South Carolina" named Irma, toward the end.[38]

Several contemporary female labor poets have focused on the Triangle Fire as a powerful marker of injustice, bringing gender and class together as the double sources of women workers' oppression.[39] Their poetry is explicitly political. Chris Llewellyn, who, as mentioned, wrote an entire book of poems on the Triangle Fire, encountered the incident when she was doing research for International Women's Day in 1978.[40] Her book, *Fragments from the Fire*, which won the Walt Whitman Award for 1986, presents the experience through the eyes of the working-class women who were its victims, as do the other female poets. This poetry reflects the ongoing working-class appropriation of the Triangle Fire as well as the rediscovery of its gendered dimensions. As Janet Zandy, who has identified a phenomenon she has labeled "fire poetry," notes, "The Triangle Fire seems to tap a collective memory of class oppression and injustice—especially for women. What is distinctive about the 'fire poetry' is that most of the contemporary writers do not work in the garment trade, nor are they from New York City nor of the same race or ethnicity as the workers. What the writers have in common is gender and class, a connection to other female workers, and a call to tell the story so it won't be forgotten . . . This event . . . becomes through memory and language and history a catalyst for breaking silence and recovering working-class identity."[41]

When poets tell the story, history takes second place to artistic or ideological considerations. All of the poets, including Pinsky, ignore some of the factual evidence, claiming variously that there were no fire escapes or that all the doors of the factory were locked. These inaccuracies serve as another example of the disjuncture of history and memory.

Despite the popular lack of concern with historical accuracy in literary reflections on the fire, historians have also preserved, and shaped, the memory of the fire for several communities of students and scholars. The scholarly memory of the fire has mirrored the original constituencies touched by the event: Historians of labor, the garment industry, immigrant Jewry, and women have explored the fire and its significance or mentioned it in passing in their work.[42] All historians who have studied the fire have focused on the victimization of workers in the age of unregulated capitalism and on the fire's impact in mobilizing immigrant workers, including women, on behalf of the union movement in the garment industry. Although the Jewishness of the majority of the victims is acknowledged, to general historians it is an incidental attribute, of no great interest.

For American historians who are sensitive to the multi-ethnic and class dimensions of their field, the fire is an American story, indeed one of the most dramatic in American history. With contemporary emphasis on social, labor, and women's history, the Triangle fire has been integrated into the narrative of American history. For example, *The Way We Lived: Essays and Documents in American Social History*, a 1988 collection, includes in its second volume a reference related to the fire. (On the other hand, an older textbook on American labor history, *Labor in America*, which focuses on institutional and political change in the labor movement from the top down, does not mention the Triangle Fire at all).[43] A recent documentary sourcebook for college students, entitled *The Triangle Strike and Fire*, points out that the Triangle strike and fire "are key events in various approaches to U.S. history: women's studies, labor history, cultural studies, and ethnic studies. *The Triangle Strike and Fire* is an appropriate supplement for courses related to the areas listed above, as well as survey courses and courses in Twentieth-Century U.S. and the Progressive era."[44] Despite the nod to ethnic studies, none of the documents in the book is drawn from a Yiddish or Italian source. Further, the collection of sources appears to address directly only issues in labor history and the role of reformers in improving the conditions of workers.

Labor historians, concerned with the lessons of the fire for contemporary working conditions in the garment industry, have pioneered disseminating material about the fire to students. The Kheel Center for Labor-Management Documentation and Archives of Cornell University, in cooperation with UNITE (the Union of Needletrades, Industrial and Textile Employees, the successor union forged from the merger of the ILGWU and the Amalgamated Clothing Workers), has prepared a multi-page web site that contains textual and visual documents, such as newspaper coverage of the fire and the subsequent investigation, oral histories, photographs, and political cartoons, as well as a substantial bibliography of primary and secondary sources on sweatshops, the fire, and the labor movement. Its target audience is high school students who might seek to write a term paper on the incident. Such a site, with its concern for contextualization and its attention to how documents must be used in research, asserts that knowledge about the fire is central to an understanding of the experience of the American working class and of the growth of the American labor movement.[45]

Most surprising is the range of contemporary references to the fire in unlikely places, for example, in a publication on causality in industrial accidents, which highlighted the fire as its central example, and in recent articles in journals of law and building safety.[46] Nor did I expect to find a 1997 essay by Stephen Jay Gould in *Natural History* that reflects extensively on the fire in a consideration of the misapplication of principles of biological evolution by social Darwinists.[47] Beginning with the personal—his office in the Brown Building and the fact that his grandmother worked in a garment factory in New York City in 1911 (but luckily not the Triangle Factory)—Gould proceeds to use the fire to illustrate how social Darwinists, in arguing that social inequality was natural and inevitable, succeeded in preventing the "regulation of industry to insure better working conditions for laborers."[48]

The Triangle Shirtwaist Fire has long moved beyond the confines of the Lower East Side and its Jewish community. It is an event in American history—its memory and commemoration carried on by those who feel a close connection to its victims because they presume to share the most important aspect of their experience: their class or their gender or both. Ironically, at the end of the twentieth century it is not primarily Jews, for the most part comfortably settled in the middle class, who remember the travails of their working-class immigrant forbears. For American Jews, the Triangle Shirtwaist Fire is no longer a central evocative symbol. American Jews are far removed from their working-class past, and the Lower East Side they seek to remember is suffused with nostalgia, but not with pain. It is the mythic launching pad for success, not the site of suffering. In the category of twentieth-century horrors that American Jews do remember and commemorate, the Triangle Shirtwaist Fire can be only a footnote.

NOTES

1. Twenty men were among the victims of the fire. See Janet Zandy, "Fire Poetry on the Triangle Shirtwaist Company Fire of March 25, 1911," *College Literature* 24, no. 3 (October 1997): 33.

2. *Forverts*, March 26, 1911, p. 1.

3. On the female activists involved in the unionization drive, see Annelise

Orleck, *Common Sense and a Little Fire: Women and Working-Class Politics, 1900–1965* (Chapel Hill: University of North Carolina Press, 1995).

4. *Forverts*, March 27, 1911, p. 1.

5. As printed in Leon Stein, *The Triangle Fire* (Philadelphia and New York: J. B. Lippincott, 1962), pp. 145–146. A member of the ILGWU and the editor of *Justice*, Stein wrote what remains the only comprehensive study of the fire and its aftermath.

6. *Forverts*, March 27, 1911, p. 5.

7. Ibid., p. 1; *Forverts*, March 28, 1911, p. 1, and March 30, 1911, p. 8.

8. Poster for the song, in my possession. See also Mark Slobin, *Tenement Songs: The Popular Music of the Jewish Immigrants* (Urbana: University of Illinois Press, 1982), pp. 134–135. The song title was (mis)translated as "Including an Elegy to the Triangle Fire Victims."

9. Yitzhok Shloyme Meyer, "Material and Notices: American Tekhines" [Yiddish], *YIVO Bleter* 39 (1955): 272–274.

10. Arthur Aryeh Goren, "Sacred and Secular: The Place of Public Funerals in the Immigrant Life of American Jews," *Jewish History* 8, no. 1–2 (1994): 284–286. Subsequently, one of the eight was identified by a family member. The leaflet is reproduced in *Justice*, March 15, 1961, p. 1.

11. Rose Schneiderman (1882–1972) was a prominent Jewish labor leader who became president of the WTUL and the only woman on the Labor Advisory Board of Franklin Roosevelt's National Recovery Administration. See her autobiography, *All for One* (with Lucy Goldthwaite) (New York: Paul S. Eriksson, 1967), and Orleck, *Common Sense and a Little Fire*. On the WTUL and Schneiderman's involvement, see Nancy Schrom Dye, *As Equals and as Sisters: Feminism, Unionism, and the Women's Trade Union League of New York* (New York: Columbia University Press, 1980), and Elizabeth Anne Payne, *Reform, Labor, and Feminism: Margaret Dreier Robins and the Women's Trade Union League* (Urbana: University of Illinois Press, 1988). See also Diane Kirby, "'The Wage Earning Woman and the State': The National Women's Trade Union League and Protective Labor Legislation, 1903–1923," *Labor History* 28, no. 1 (1978): 54–74.

12. Stein, *Triangle Fire*, pp. 138–139. The other speakers were Meyer London and Morris Hillquit.

13. Ibid., pp. 135–136.

14. See, for example, Elizabeth Dutcher, "Budget of the Triangle Fire Victims," *Life and Labor* 2 (September 1912); Report of the Joint Relief Committee, January 12, 1913, Tamiment Library, NYU.

15. Report of the Joint Relief Committee, pp. 142–143; *ILGWU News—History 1910–1911*, Tamiment Library, NYU.

16. *Automatic Sprinkler Bulletin*, Special Edition on the Triangle Fire, 1911, Tamiment Library, NYU.

17. "Murdered by Incompetent Government," editorial, *New York World*, March 27, 1911; *New York Daily Tribune*, March 27, March 29, April 3, 1911; *New York Herald*, March 27, 1911.

18. Phillips Russell, *International Socialist Review* 12, no. 8 (February 1912): 472–473. An earlier article in the same journal, 11, no. 11 (May 1911): 666–673, was entitled "The Murder of the Shirt Waist Makers."

19. Goren, "Sacred and Secular," pp. 284–286; Stein, *Triangle Fire*, p. 156.

20. For a recent commemoration, see *New York Times*, March 26, 1998.

21. As cited in Gerald Sorin, *A Time for Building: The Third Migration* (Baltimore: Johns Hopkins University Press, 1992), p. 130, and his *The Prophetic Minority: American Jewish Immigrant Radicals, 1880–1920* (Bloomington: Indiana University Press, 1985), p. 85. On Fannia Cohn, see Orleck, *Common Sense and a Little Fire*.

22. Elizabeth Hasanovitz, *One of Them: Chapters from a Passionate Autobiography* (Boston and New York: Houghton Mifflin, 1918), pp. 213–223.

23. Orleck, *Common Sense and a Little Fire*, p. 130.

24. *New York Times*, April 3, 1911. Cited in Stein, *Triangle Fire*, pp. 144–145. Ironically, Schneiderman became an important figure in the cross-class Women's Trade Union League.

25. Fannia Cohn, "Triangle Memory Lives Again," *Justice*, April 1934, p. 13.

26. *New York Times*, March 26, 1961, pp. 1, 66; *Justice*, April 1, 1961, p. 1; article by Esther Peterson, Assistant to the Secretary of Labor, *RWDSU Record*, March 26, 1961.

27. For example, flyers for ILGWU exhibits in 1986 and 1992, Tamiment Library, NYU.

28. Deborah E. Bernhardt, in *CRM—National Park Service*, vol. 17, pp. 33–34; *Labor's Heritage*, 6, no. 4 (Spring 1995): 41.

29. "The Triangle Fire Tragedy Forged the New York State Department of Labor," Flyer, March 1994, Tamiment Library, NYU.

30. Flyer, March 1994, Tamiment Library, NYU.

31. "No Sweat: Help End Sweatshop Conditions for American Workers": http://www.dol.gov/dol/opa/public/nosweat/offback.htm

32. Flyer, Tamiment Library, NYU.

33. Chris Llewellyn, *Fragments from the Fire* (New York: Viking Penguin, 1987), p. vii.

34. Zachary Kent, *The Story of the Triangle Factory Fire* (Chicago: Children's Press, 1989), p. 31.

35. Holly Littlefield, *Fire at the Triangle Factory* (Minneapolis: Carolrhoda Books, 1996).

36. *The Triangle Factory Fire Scandal*, directed by Mel Stuart, released in 1979 and broadcast on ABC, National Jewish Archive of Broadcasting, New York City.

37. Discovery Channel Online, "The Great Triangle Fire": http://www.discovery. com/DCO/doc/1012/world/history/trianglefire/weblinks.html

38. Robert Pinsky, *The Figured Wheel: New and Collected Poems, 1966–1996* (New York: Farrar, Straus and Giroux, 1996), pp. 84–85. The poem was first published in 1990.

39. Janet Zandy, "The Fire Poems," *Women's Studies Quarterly* 1 and 2 (1995): 169–170, followed by Carol Tarlen's poem "Sisters in the Flames," pp. 171–172, and Safiya Henderson-Holmes's poem "rituals of spring," pp. 173–177. For a longer analysis of the fire poetry, see Janet Zandy, "Fire Poetry," pp. 33–54.

40. *Service Employees Union* 3, no.1 (February/March 1989); Llewellyn, *Fragments from the Fire*.

41. Zandy, "Fire Poems," p. 170.

42. See, for example, Irving Howe, *World of Our Fathers: The Journey of the East European Jews to America and the Life They Found and Made* (New York: Simon and

Schuster, 1976); Sorin, *A Time for Building*; Alice Kessler-Harris, "Organizing the Unorganizable: Three Jewish Women and Their Union," *Labor History* 17 (Winter 1976): 5–23; Susan Glenn, *Daughters of the Shtetl: Life and Labor in the Immigrant Generation* (Ithaca, N.Y.: Cornell University Press, 1990); Orleck, *Common Sense*; Melvyn Dubofsky, *When Workers Organize* (Amherst: University of Massachusetts Press, 1968); Leon Stein, ed., *Out of the Sweatshop: The Struggle for Industrial Democracy* (New York: Quadrangle/The New York Times Book Co., 1977); Meredith Tax, *The Rising of the Women: Feminist Solidarity and Class Conflict, 1880–1917* (New York and London: Monthly Review Press, 1980); Sara Eisenstein, *Give Us Bread but Give Us Roses: Working Class Women's Consciousness in the United States, 1890 to the First World War* (London and Boston: Routledge and Kegan Paul, 1983); Joan M. Jensen and Sue Davidson, eds., *A Needle, a Bobbin, a Strike: Women Needleworkers in America* (Philadelphia: Temple University Press, 1984); Carolyn Daniel McCreesh, *Women in the Campaign to Organize Garment Workers, 1880–1917* (New York: Garland Press, 1985); Payne, *Reform, Labor, and Feminism*; and Noralee Frankel and Nancy S. Dye, eds., *Gender, Class, Race, and Reform in the Progressive Era* (Lexington: University of Kentucky Press, 1991).

43. Frederick M. Binder and David M. Reimers, eds., *The Way We Lived: Essays and Documents in American Social History* (Lexington, Mass.: D. C. Heath, 1988). The 4th edition of *Labor in America: A History* (Arlington Heights, Ill.: Harlan Davidson), by Foster Rhea Dulles and Melvyn Dubofsky, was published in 1984.

44. Promotional leaflet distributed by Harcourt Brace for John F. McClymer's new book, *The Triangle Strike and Fire* (New York: Harcourt Brace, 1997).

45. "The Triangle Shirtwaist Factory Fire," Kheel Center, Cornell University: http://www.ilr.cornell.edu/trianglefire/cover.html
A smaller web site has been prepared by the *Encyclopedia Britannica*. See "Triangle Shirtwaist Company Fire," Women in American History by Encyclopedia Britannica: http://women.eb.com/women/articles/Triangle_Shirtwaist_Company_fire.html

46. Arthur F. McEvoy, *The Triangle Shirtwaist Factory Fire of 1911: Social Change, Industrial Accidents, and the Evolution of Commonsense Causality* (Chicago: American Bar Association, 1994); "Building Codes and Life Safety," *Building Renovation* (Winter 1994): 43–46; Mary Galvin, "The New Fire Triangle: Putting the Prosecutor on the Team," *Police Chief* 97, no. 12 (December 1990): 50; Marcia Chambers, "Lessons from the Triangle Factory Fire," *National Law Journal* 12, no. 38 (May 28, 1990): 13.

47. Stephen Jay Gould, "A Tale of Two Worksites," *Natural History* 106, no. 9 (October 1997): 18, 20, 22, 29, 62, 64–68.

48. Ibid., p. 67.

The Ghetto Girl
and the Erasure
of Memory

Riv-Ellen Prell

In his masterful meditation on twentieth-century fieldwork among the indigenous people of Brazil, *Tristes Tropiques*, the anthropologist Claude Lévi-Strauss posed the dilemma of historical and ethnographic knowledge. Arguing in 1955 that the world of "primitive" civilization was lost forever to the creeping "monoculture" of modern society, he wrote, "I am subject to a double infirmity: All that I perceive offends me and I constantly reproach myself for not seeing as much as I should."[1] He lamented that what he observed was a tragic diminishment of a once vital world, yet paradoxically scholars of the future would in turn decry their inability to have seen at least as much as he did.

Lévi-Strauss posed another dilemma. Even were he to have access to that lost world, he still could not understand it. "For every five years I move back in time, I am able to save a custom, gain a ceremony or share in another belief," he wrote. "But I know the texts too well not to realize that going back a century, I am forgoing data and lines of inquiry which would offer intellectual enrichment."[2] Without the tools of analysis and contemporary theory, he suggested, the world he longed to understand would nevertheless remain inaccessible.

Chroniclers of the vital world of New York's immigrant Lower East Side appear to share few of Lévi-Strauss's dilemmas. It was a world neither pristine nor remote. Historians, social scientists, and writers may readily look to a wide variety of sources to reconstruct the story of that time and place. Through print, photography and film, they can "see" what was seen by journalists, writers, social welfare workers, and others who believed that they "captured" what was most important about that classic site of Jewish immigrant life.

Nevertheless, the record that remains hardly resolves this conundrum; rather, it allows us to ask more forcefully, what did those who described and analyzed the Lower East Side see, and why? How do we interpret what a great number of experts claimed to know? How do the more contemporary "lines of inquiry" of feminist and cultural studies scholarship help us to understand what we might have seen had we been there?

I pose this problem in order to understand not *how* the paradigmatic world of immigrant New York is remembered, but to learn *what* about that world has been forgotten. In my reconstruction and deconstruction of the Ghetto Girl, a long-forgotten stereotype of that period, I find clues to that process. "She" was a young working woman whose taste was too conspicuous, her clothing too garish, and her makeup too excessive; she was betrayed by the cheapness of what she purchased and wore. Her wages financed her own excess, making her autonomous and beyond the control of the family. She was loud in public and immodest.

All of the names for this stereotypical "girl" tied her to a place. Whether she was described as an "East Side Girl" or a "Ghetto Girl," even on the rare occasions when her better qualities were invoked, she was always known by a geographic locale. Indeed, American-born journalists and writers discussed her well into the 1920s when the vast majority of Eastern European immigrants and their children had left the Lower East Side. Still, those undesirable qualities were associated with a place and a gender, which became inseparable in the stereotype. What was undesirable was attached to the experience of being an "outsider," a person yearning to get into the center who was constantly betrayed by qualities that she could not shed. In the eyes of Jews embarrassed by her "vulgarity," the ghetto clung to the skirts and hat feathers of a young woman with dreams for her future. As the Lower East Side was more than a place, and a Ghetto Girl not simply a woman from the ghetto, we look to both in order to understand why they were, when combined, so "dangerous" to other Jews.[3]

The Ghetto Girl served as a complex trope for the process of Americanization. The period's anxieties rested quite deliberately on the image of the body and desires of a young, autonomous, unmarried woman from the Lower East Side. Memory of "her" was erased when class mobility reconfigured American Jewish identity and anxiety differently. To understand why she was forgotten takes us to the crossroads of what Lévi-Strauss identified as both what we were unable to see and what, lacking key analytic frameworks, we would not have been able to comprehend. We should not be surprised to find gender, representation, and anxiety standing at that conceptual meeting-place in understanding New York's turn-of-the-century Lower East Side.[4]

Ironically, the monoculture that Lévi-Strauss had reason to decry, because it helped to create the urban slums and homogenized cultures of Brazil, is hardly divorced from the milieu of the Ghetto Girl. The anxieties that created her image were largely the making of a capitalist bourgeois culture. The discipline of the industrial work force, the intolerance for diversity, the anxiety about women's autonomy, and the emerging power of consumerist desire—all social processes that shaped the stereotype—were critical to Jews' experience of Americanization and their struggle with its effects.

An Anxious Image

The Ghetto Girl was the nightmare of excessive Americanization and desire projected by professionals and middle-class Jews onto young working-class Jewish women. To a lesser extent, it was also an image used by East Side male journalists. Neither their male contemporaries, nor the German Jewish young men and women who had come more than a half century before them, offered such a powerful and complex image of immigrant, American Jewish life. The "Ghetto Girl," in journalism, philanthropy, social work, and drama, to mention only a few of the settings where this image was circulated, was a lightning rod for the sentiments and anxieties that beset those undertaking Americanization. All those threatened by the image of the Ghetto Girl were concerned about being barred in one or another way from the nation because they were Jews.

The Ghetto Girl stereotype emerged in the early years of the twentieth century with the first signs of economic optimism on the Lower East Side following the late-nineteenth-century economic depression in the United States. Rising economic hopefulness was partially realized in the emergence of a small middle class of immigrant Jews on the

East Side. Irving Howe noted that the Lower East Side's "social land-scape" grew far more complex in this period.[5] No longer a flat world of shared impoverishment, it now held a variety of complex, internal distinctions determined by length of residence, occupation, income, education, and an Americanization measured by style, manners, and language.

What complicated that landscape poignantly was the extent to which its markers of difference sometimes reflected the various accusations of those who sought to restrict immigration from Eastern Europe and to impose barriers on Jews' access to the nation's institutions.[6] Classic stereotypes of Jewish avarice, cunning, and incivility, among others, were the stuff not only of antisemitic slurs, but also of cultural differentiation among Jews. If a young Jewish woman living in the ghetto was portrayed by other Jews as lacking taste, as overly acquisitive, or as not fitting in with American values, what was said of her and her home were the very rationales used to exclude all Eastern European Jews from American citizenship.[7]

The Ghetto Girl came to life just as East Side immigrants began more fully to imagine that others like them could Americanize and join the middle class. Such aspirations did not make these Jews more tolerable to Uptown German Jews, for whom the East Side became a nightmare as American society increasingly placed affluent Jews outside a circle of social acceptance. Once embraced by an elite Protestant American society, they were now rejected when the ideology of Anglo-Saxon purity emerged to cement a new alliance between entrepreneurs and old-stock Americans against German Jews.[8] Increasingly, affluent Uptown German Jews were portrayed as indistinguishable from Downtown immigrant Jews with whom they felt little or no kinship.

This antisemitism intensified conflicts among Jews. Not only did middle-class Jews see in their poor and working-class counterparts liabilities to acculturation, but Jewish men often accused Jewish women of vulgarity, a term with which the patrician class branded them. One group of Jews' effort to embrace and then hold dear the propriety of bourgeois life was undermined by another group. "Jew" became a frightening phantom that could haunt those Jewish men and women who aspired to, or felt well rooted in, America's tolerant and liberal middle class.

This volatile mix found expression in the representation of the body of the young Jewish woman from the Lower East Side whose style, appearance, and desires became an alternative stage on which Jews and Christian Americans anxiously debated what it meant to be an American and a Jew. In the period of American Jewish experience often called the Age of Optimism, because of expanding economic opportunities and the development of an organizational life, this Jewish gender stereotype revealed the extent and complexity of Jewish anxiety as Jews Americanized.[9]

The danger of a "vulgar" Jewish woman for established Jews lay in the fact that if any Jew's life whispered excess, or the open pursuit of pleasure, non-Jews might more aggressively enforce their boundaries between insiders and outsiders. In an environment of increased discrimination and multiplying stereotypes whose racism erased intra-Jewish differences, the Ghetto Girl image emerged and crossed over—between Jews and Jews, and Jews and non-Jews, within and across class, between women and among them—to articulate the deep anxieties of being a Jew in New York and the nation.[10]

The Bourgeois Response: Containing Jewish Desire

In 1900, a *New York Tribune* journalist, interested in new immigrants, compared Jewish women on the Lower East Side to those who lived in fashionable upper Manhattan.

> Does Broadway (upper New York) wear a feather? Grand Street (lower Eastside) dons two, without loss of time. Are trailing skirts seen in Fifth-ave.? Grand-st. trails its yards with a dignity all its own. Are daring color effects sent over from Paris? The rainbow hides its diminished head before Grand-st. on a Sunday afternoon.
>
> If my lady wears a velvet gown, put together for her in an East Side sweat shop, may not the girl whose tired fingers fashioned it rejoice her soul by astonishing Grand-st. with a copy of it on the next Sunday? My lady's is in velvet, and the East Side girl's is in the cheapest of cloth, but it's the style that counts![11]

By turns sympathetic and ironic, the journalist suggested that East Side young Jewish seamstresses were doomed in their efforts to imitate the wealthy. The pattern failed to provide the good taste. They substituted excess for style, the inexpensive for the elegant, and hence failed in their pretense. Ghetto Girls were inseparable, mirror images of outsiders who failed to measure up to American life.

A journalist for the English-language Jewish press approached the young, female perpetrator of excess differently. Writing not with the detached, ironic tone of the American writer, she expressed "shame . . . anger (and) hurt" at seeing the behavior of East Side Jewish women:

> the fashionable dress of the East-side girls shrieks its cheapness and mimicry of the real thing. . . . Her exaggerated coiffure, with its imitation curls and soaped curves that stick out at the side of the head like fantastic gargoyles, is an offense to the eye. Her plated gold jewelry with paste stones, bought from

"DID I PUT TOO MUCH ON, POP?"

Fig. 4.1 This cartoon, a weekly feature known as "East-Sidelights," appeared in the *Jewish Daily Forward* on 17 July 1927. The young woman, dressed as a flapper, asks a janitor if her makeup is excessive. The cartoonist draws both of his characters—a worker at the bottom of occupations and a "new" woman—unsympathetically. Her use of slang, her makeup, and her style all mark her as undesirable. Courtesy of The Forward Association, Inc.

the Grand Street peddlers on pay-day reveals its cheapness by its very extravagance. What is the matter with this girl? Is this bad taste acquired? Is it inherent in her character? Or is it simply a transient mood of the immigrant? Or perhaps is the East-side girl quite normal in taste and all this talk just prejudice? These questions I have heard wrangled and argued so often.[12]

Marion Golde suggested (in 1918) that a Jew's anxiety over the issue was not shared by others who were confronted with a Ghetto or East Side girl. Whether the Ghetto Girl's taste was the product of an "inherent" weakness or a stage in Americanization, Jews' "racial" kinship made the Ghetto Girl a problem for the entire group. The Ghetto Girl failed to meet the ideal of an American woman who should be coquettish but not excessive, and fashionable without being garish. She failed as a Jew because her exaggeration brought pain to her "race."[13]

In addition to those who wrote in English, bourgeois Yiddish writers and journalists remarked upon the styles and excesses of Jewish women, and advocated for the need for good taste and restraint for Jewish immigrants. Tashrak, the pen name of Israel Zevin, a journalist, humorist, and the author of a popular etiquette book for Yiddish-speaking immigrants, wrote about women's dress:

It is actually among the poorer classes that women blindly follow the dictates of fashion. . . . It is awful what poor taste most Jewish girls have. Consider the garish colors you can see on a Saturday or a holiday on Jewish streets. If fashion decrees that women should wear red (this season), does it follow that a woman with red hair and freckles must dress in a color that makes her look like a scarecrow?[14]

Tashrak did not recoil with shame and horror or call upon his race to deal with the problem of fashion. But he singled out young Jewish women for being unable to discern the difference between good taste and fashion.

Not surprisingly, even rabbis commented on the subject. In 1916, Rabbi Israel Levinthal of Petach Tikvah synagogue in Brooklyn, New York, delivered to his newly middle-class congregants a sermon that he titled "Style." He told the story of Dina, Jacob's daughter, who was raped by a prince of the Hivite people where Jacob's family was visiting (Genesis 34). Rabbi Levinthal told his congregants that "great Jewish sages" had already noted that Dina's misfortune came "because she went out to copy the fashions of the daughters of the land." He went on to exhort his congregants that "it was style, the fashion that reigned among the daughters of the land that fascinated her. What more needed lesson for our daughters, for our women of today. If I had the power I would have read aloud in every Jewish home the portion of the

Torah which contains our text and have them placed before every mother's eyes!"[15] The rabbi's biblical text underlined the dangerous path awaiting women who were interested in style.

Few articles or comments about Ghetto Girls were written simply as colorful descriptions of the new immigrants. In the reformist mood of the time, they normally carried a moral lesson, if not solutions to the "problem." Social workers and settlement-house professionals often evoked this image in their work. Lillian Wald, long-time director of New York's Henry Street Settlement House, reflected in her memoirs how she handled the excesses of the Ghetto Girl in the century's first decades. Like other reformers, Wald devoted most of her energies to Americanizing immigrants. She told "Bessie's story" in order to illustrate her methods for dealing with the troublesome habits of immigrant women. Wald invited Bessie to the "cozy intimacy of my sitting room." She wrote that the young woman immediately guessed that the summons was "on account of my yellow waist" (the shirtwaist was a popular style of blouse produced by garment workers, many of whom were young Jewish women). Wald continued, "It was easy to follow up her introduction by pointing out that pronounced lack of modesty in dressing was one of several signs; that their dancing, their talk, their freedom of manner all combined to render them conspicuous and to cause their friends anxiety."[16]

Wald believed that Bessie could conform to the vision of American womanhood she advocated—modesty, simplicity, and circumspect behavior—only by abandoning the garish waist. When Bessie protested that she could not simply throw away an item of clothing that she had recently purchased, Wald offered to buy the waist for what was at the time a large sum, the five dollars that Bessie had paid. Wald reported that her offer to buy the waist and burn it because Bessie's dignity was worth more than five dollars had considerable effect. Bessie responded to Wald's offer saying, "That strikes me as something grand. I wouldn't let you do it, but I'll never wear the waist again."[17]

Wald taught new values to immigrants by showing the Bessies of the Lower East Side just how highly she valued good taste. Young women's display of bright and "vulgar" clothes signaled to the middle class and to professional enforcers of middle-class values (social workers and teachers) that their most important lessons went unheeded. Hard work, thrift, and moderation were key to becoming good Americans. Curbing young women's desires was one of the most important foundations for this transformation.[18] In order to be accepted, Jews needed to be better, and Jewish women needed to be more exemplary than other women as they pursued an American life.[19]

Lillian Wald's memoir refers only indirectly to the gravest danger facing Bessie. Social service workers of the period were more anxious about unmarried women's sexual activity than about virtually any other vulnerability. An article on Jewish immigrant girls in Chicago by Viola Paradise, a social worker writing in 1913 for *Survey* (the first professional social workers' journal), was one of the few that explicitly linked immigrant women's consumer patterns and sexual desires. Paradise analyzed the Jewish woman's desire to "look stylish":

> The danger comes later when the girl realizes that she will never be able to afford as many and as nice clothes as she wants. Then she is in danger of taking a wrong way to get the luxuries which America has taught her to crave.[20]

Paradise was concerned that the Ghetto Girl would turn "the wrong way"—toward prostitution to support her taste for extravagance.[21] Many Progressives believed that "white slavery" or white women's prostitution preyed disproportionately on Jewish women.[22] The middle class was required to guard young women vigilantly by monitoring their clothing, behavior, and associations.

Reformers' fears of women's prostitution, rather than sexual pleasure, reflected their sense of the dangerous attraction of the trappings of Americanization. Immigrants' experience of America was, at least in part, powerfully tied to the consumer economy and the availability of an unprecedented number of attractive and novel items. In the minds of the reformers, the erotic appeared to serve the wish to consume.[23] Desire may have put immigrant women at risk, but at the same time it made them Americans. Social workers like Paradise and Wald, and philanthropists like the founders of residences for immigrant women, confronted the problem by attacking desire, which they represented as the tragic flaw of the young Jewish woman. However they may have criticized the corrupt institutions of American life, these reformers never abandoned their conviction that the greatest threat to a young woman's virtue and ability to Americanize was her own desire to consume.

The Jewish Working-Class Response: Holding Tight

Ghetto Girls were not only condemned by Americans and the Jewish bourgeoisie. The Yiddish socialist press, in addition to engaging in a class war, offered its own version of gender warfare. What troubled male writers was, to use a popular phrase of the day, "what women wanted." Where the Jewish middle class saw vulgarity and acquisitiveness, Jewish working men saw dangerous and excessive desires.

The *Jewish Daily Forward*, for example, frequently dissected young women's pleasures and characterized the women of the East Side as "Trolly Car Girls with Rolls Royce Tastes."[24] Though these women lived in tenements, "their hearts are bent on palaces."[25] They are "gripped by the current mania for speed and pleasure." An article by Leo Robbins in 1923 promised "disaster" for these "little girls" who passed up marriage proposals from poor Jewish men to wait for a rich man's offer that would never materialize.[26] Commentators repeatedly suggested that these inflated desires led women to pursue impossible dreams beyond their workplace or home. The illegitimacy of their desires showed in their "bad taste," which one writer suggested "shriek[ed] louder than the whine of the beggars' tatters."[27]

Members of her own community projected onto the Ghetto Girl stereotype their fear that young Jewish women would abandon them. The Lower East Side had no Prince Charmings with wealth to underwrite palaces, fancy cars, and other pleasures. Beneath the ridicule of these young women is an unmistakable anxiety about women not staying behind to share with their peers a life without such possibilities.

Community members expressed a second anxiety as well, that working-class daughters' love of pleasure threatened their families if it took away their wages and their affection. "Our girls" became Ghetto Girls when writers and leaders imagined the young women's heartless indifference to their kin. This concern appeared not to be founded in reality, for most immigrant Jewish families were supported by young adult family members.[28] Young women shared their wages with their families. A Bureau of Labor study of wages from 1900 to 1910 indicated that in Jewish families working daughters produced almost 40 percent of the families' total yearly earnings on average. Jewish daughters sometimes turned over as much as 100 percent of their wages to their parents, though the average was about 89 percent, in contrast to Jewish sons, who gave only 70 percent.[29]

East European Jewish women joined an American work force that had begun to integrate women in the early nineteenth century. The entry of native and "new immigrant" women from northern and western Europe and Ireland into the labor force caused changes in relations between wives and husbands and between the generations. A similar process occurred within Jewish families when Jewish women went to work. Working-class Jewish men, many of whom worked in seasonal employment that typified the garment industry, earned too little to be the sole support of their families. Unmarried Jewish daughters' wages made a significant contribution to the family's income. This left working-class unmarried Jewish women, like other young women workers, relatively free from many forms of traditional authority for five or six years before marriage and gave them particular autonomy in spending the wages that they earned.[30]

Ghetto Girls evoked precisely the same anxieties as did American working-class women in the mid-nineteenth century. Often forced to work by their fathers' inability to support families, the earlier American women constituted the first group of autonomous urban women whose freedoms were continually attacked by the same types of journalists, moralists, and philanthropists who worried over Ghetto Girls. Their sexuality, autonomy, and display were also conflated into a single image of a dangerous and out-of-control woman. However, the anxieties expressed by immigrant Jews in the press were a particular version of the fear of independent women: Jews were frightened that with the Ghetto Girl's alienation from her parents she might withdraw her wages and leave her family.

Writers in the Yiddish press associated young working women's love of fashion with a diversion of wages to buy fine clothes. These earnings could instead have been used to help their families. Zelda, a regular columnist for the English page of the *Jewish Daily News*, wrote in 1903 about the evils of this behavior:

> You, working girls, listen to the voice of one of you—don't endeavor to mimic the pampered pet of material fortune. Those luxuries are beyond the station of a working girl. For the price of one silken rag, your mother, your toiling father and your little sisters and brothers can have better, purer food, warmer and better garments, comfortable rooms in a better neighborhood and a dozen other things that they haven't now, and suffer because of the lack of it.[31]

The Jewish immigrant family's economic vulnerability and cultural displacement explain why the Ghetto Girl was a powerful symbol of their fear. Jewish immigrant and second-generation literature, so often devoted to the struggles between sons and their immigrant parents, pointed to the second generation's yearning for consumer items, clothing, and pleasure that threatened to disrupt the economic basis of the family, as well as the ties of connection among its members. The Ghetto Girl personified the danger of a desire that alienated her from her parents as well as from the men of her generation. While sons were always moving toward separation from their families, daughters were considered more in the control of their families until marriage. This patriarchal formulation made unmarried daughters' autonomy more threatening.

Debating the Sources of the Ghetto Girl

The Ghetto Girl stereotype was powerful and widespread enough to generate debates within each battalion of accusers. Journalists for the mainstream press sometimes countered the image with another. One reporter for the *New York Herald Tribune* in 1900, for example, sympathetically reported precisely how a young working woman managed to put together her outfit for her Sunday promenade. He wrote, "To the uninitiated the costume represented an outlay of $20.00 at least, although she had achieved it at an expense of $3.30, and was able to go abroad without proclaiming her dire poverty at home." He revealed that by denying herself luxuries, the young seamstress could buy a few items, use scraps given to her by other relatives in the garment industry, and make her fashionable outfit by herself.[32] He portrayed her as a model of economy and sacrifice rather than of excess and self-indulgence.

Other journalists in the English-language Jewish press defended, rather than condemned, the Ghetto Girl. Miriam Shomer Zunser, writing for the *American Jewish News*, declared the picture of the Ghetto Girl exaggerated: "Notwithstanding the fact that many excellent folks have already discussed this creature, and have already doomed her to eternal glory or disgrace (most likely disgrace, if prevalence of opinion counts). The 'Ghetto girl' is in fact like the girls in any other community except that she bears within her heart the sorrow she borrowed from her race."[33]

Sophie Irene Loeb, a journalist for the *Evening World*, explained to a writer for the Jewish press in 1918 that the young Jewish immigrant woman was simply taking an early step in her evolution toward Americanization.

> Naturally, you will find a certain amount of crude-dressing on the East-side, but this is not an inherited trait. Good taste in dressing is acquired like any other of education, and what showiness these girls exhibit is but the elementary stage in the acquirement of this education. . . . Many of the girls come from a miserably paid position in the old country to a well-paid position in New York, and the change may have made them a little reckless. They may have spent too much money with too little judgment, but this failing is transitory and the girls emerge from it with a refinement equaling the best.[34]

These journalists, representing different positions as American-born, educated Jewish immigrants and children of immigrants, dismissed the Ghetto Girl's excesses as misunderstood or as an evolutionary step toward full Americanization. Sympathetic and compassionate, they appealed for better information and understanding from those who took offense.

Only a radical feminist activist like Margaret Sanger simply condemned the entire discussion as irrelevant. In one of her pamphlets on women's health that was translated into Yiddish, she criticized social reformers for their attack on young women's pleasures. She argued that they denounced women's clothes as "frivolous" and wasteful because of their own patrician backgrounds, and she urged the reformers to pay attention to the injustices that they perpetuated, rather than to concentrate on working women's love of clothing.[35]

However, the vast majority of articles in the press about these women condemned them. In an interview, Mrs. Sholom Asch, wife of the famed Yiddish writer, said that she had inquired of her non-Jewish friends why these "girls" were so extravagant.[36] They attributed these habits to the girls' lack of education. Mrs. Asch contended rather improbably that these immigrant girls encountered "freedom" in America. "No restrictions, no encumbrances, they were perfectly free to do as they pleased, and had plenty of money to spend as they pleased."[37] In this unrealistic version of immigrant reality, the luxuries and freedoms of young working-class women could only be tamed by the educations they refused to pursue.

The most forceful critic of Ghetto Girls was one of the most well-known Jewish woman of her day, the writer Fanny Hurst.[38] In an interview given to the *American Jewish News* for its 1918 article on "The Modern Ghetto Girl," Miss Hurst gave her impression of the East Side girl: "When I go down to the East-side and look upon those pasty, white faces and the hopelessly vulgar, stupid dresses, I am filled with wonder and admiration that these girls with all their vulgarity, should rise to the heights that some of them do and be so great in achievement."[39] The journalist Marion Golde asked Hurst to name the cause of "this extravagance in dress and taste." Golde characterized Fanny Hurst's response as "striking."

> It is due to the vivid, aggressive temperament and imagination of the Jew. The girl walks down Fifth Avenue. She sees a latest model dress or hat, or the latest modes in coiffures, and immediately her aggressive imagination fastens upon these modes. She goes home and models her own style on them, but not possessing the good taste that prompted the original mode, a contorted exaggeration results. It is the reaction to a vivid imagination and temperament that lacks the restraining force of instinctive good taste.[40]

In short, the Ghetto Girl was, as Hurst phrased it, "a contorted exaggeration." To her accusers, it was the Jewish working woman who created a self that was out of proportion to the norm.

But the real contorted exaggeration was in the work of those who circulated the representation. The frantic, panicked rendering of young Jewish womanhood was created by Jews who felt threatened by non-Jews, men threatened by women, the middle class threatened by working women, native-born Protestant Americans frightened of a nation of immigrants, and participants in a changing economy frightened by their own attraction to consumption and leisure. Each of these groups fought to define community, nation, and class by exclusion. The Ghetto Girl represented that which threatened the order of each category.[41]

The various faces of this stereotype suggest nuanced differences in the anxieties to which the Ghetto Girl spoke. The vulgarity that haunted Fannie Hurst, an acculturated Jew, was a different threat than that experienced by the young male readers of the *Forward's* English page who feared the autonomy of young Jewish working women. Progressives' anxieties that required the control of young women certainly paralleled their other concerns about creating a homogenous American nation. Nativists' obsession with an agrarian America endangered by the city and leisure were threatened by urban working women who controlled their own resources and exercised their own taste.

What unified the different versions of the Ghetto Girl was her desire. Her accusers who stood across her class and within her culture were joined by nothing other than their condemnation of her "excessive" and "undeserved" wants. Her illegitimate desires might make her vulnerable to sexual predators, deprive her family of its needs, reveal her as a cheap imitator of style, or betray her class in her search for a fortune. Although the Ghetto Girl was always portrayed as a working woman, paradoxically her wanting was never connected to her own productivity. She sought either what was wrong, or things to which she was not entitled. Her desire was the meeting ground of anxieties about Americanization, class status, and gender. Her *Jewishness* was the source of her excess and her marginality. The Jew in the woman and the woman in the Jew were condensed into the cultural representation of the Ghetto Girl. The Jew was the alien to the nation, avaricious, and aggressive. The woman was marked by her desire, in this setting defined primarily by consumer items of fashion and leisure. Her class was marked by the illegitimacy of that desire, for she wanted those things to which others, but not she, were entitled.

The Ghetto Girl, like stereotypes of other autonomous women, blurred all of these boundaries. Desire, a sexual impulse, became inseparable from an economic relationship between men and women that enabled consumption. While middle-class women of this period were increasingly defined as consumers, Ghetto Girls were prohibited from these very desires because they were unmarried and not members of the middle class. As marriage regulated sex, so, in capitalist societies, it regulated consumption since marriage legitimated both of them.

East European Jews were newcomers, at best, to both this division of labor and practice of consumption, which most of them fully embraced as they entered the middle class. The Jewish and non-Jewish bourgeoisie were constantly frustrated by the Ghetto Girl's sense of entitlement to the pleasures of freedom and consumption, which eventually stood for all the anxieties provoked by Americanization, antisemites, and the consumer society.[42]

The Jewish woman's body became a cultural terrain subject to Americanization. The Ghetto Girl violated the nation. She challenged a Protestant American commitment to restraint, to the separation of classes and the regulation of sexuality. Therefore, Jews policed one another, watched, condemned, and constrained their own use of display in their ongoing effort to find a niche for themselves. Clothing, jewelry, hairstyles, shoes—no element of decoration was too small to worry over as a sign of vulgarity or acceptability.

Dangerous Mirrors: Ghetto Girls in the Eyes of the Beholder

Jewish qualities were of course those that were feared by Jews who were seeking a secure place in America. Not surprisingly then, the wealthy Jewish women of the late nineteenth century were targets of the same accusations that they so often leveled at new immigrants.

Unflattering antisemitic portraits of affluent Jewish women appeared in the American press in the nineteenth and twentieth centuries. After 1875, the American dominant culture's preoccupation with how Jews dressed, spoke, and amused themselves formed the crucial justification for social discrimination.[43] In 1880, for example, in *Harper's Bazaar*, a light-hearted article was devoted to school girls cheating on their compositions. The girls received their comeuppance for their plagiarism when the friend they had relied on for help gave each of them, unbeknown to one another, the same essay. Their guilt was revealed when girl after girl read the essay "Women Jews," which began,

> Women Jews—By this term we do not mean Jewish women—those pretty, black-eyed daughters of Israel, conspicuous chiefly for their inordinate fondness for cheap jewelry and proportionate distaste for swine's flesh. No, it is not of those we would speak, but of that class of women, be they olive-skinned descendants of Abraham or pale-faced American Gentiles, who habitually ask and expect a dealer to "fall" a few cents on the stated price of every article for purchase.[44]

So conventional were these stereotypes that they were merely the backdrop of the story, and more importantly, what could be antisemitic about a work that suggested these qualities were detachable from Jewish women? If only behavior could change, antisemites would certainly disappear, at least according to popular magazines of middle-class America.

Affluent Jewish women's behavior, then, was constantly criticized in the writing and speeches of Jewish men who were doggedly pursuing acceptance. They strongly condemned women who dressed up and wore jewelry, and they often lamented how such behavior influenced the opinions of Christians.[45] An etiquette note concerning summer resort dress from an English-language Jewish newspaper in 1883, the *Jewish Messenger,* offered a typical, if sarcastic, admonition: "The more richly you dress, the more rightly you can claim to be refined. Hang out a diamond from every finger. Nothing is daintier than to see diamonds flashing amid griddle cakes and syrup."[46]

In the stereotypes, Jewish women consumed too much, but Jewish men were unnaturally productive, either as a result of their business success or criminality. By their genders, they were a matched set of aliens to American life. Before Americans created quotas limiting Jews' access to education, workplaces, and leisure settings, Jewish men served as foils against national values. They personified materialism and acquisitiveness, attributes thought to be the opposite of American virtues.[47] For example, Robert Woods and Albert Kennedy's *Zones of Emergence,* written around 1910, described the Jews of Boston as "born real estate speculators" and "natural traders" whose neighborhoods, by contrast with the Italians', were "crude" and "riotous."[48]

Antisemites saw these mercantilist tendencies underlining the Jews' supposed lack of physical ability. Their labor was never the honest work produced through sweat. As early as 1820, for example, a far more benevolent time in Jewish-Christian relations in the United States, the news magazine *Nile's Weekly Register* speculated why American Jews were denied civil rights that other men were granted. The writer concluded, "they create nothing and are mere consumers. They will not cultivate the earth, nor work at mechanical trades, preferring to live by their wit in dealing, and acting as if they had a home no where."[49]

In far less empathic terms, and nearly a century later, Theodore Bingham, New York's police commissioner in 1907, suggested that the city's Jewish population accounted for half of its criminals, a fact he attributed to the Jews' lack of physical fitness for "hard labor."[50] Then in the 1920s, at the height of anti-immigration hysteria, a popular novelist suggested that the fact that Jews "live by their wits alone" made them one of the most "undesirable" races to crowd into America's cities.[51]

Productive without working, consumers rather than laborers, traders by "racial instinct," and hence "obsessed with bargaining," Jewish men in a more tolerant nineteenth-century America, as well as in an increasingly intolerant nation of the early twentieth century, appeared to share a striking number of traits with Ghetto Girls. Jewish men and women's behavior, however, was differentiated by gender as well as by social class. Therefore, activities related to both of these categories—clothing, manners, and appearances—were subject to men and women constantly monitoring one another.

Jewish women's "behavior" was policed by Jewish men to remove its affronts, and Jewish women commented on one another's actions for the same reason. Jewish women enforced their conformity to Anglo-Protestant, bourgeois ideals in their own English-language Jewish press, which was a crucial organ for maintaining Jewish identity within an upwardly mobile Jewish population committed to rapid Americanization.[52] Women's pages typically juxtaposed advice about style, fashion, and beauty with lessons in Jewish womanhood and the responsibilities of Jewish women to maintain Judaism. These pages contained articles on the improvement of firmly established middle-class Jews of both German and East European descent more often than they prescribed ways to reform Ghetto Girls. Nonetheless, these columns bristled with anxiety.

For example, in 1918 Julia Weber's column "Woman and Her Home," in the *American Jewish News*, was devoted to the question "Have You a Pleasing Voice?"

Weber told of standing at a railroad station where a Jewish girl greeted her companions "each boisterously and in a loud voice, arousing criticism all about her." She recounts that her companion said about "this type of Jewish girl,"

> She knew how to buy good clothes and how to wear them, but this type of girl, with such a manner and voice, will never be accepted in good society, no matter how many redeeming qualities she may have. While there are thousands of splendid Jewish girls who are ladies in every sense of the word, yet there are others who, like this girl, help bring severe criticism upon all Jewish girls. Her voice is either loud and harsh or shrill. She does not realize that this stamps her as uncultured and vulgar.[53]

Her "friend" could claim expertise because she was a "professional reader," an actress who recited on social occasions. Her solution was the following:

A girl should speak in low and well modulated tones and for the benefit of her listeners only. She should be careful not to speak in the throat or she will swallow her words. If she talks through her nose in that shrill tone she produces the same disagreeable sound as is produced by speaking with the nostrils pinched together. . . . She should speak so that every word is heard yet is modulated with a view to a pleasing, clear and forceful expression of thought and feeling. Just a simple exercise on the vowels a-e-i-o-u will produce excellent results.[54]

Sandwiched between advice about how to equip a bathroom, the value of fish in the diet, and an explanation of the symbolism of the *Mezuzah*, the "Woman and Her Home" column revealed that good taste in clothing was insufficient proof of the acceptability of a Jewish woman. She could still be betrayed by her voice, her nasal tones, and her volume, all of which were tell-tale signs of coarseness that kept her from "good society," in other words, from acceptability to the non-Jewish world.[55]

The parallel between this article and one in the Yiddish press, directed to the children of immigrants, is striking.

Have you ever been on a street-car when the theatre-goers are homeward bound? Have you ever been in a restaurant when the workers are at their noon-day meal? If so, you have surely been struck by the loud talking and laughing of some girl. You, no doubt, immediately called her unrefined and vulgar. Would you want another to class you the same way simply because you forget to control your voice?

And you and I have a double responsibility as Jewish girls. Not only we as individuals are judged, but indeed the whole nation is judged by each of us. If you are known as unrefined in your small circle, and I undignified in mine, why then is it said: "the Jews are loud and unrefined." So remember, girls, how much depends on you and me.[56]

Yiddish writers who established etiquette for immigrants offered the same advice. Tashrak wrote that no matter how well dressed a woman was, a "shrieking laugh" gave away the fact that she was "no lady" (a *proste yente*, or a common gossip).[57] Jewish well-being across classes depended on containing the vulgar wants and behaviors of Jewish women.

Other commentators repeatedly returned to the Jewish woman's body as the key to her problem. By contrasting the styles of Fifth Avenue and East Side women, the cartoonist Foshko suggested that taste ran well beyond education to the core problem for the Ghetto Girl. As he explained to a journalist,

You may say that such crazes in fashion are worn by the Fifth Avenue girl and that they become her, but there is this difference. The Fifth Avenue girl lives in an atmosphere of her own—a rich atmosphere with leisure and luxury. Her body has acquired the mold of her life. The girl on the East side also lives in an atmosphere of her own and her life has fashioned her body in harmony with it. What would therefore become the Fifth Avenue girl looks out of place on the East side girl. Realize that the make-up of a girl on Clinton Street who works at a machine cannot be the same as the make-up of a girl from Fifth Avenue![58]

As Ghetto Girls were less often featured in the press because the numbers of Jews in the ghettos diminished, her phantom qualities still persisted and required careful monitoring, most often by other women. An anonymous female writer for the Yiddish newspaper *The Day* suggested in 1930 that Jewish women's bodies were a special burden to them in their efforts to dress well for work. She asserted that Jewish women were not extravagant when they purchased clothing and stockings because "the average working girl in New York City has got to look smart and trim if she wants to keep her job." This requirement is not a hardship for the "Gentile girl who usually has small features, light eyes, and a slim figure. This girl will look neat and pleasing in almost any dress she puts on, and her hats, even if in some popular and rather extreme mode, will not make her conspicuous. Jewish women, on the other hand, must be careful in the clothing they wear because they are easily 'typed' as flamboyant and 'conspicuous.'"

The writer continued:

> Many Jewish girls are of the oriental type of physique. This may be very beautiful in its proper setting, but in an Occidental, Gentile country a really graceful curved nose is regarded as a "hooked nose," the vivid coloring black eyes, full mouth, black hair, appears "common" and "loud," the full well-developed figure is "blowsy" or "fat." To dress herself in accord with the ideals of Americans, the Jewish girl must offset these intimations of vulgarity by making it her rule to wear the simplest clothes possible. But alas, as we all know by this time, the simplest clothes are the most expensive![59]

An Oriental body was not a Jewish woman's only problem. A 1929 article in *The Day*'s English section warned that the Jewish woman's "style" might lead her to lose her job. The writer recounted her story of a Jewish girl who "obtained an excellent position in the office of an ad man." The "Jewish girl" was unusually clever, but nevertheless, her boss had to fire her. She wore "low necked afternoon dresses of beaded silk," "high heeled satin shoes," and excessive makeup. "It was cheaper for him to get a less brilliant worker than to destroy the carefully built up impressiveness of his reception room."[60] Terry Selber, writing for the same newspaper in 1926, had commented on a similar problem and quoted a non-Jewish expert who explained that Jewish women's "intensity manifests itself in their clothes."[61]

Affluent Jewish women were haunted by the same phantom of excessive desire. As journalists lectured the aspiring middle-class Jewish woman, so too did they write to constrain the successful Jew. Another "Woman and Her Home" column in 1918 exhorted its fashionable readers to learn that "good dressing does not mean exaggeration; that the exhibition of a veritable shop of jewels cannot hide untidy hair and an over-painted face, . . . that impeccable tidiness of nails, hair, teeth, and shoes are more desirable than a five hundred dollar fur cape and a pair of diamond earrings."[62] These gender stereotypes conspired to suggest that something was wrong with Jewish women.

Not Me—Not Them

The more Americanized that Jewish women became—whether they sought "ostentatious" or well-tailored clothing—the more likely it seemed that they were to betray their Jewishness. Desire doomed them because it could not erase what was stubbornly and persistently "wrong" with them, that they were outsiders and Jews.

Beginning in the late nineteenth century, cleavages among Jews living in America led to infighting. Affluent Jewish men maintained a ceaseless assault on the perceived consumer excesses by Jewish women. Wealthy German Jews, suddenly considered dangerous to America, turned on East European Jewish women and men, attacking their vulgarity. Jewish men ridiculed Jewish women. Rich Jews attacked poor Jews. The more established Jews condemned Jews who had recently emigrated. Jews were at once too American in their dress and too Jewish in their demeanor; in either case, Jews were considered fundamentally wrong. Each group of Jews differentiated the others by social class, gender, region of origin, and religious practice and condemned one another's bodies and styles to demonstrate their own respectability in a world that questioned their suitability for the middle class and citizenship in the nation. The tasks of acculturation, involving either rapid or gradual change, turned Jews against each other.

Americanization required men and women to distance themselves from what they perceived as undesirable former selves. Immigrants tried, sometimes desperately, to Americanize by changing their language and their appearance. The process seemed to require them to differentiate themselves from some other group or gender of Jews. To distance oneself from a vulgar, noisy Jewish woman was a way to assert one's status as an American.

Their ability to become American required Jews to make minute distinctions in an antisemitic world. Jews' apparent ability to assimilate to the white, Christian world around them only heightened the sense that difference was dangerous.[63] Because, like other Americans, young

105

Jewish women could buy what they wanted with the money they earned, what they purchased was constantly condemned as lacking in taste, proving that they were not successful imitators. A writer for a Yiddish daily commented in 1902 how much the "shop girl" tried to copy the rich. "The very latest style of hat, or cloak, or gown is just as likely to be worn on Grand street as on Fifth avenue. The great middle class does not put on the newest styles until they have been thoroughly exploited by Madam Millionaire of Fifth avenue and Miss Operator of Essex street."[64] From the point of view of the Jews of the Lower East Side, the shop girl was as attuned to style as were the wealthy. To the Jews of the "great middle class," this behavior, by contrast, had to be constantly controlled to protect against embarrassing imitation. Their place in that class remained vulnerable despite their economic standing.

The need for ever-increasing precision to keep some people *out* and some people *in* the mainstream because of their manners and style rather than their ability to consume, placed Jews in conflict with each other, and placed both Jewish women and men, and the Jewish working class and middle class, in particular struggle.[65]

The period in which the Ghetto Girl served as a potent stereotype for Jews coincided with Americans' struggles to create an urban and pluralistic society, their ambivalence about capitalism and industrialization, and their anxieties about changing roles of women and the family. The Ghetto Girl provided a cultural meeting ground for American fears, if not for open antisemitism, and American Jews' own evolving sense of their identities as participants in the nation's middle class. For the dominant culture, bourgeois norms allowed them to draw the boundaries of society to exclude outsiders by color. If Jews were harder to categorize, then their unsuitability was established by other measures embodied in the stereotype that placed them beyond white, genteel society.

For young Jewish women and men who wanted a life in the American middle class, the need to shape and contain consumer desire made the Ghetto Girl a representation of scorn and fear. Jews consequently rejected characteristics that were "Jewish."

As Beth Wenger argues, by the 1920s and 1930s the Lower East Side was the source of both nostalgia and forgetting.[66] The fear that the ghetto clung to Jews was potent. The Lower East Side as a site of dirt, repulsive odors, bad manners, avarice, and unsavory business practices persisted throughout the period of the Ghetto Girl stereotype. Jewishness and gender were inseparable in this image. The ghetto carried the onus of Jewishness, and the "girl" stood for the myriad of anxieties raised by women for all Americans, as well as Jewish Americans.

Whatever differences divided Jews, the shame, pain, embarrassment, and rage created by the stereotyped image of an autonomous and desiring Jewish woman from the ghetto were the product of America's reluctance to allow those marked as "different" to join the nation on their own terms. The Ghetto Girl's qualities—vulgarity, excess, and desire—figured into intra-ethnic gender stereotypes for the remainder of the twentieth century because Jews' difference from others in the nation continued to find expression, represented primarily by an unattractive Jewish woman from the Lower East Side. Her capacity to embody what was both frightening and desirable about America—consumption, freedom, economic dependence through marriage, and display—cast her in this problematic role as an icon of Americanization.

Erased Memory

The Ghetto Girl has disappeared from the contemporary pantheon of immigrant images of this period. The Yiddish and English language literatures of Jewish immigrants have kept alive the "Alrightnik," the Socialist dreamer, and various images of the Jewish family. Nostalgic memories of that time and place may evoke pious Jewish men and perhaps saintly mothers (however, the Jewish Mother is evoked today in media and humor as monster and meddler, rather than as self-sacrificing and beloved to her children). Jewish women have not been remembered culturally. Few of them have been evoked as the great leaders of American Jewry. The field of Jewish women's history has been in large measure a process of recovery, both of remarkable women and the sheer presence of women as actors in Jewish life.

The absolute centrality of social class to the creation of an American Jewish identity is, then, illustrated by the creation and erasure of the Ghetto Girl. But there is more to her story than that. The ability or inability to see the gender dimension of experience is the very infirmity of which Lévi-Strauss wrote. Seeing is enabled by certain tools of analysis. The Ghetto Girl is forgotten, but her characteristics—illegitimate desire, an embodiment that betrays her difference, and her danger to other Jews—have appeared repeatedly in the self-hating representations that have dominated American Jewish life since the end of World War II. What the erasure of Lower East Side memory teaches us is that the anxieties that shape Jewish self-representation are inaccessible to us if we lack an understanding about the intersection of gender and class in the making of American Jews.

NOTES

This essay is derived from "Ghetto Girls and Jewish Immigrant Desire," Chapter 1 of Riv-Ellen Prell, *Fighting to Become Americans: Jews, Gender and the Anxiety of Assimilation* (Boston: Beacon Press, 1999). Copyright © 1999 by Riv-Ellen Prell. Reprinted by permission of Beacon Press, Boston.

1. Claude Lévi-Strauss, *Tristes Topiques*, trans. John and Doreen Eightman (New York: Atheneum Press, 1974), p. 41.

2. Ibid.

3. The Ghetto Girl was an English-language, rather than Yiddish-language, image. I found references to "her" as early as 1902 in the English-language page of the *Jewish Daily News*, vol. 16, English Department. Paula Hyman's *Gender and Assimilation in Modern Jewish History: The Roles and Representations of Women* (Seattle: University of Washington Press, 1995) draws attention to the role of gender representation in the analysis of modern Jewish culture. This work is indebted to that fundamental insight of hers.

4. The notion of forgotten memory in relationship to the Lower East Side is the subject of essays by Jonathan Boyarin, "The Lower East Side: A Place of Forgetting," in *Storm from Paradise: The Politics of Jewish Memory* (Minneapolis: University of Minnesota Press, 1991), and Beth Wenger, "Memory as Identity: The Invention of the Lower East Side," *American Jewish History* 85 (March 1997): 3–26. Both emphasize that "forgetting" was part of the process of upward mobility.

5. Irving Howe, *World of Our Fathers: The Journey of the East European Jews to America and the Life They Found and Made* (New York: Touchstone Books, 1976), p. 121.

6. For a concise history of American efforts to restrict immigration see John Higham, *Send These to Me: Immigrants in Urban America*, revised ed. (Baltimore: Johns Hopkins University Press, 1984), pp. 29–70.

7. Benjamin Ginsberg, *The Fatal Embrace: Jews and the State* (Chicago: University of Chicago Press 1994), pp. 75–87; John Higham, *Send These to Me*, pp. 95–116.

8. Benjamin Ginsberg, *The Fatal Embrace*, pp. 81–87. Frederic Cople Jaher demonstrates that prior to this period, through the 1850s, fiction, drama, newspapers, and even guidebooks to New York employed classical Christian antisemitism. *A Scapegoat in the New Wilderness: The Origins and Rise of Anti-Semitism in America* (Cambridge, Mass.: Harvard University Press, 1994), pp. 211–241. Michael Dobkowski, *The Tarnished Dream: The Basis of American Anti-Semitism* (Westport, Conn.: Greenwood Press, 1979), provides evidence for this perspective as well.

9. Evyatar Friesel, "The Age of Optimism in American Judaism, 1900–1920," in *A Bicentennial Festschrift for Jacob Rader Marcus*, ed. Bertram Wallace Korn (New York: Ktav Press, 1976), pp. 131–154.

10. Ironically, the most famous observer of the "the ghetto" of this period, Hutchins Hapgood, found no evidence of her in his sketches of urban Jewish life in New York. His typologies of Jewish women included Old World women as well as those interested in Americanization, but the vulgar, overdressed, and excessive young woman that created such anxiety made no appearance in his work. Hutchins Hapgood, *The Spirit of the Ghetto*, ed. Moses Rischin (Cambridge, Mass.: Harvard University Press, 1967).

11. Anonymous, "East Side Fashions. They Keep Pace with Those of Fifth Avenue, and Perhaps Outshine them a Little," in Jacob Rader Marcus, *The American Jewish Woman: A Documentary History* (Cincinnati: American Jewish Archive, 1981), pp. 497–501.

12. Marion Golde, "The Modern Ghetto Girl: Does She Lack Refinement?" *American Jewish News* 1 (22 March 1918): 11.

13. For a discussion of Jewish racial identity in the late nineteenth century, see Eric L. Goldstein, "'Different Blood Flows in Our Veins': Race and Jewish Self-Definition in Late Nineteenth-Century America," *American Jewish History* 85 (March 1997): 29–56. For a discussion of Jews, eugenics, and the Americanization movement in this period, see Robert Singerman, "The Jew as Racial Alien," in David Gerber, ed., *Anti-Semitism in American History* (Urbana: University of Illinois Press, 1986), pp. 103–128.

14. Cited in Eli Lederhendler, "Guide for the Perplexed: Sex, Manners, and Mores for the Yiddish Reader in America," *Modern Judaism* 11 (1991): 333.

15. Rabbi Israel Levinthal, "Style," a sermon delivered December 26, 1916, pp. 2–4. Israel Levinthal Papers, Box 2, Ratner Center for American Jewish Experience, Jewish Theological Seminary, New York City.

16. Lillian Wald, *The House on Henry Street* (New York: H. Holt, 1915), p. 190.

17. Ibid., p.191.

18. In contrast, Margaret Sanger, who pioneered birth control for women, was quite critical of Progressives. In a Yiddish pamphlet in which she wrote about how to raise a modern American girl, she was impatient with those who stifled and inhibited young women's desire for self-adornment and self-expression. Lederhendler, "Guide for the Perplexed," p. 327.

19. Naomi Cohen, *Encounter with Emancipation: The German Jews in the United States, 1830–1912* (Philadelphia: Jewish Publication Society, 1984), discusses German Jews' strategies for expecting their behavior to be "at least as good as everybody else," p. 110.

20. Viola Paradise, "The Jewish Immigrant Girl in Chicago," *Survey* 30 (16 September 1913): 704.

21. For scholarly discussions of issues connected to Jewish women and prostitution, see "Introduction," in *The Mamie Papers*, ed. Ruth Rosen and Sue Davidson (Bloomington: Indiana University Press, 1977); Reena Sigman Friedman, "'Send Me My Husband Who Is in New York City': Husband Desertion in the American Jewish Immigrant Community, 1900–1926," *Jewish Social Studies* 44 (1982): 7–8; and Egal Feldman, "Prostitution, the Alien Woman and the Progressive Imagination, 1910–1915," *American Quarterly* 19 (1967): 192–206. Naomi Cohen also discusses the profound anxieties of German Jews about the Jewish problem of white slavery, *Encounter with Emancipation*, p. 32.

22. Jewish commentators publishing in Jewish newspapers were reluctant to write about sex and promiscuity. They might well have feared the judgments of others, or they might have hesitated to discuss sexuality because of religious concerns for "modesty" that prohibited public speech about sexual matters. In either case, Jewish publications avoided the conclusions that Viola Paradise advanced.

23. Kathy Peiss's important work on early-twentieth-century urban working

women's culture underlines the fact that women supplemented their wages by men's gifts, often bought at the price of their consent to trade sexual favors. *Cheap Amusements: Working Women and Leisure Time in Turn-of-the-Century New York* (Philadelphia: Temple University Press, 1986).

24. Leo Robbins, "Trolly Car Girls with Rolls Royce Tastes," *Jewish Daily Forward* 26 (13 May 1923): 3.

25. Ibid.

26. Ibid.

27. Leopold Lazarus, "Do Our Eastsiders Know How to Dress?" *Jewish Daily Forward* 26 (13 April 1924): 3

28. The 1910 U.S. census measured the number of earners in the nuclear family. The Yiddish-speaking households contained a higher mean number of earners in the nuclear family (1.7) than Italian and other East European households who had immigrated at a similar time (1.4) and than households of native-born Americans (1.4).

29. Susan Glenn, *Daughters of the Shtetl: Life and Labor in the Immigrant Generation* (Ithaca, N.Y.: Cornell University Press, 1990), p. 84. Glenn draws her information on wages from the "Report on Condition of Woman and Child Wage-Earners," vol. 1: "Men's Ready-Made Clothing Industry." Daughters and sons, rather than mothers, supplemented fathers' wages. Daughters also used their wages to bring family members from Europe. Elizabeth Ewen, *Immigrant Women in the Land of Dollars: Life and Culture on the Lower East Side, 1890–1925* (New York: Monthly Review Press, 1985).

30. See Christine Stansell, *City of Women: Sex and Class in New York, 1789–1860* (Urbana: University of Illinois Press, 1987), pp. 76–78, 89–91,115–117, for a discussion of these relations among New York working women in the eighteenth and nineteenth centuries.

31. Zelda, "Just between Ourselves Girls," *Jewish Daily News* 17 (22 December 1903), English Department.

32. Cited in Jacob Rader Marcus, *The American Jewish Woman: A Documentary History* (Cincinnati: American Jewish Archive, 1981), p. 500. Lillian Wald commented on this same phenomenon in her memoir. She responded to a newspaper editorial on the stylish appearance of working women by asking a young woman how she afforded her clothing, and learned about her frugal and efficient purchases. She declared that the young woman was able "to show excellent discretion in the expenditure of income." *House on Henry Street*, pp. 194–195.

33. Miriam Shomer Zunser, "The Ghetto Girl Again," *American Jewish News* 1 (19 April 1918): 15.

34. Golde, "The Modern Ghetto Girl," p. 11.

35. Cited in Lederhendler, "Guide to the Perplexed," p. 327.

36. Mrs. Asch was born Matilda Spiro in Lodz, Poland, in approximately 1883. She was from an urban, cosmopolitan family. Personal communication, David Mazower. Clearly her class bias is revealed in her reaction to immigrant women.

37. Golde, "The Modern Ghetto Girl," p. 11.

38. For a recent biography of Fannie Hurst in the context of American Jewish women's history, see Joyce Antler, *The Journey Home: Jewish Women and the American Century* (New York: Free Press, 1997), pp. 150–172. For a recent consideration of

Fanny Hurst's writing in relationship to her family, see Janet Handler Burstein, *Writing Mothers, Writing Daughters: Tracing the Maternal in Stories by American Jewish Women* (Urbana: University of Illinois Press, 1996), pp. 50–59.

39. Golde, "The Modern Ghetto Girl," p. 11.

40. Ibid. Fanny Hurst ultimately acknowledged the antisemitic nature of her remarks about East European Jews in her autobiography *Anatomy of Me: A Wonderer in Search of Herself* (New York: Doubleday, 1958), p. 350. Janet Burstein brought this reflection of Hurst's to my attention.

41. As George Mosse noted in his work on nationalism and sexuality, both nationalism and ideas about "respectability" provided a sense of order and normality. Whatever threatened those categories also threatened order. Distinctions between men were crucial to that orderliness. *Nationalism and Sexuality: Middle-Class Morality and Sexual Norms in Modern Europe* (Madison: University of Wisconsin Press, 1985), p. 16.

42. T. J. Jackson Lears, "From Salvation to Self-Realization: Advertising and the Therapeutic Roots of the Consumer Culture, 1880–1930," in *The Culture of Consumption: Critical Essays in American History, 1880–1930,* ed. Richard Wrightman Fox and T. J. Jackson Lears (New York: Pantheon Books, 1983), p. xi.

43. Cohen, *Encounter with Emancipation,* p. 112, and Higham, *Send These to Me,* 1984, pp. 117–152.

44. "A School-Girl's Stratagem," *Harper's Bazaar* 13 (31 July 1880): 490.

45. Rudolf Glanz, *The Jewish Woman in America: Two Female Immigrant Generations, 1820–1929,* vol. 2: *The German-Jewish Woman* (New York: Ktav Press, 1976), p. 55; Cohen, *Encounter with Emancipation,* p. 112.

46. Cited in Glanz, *The Jewish Woman in America,* vol. 2, p. 56.

47. Hasia R. Diner, *A Time for Gathering: The Second Migration, 1820–1880* (Baltimore: Johns Hopkins University Press, 1990), pp. 189–190.

48. Robert A. Woods and Albert J. Kennedy, eds., and abridged by Sam Bass Warner, *Zones of Emergence* (Cambridge, Mass.: Harvard University Press, 1962), pp. 167, 173. Dobkowski, *The Tarnished Dream,* discusses the continuing stereotype of the Jew as Shylock, the miser and thief, throughout the late nineteenth and early twentieth centuries in the United States.

49. Quoted in Higham, *Send These to Me,* pp. 160–161.

50. "Foreign Criminals in New York," *North American Review* 634 (September 1908): 383. This accusation was the source of a major protest, and Bingham ultimately recanted the extent of the accusation.

51. Kenneth L. Roberts, "Why Europe Leaves Home," cited in Dobkowski, *The Tarnished Dream,* p. 102.

52. Arthur Goren, "The Jewish Press," in *The Ethnic Press in the United States: A Historical Analysis and Handbook,* ed. Sally M. Miller (New York: Greenwood Press, 1987).

53. Julia Weber, "Have You a Pleasing Voice?" *American Jewish News* 1 (26 July 1918): 368.

54. Weber, "Have You a Pleasing Voice," p. 368. Sander Gilman's book *The Jew's Body* (New York: Routledge, 1991) discusses the Jewish voice in the context of long standing anti-Jewish accusations of a secret Jewish language.

55. The voice continued to haunt Jewish women throughout the first half of the century. Ruth Jacknow Markowitz's study of Jewish women enrolled at New York's public Hunter College recounted that women feared that they would not be certified for teaching because of their failure to speak English properly. All students were subjected to oral exams and the possibility of remedial courses to correct accented speech. *My Daughter the Teacher: Jewish Teachers in the New York City Schools* (New Brunswick, N.J.: Rutgers University Press, 1993).

56. "Voice Influence," *Jewish Daily News* 31 (1915), English Department.

57. Cited in Lederhendler, "Guide to the Perplexed," p. 333.

58. Golde, "The Modern Ghetto Girl," p. 11.

59. "The City Business Girl Must be Good-Looking," *The Day* 16 (23 February 1929), English Section.

60. Ibid.

61. Terry Selber, "As Many Employers See Our Taste in Clothes," *The Day* (10 October 1926), English Section.

62. M. S., "By Their Dress Shall You Know Them," *American Weekly Jewish News* 1 (26 December 1918): 704.

63. Daniel Itzkovitz explores the issue of Jews' differences from the dominant culture in "Secret Temples," in Jonathan Boyarin and Daniel Boyarin, eds., *Jews and Other Differences: The New Jewish Cultural Studies* (Minneapolis: University of Minnesota Press, 1997), pp. 197–202.

64. The Observer, *The Jewish Daily News* 17 (13 January 1902), English Department.

65. Women provided a particularly powerful source of intra-ethnic representation that transected class. Men did, however, briefly serve as a far less elaborated intra-ethnic stereotype parallel to the Ghetto Girl in the Yiddish press. See Riv-Ellen Prell, *Fighting to Become Americans: Jews, Gender, and the Anxiety of Assimilation* (Boston: Beacon Press, 1999), chapter 1, for a discussion of some of these images.

66. Wenger, "Memory as Identity," p. 27.

Constructions of Memory: The Synagogues of the Lower East Side

David Kaufman

In the landscape of the American Jewish past, no space is more packed with memory than the Lower East Side of New York City. Tenements and pushcarts, sweatshops and settlement houses, *landsmanschafts* and labor unions, Yiddish theaters and coffeehouses are but a few of the images evoked by the archetypal immigrant neighborhood. Yet of all the kaleidoscopic images of the historic Lower East Side, the immigrant synagogue—*shul* in colloquial Yiddish—stands out as especially enigmatic.[1] Though in most instances a key institution of Jewish communal life, the synagogue was not necessarily central to life in the immigrant ghetto. As an image of Lower East Side memory, therefore, the synagogue has been represented in widely divergent ways. Some observers assign the synagogue minimal importance in the overall scheme of immigrant life and Yiddish culture; witness, accordingly, its relative exclusion from academic treatments of Lower East Side history. Others tend to emphasize the centrality of the synagogue, projecting the current religiosity into the more secular past and thus privileging the role of the house of worship. This dichotomy is embodied by the two leading tourist sites on the Lower East Side today, the Tenement Museum and the Eldridge Street Synagogue Project, one downplaying the Jewishness of the Lower East Side, the other highlighting the Judaism of the immigrant community.

How are we to reconcile these antithetical positions? How to explain the tension between the historical view of synagogues as peripheral to the immigrant experience and a communal memory focused upon the "sacred space" of synagogues?

The tension runs throughout the history of Lower East Side representation. Take, for example, two very different maps of the East Side neighborhood. One is the familiar map from Moses Rischin's *The Promised City*, first published in 1962 (fig. 5.1).[2] In delineating thirty-six key institutions of "New York's Jews," Rischin lists just one synagogue: Beth Hamedrash Hagadol, which he notes for its "catholicity," and then quotes from its literature: "In dispensing money and matzos to the poor, all are recognized as the children of one Father, and no lines are drawn between natives of different countries."[3] In other words, Beth Hamedrash Hagadol was a civilized counterpoint to the divisive "landsmanschaft shul,"[4] and as such, deserved its place on the map.

Compare this with a more recent map, entitled "Hester Street," in Eric Homberger's *Historical Atlas of New York City*—published more than thirty years after Rischin's work (see fig. 5.2). Clearly much had changed in the interim. Homberger writes that despite "shocking conditions . . . Jewish culture and religion flourished. Hundreds of synagogues and religious schools were established, ritual baths built, and religious goods manufactured."[5] Though he does not expand on the theme of the synagogue in his text, his "visual celebration" tells another story. Tiny blue Stars of David represent synagogues, and the map is literally strewn with them. Color blocks represent population density, and the superimposed blue stars represent religious density. Obviously, then, there is a wide divergence between the views of Rischin and Homberger, whose emphases represent two conflicting understandings of the history of the immigrant Jewish community.

How may we explain the discrepancy? One possibility lies in the failure to correlate the greater picture of immigrant demographics with the familiar narrative of the founding of a myriad of synagogues during the immigrant era. Such a narrative may be found, for instance, in Gerard Wolfe's book *The Synagogues of New York's Lower East Side* (1978), in which he writes: "It is estimated that between 1880 and

25 Public School 63
26 Music School Settlement
27 Asch Building
28 Astor Library
29 Cooper Union
30 Hebrew Technical School for Boys
31 Labor Temple
32 Rand School
33 Hebrew Charities Building
34 Metropolitan Life Building
35 Madison Square Garden
36 City College

Boundaries of sub-ethnic districts
...... Hungarian
—+— Galician
+-o-+ Rumanian
∿∿∿ Levantine
--- Russian

Shaded blocks indicate Tenth Ward

0   ¼ MILE

THE LOWER EAST SIDE

1 Newspaper Row
2 World Building
3 Chatham Sq. Library
4 Beth Israel Hospital
5 Israel Elchanan Yeshiva
6 Seward Park Library
7 Forward Building on Yiddish Newspaper Row
8 Educational Alliance
9 Henry St. Settlement and Clinton Hall
10 Machzike Talmud Torah
11 Hebrew Sheltering House
12 Hebrew Technical School for Girls
13 Home for Aged
14 Jewish Maternity Hospital
15 Young Men's Benevolent Association
16 Camp Huddleston Hospital Ship School
17 Beth Hamedrash Hagadol
18 Pro-Cathedral Mission
19 University Settlement
20 Grand Theater
21 Yiddish Rialto
22 Thalia Theater
23 People's Bath
24 Police Headquarters

77

Fig. 5.1 Map of the Lower East Side, 1962. Courtesy of Harvard University Press.

115

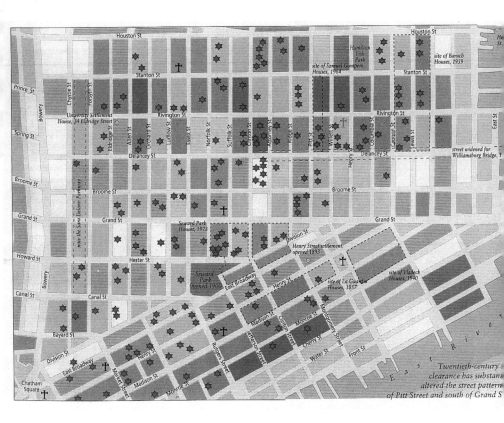

Fig. 5.2 Map of the Lower East Side, 1994.
Courtesy of Henry Holt and Company.

1915 more than five hundred Jewish houses of worship were organized in the Lower East Side. In an actual count taken in the year 1905, there were 350 congregations functioning. In all, about sixty buildings were expressly built as synagogues, including about a dozen converted churches."[6] These numbers sound impressive until we contextualize by adding population figures. For the year 1905, we may accept the approximate number of 350,000 Jews living on the Lower East Side.[7] Divided by the 350 congregations, that would make one synagogue for every one thousand Jews. In light of the fact that most were small landsmanschaft shuls with average memberships of about fifty men, this simple arithmetic reveals the American Jewish ghetto as an overwhelmingly secular place. Even when we add the families of the members, only a fraction of the neighborhood's Jews seems to have been actively engaged in synagogue life.

Most outside observers, therefore, have minimized the subject of the synagogue. But many go further still, suggesting it played no role at all in the life of the ghetto. In the initial phase of Lower East Side memory, from the 1920s to the 1960s, the synagogue was virtually absent from descriptions and observations of the downtown community. This remained the case until the 1970s, when synagogues were rediscovered, or reinvented, as the very embodiments of the Jewish immigrant past. Though clearly exaggerated, the emphasis on synagogues is understandable given the simple fact of their physical survival. Built to last, and thus established to preserve the future as well as the past, the surviving synagogue structures are vivid testimony to the continuity of Jewish life. At the same time, their very decrepitude bespeaks a lost culture. For either reason, or perhaps for both, the contemporary period has seen the near-fetishization of the "old synagogue" in the popular imagination. We have, as a result, two extremely variant views of the place of the synagogue in the history of the Lower East Side. How, when, and why did this change come about? We may gain some better understanding of the issue by surveying the representations of synagogues in various media.

Two early illustrations of the Lower East Side, both from the early 1880s, exhibit major differences in their treatment of the synagogue. The first, dating from May 1884, portrays a typical street scene, depicting what it calls the "Polish Trading Post" of downtown New York for the uptown audience of *Harper's Weekly* (fig. 5.3). It is typical in the sense that it depicts the Lower East Side in terms of its crowded street life and commercial hubbub. This secular activity would come to characterize the Lower East Side far more often than the religious world of the synagogue. Note, however, that in the center background of the illustration, partially obscured by a tree, is a synagogue. Was it intentionally chosen by the illustrator, one A. Berghaus? We do not know. But if so, then the symbolism is apt. The synagogue, once central to Jewish life, is now obscured—not by foliage alone, but also by the public business of buying and selling. This was the developing reality of the Lower East Side.

Another image dating from the same time, perhaps even the same year, is an unsigned color rendering of K'hal Adath Jeshurun, better known as the Eldridge Street Synagogue (fig. 5.4). The picture has the measured lines and perspective of an architectural drawing, and may very well have been executed by one of the synagogue's designers, Peter or Francis Herter. The Herters were tenement builders in the down-

Fig. 5.3 "Polish Trading Post."
Illustration by A. Berghaus for
Harper's magazine, 1884.
Collection of Peter Schweitzer.

Fig. 5.4 K'hal Adath Jeshurun,
Eldridge Street, built 1886.
Watercolor, 21.8 x 17.14.
Courtesy of the Museum of the
City of New York. The J.
Clarence Davies Collection.

town ghetto and should not be confused with the well-known Herter Brothers, who owned a design firm that catered to uptown society. Yet this elegant drawing, if theirs, provides evidence of aspirations to a higher status, as does the building itself. The design of the Eldridge Street Synagogue was inspired by the Moorish precedents of uptown New York synagogues.[8] The illustration, depicting an ideal downtown synagogue, perhaps as yet unbuilt, was a vision of the East Side as it could be, rather than as it was.

A combination of these two extremes is found in an 1898 drawing by W. A. Rogers for *Harper's Monthly* magazine, reprinted in Irving Howe and Ken Libo's *How We Lived* (fig. 5.5). The work contains the caption "A Lower East Side church becomes a synagogue."[9] On the one hand, the quiet dignity of the synagogue edifice and its congregants is highlighted, probably depicting an idealized Sabbath scene. At the same time, the scene is realistic, as it places the building within its urban context. Also, its subject refers to the common practice of converting former church buildings to synagogues. In this case, the influence of the Eldridge Street Synagogue can plainly be seen in the very similar ornamentation used to "convert" this church for Jewish purposes.

Consider next an illustration of an immigrant synagogue drawn by Abraham Phillips for Lillian Wald's 1915 memoir of the Henry Street Settlement (fig. 5.6). In the text, Wald emphasizes the generational changes taking place:

> Freedom and opportunity for the young make costly demands upon the bewildered elders, who cling tenaciously to their ancient religious observances. The synagogues are everywhere—imposing or shabby-looking buildings—and the *chevras*, sometimes occupying only a small room where the prescribed number meet for daily prayer . . . But though the religious life is abundantly in evidence through the synagogues and the Talmud-Torah schools and the Chedorim, . . . there is lament on the part of the pious that the house of worship and the ritualistic ceremonial of the Jewish faith have lost their hold upon the spiritual life of the younger generation.[10]

Interestingly, Phillips had chosen to illustrate a recently constructed building. The Erste Warshawer Congregation had erected this synagogue on Rivington Street in 1903, and it soon became a leading synagogue for Polish Jews, one of the "imposing" structures of Wald's description. But in Phillips's view, the synagogue was a neighborhood shul, crowded with worshippers and lively with activity. In this regard, it seems to have been somewhat of a rarity, a synagogue with synagogue-goers!

A quite different view had been offered by Jacob Epstein in his illustrations for Hutchins Hapgood's *The Spirit of the Ghetto* (1902).[11]

119

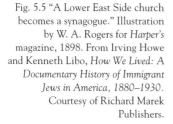

Fig. 5.5 "A Lower East Side church becomes a synagogue." Illustration by W. A. Rogers for *Harper's* magazine, 1898. From Irving Howe and Kenneth Libo, *How We Lived: A Documentary History of Immigrant Jews in America, 1880–1930*. Courtesy of Richard Marek Publishers.

Fig. 5.6 "The Synagogues Are Everywhere—Imposing or Shabby-Looking Buildings." Engraving by Abraham Phillips depicting the Warshawer Shul on Rivington Street. From Lillian D. Wald, *The House on Henry Street* (New York: Holt, Rinehart and Winston, 1915; repr. Dover Publications, 1971).

The few images that relate to synagogue life depict isolated individuals, such as in the cover illustration of a bearded man wrapped in his prayer shawl (fig. 5.7) and the sketch of a father and son "going to the synagogue." Epstein also offered two other scenes of elderly Jews at prayer, one of a woman sitting behind the *mechitzah* (the divider separating the section set aside for women), and the other of a man even more anonymous and alone in the shul pews (fig. 5.8). Rare for their intimacy, comparable perhaps to Jacob Riis's interior photographs of tenement life, these two portraits convey the impression that the synagogue is but sparsely attended and then only by the old—and we are left to wonder whether the synagogue has any future at all in America.

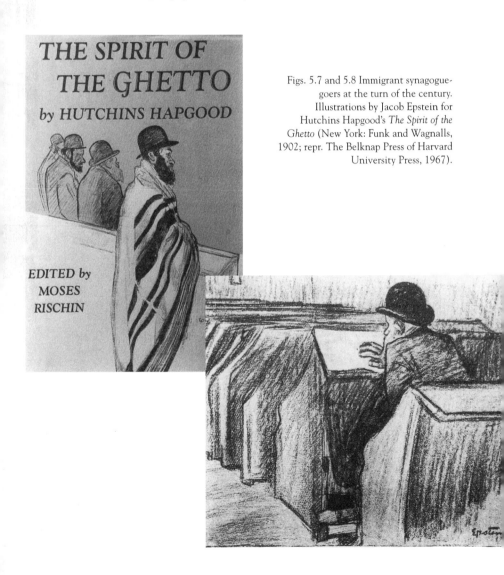

Figs. 5.7 and 5.8 Immigrant synagogue-goers at the turn of the century. Illustrations by Jacob Epstein for Hutchins Hapgood's *The Spirit of the Ghetto* (New York: Funk and Wagnalls, 1902; repr. The Belknap Press of Harvard University Press, 1967).

Concurrent with the rise of the immigrant ghetto, photography had become a principal medium of historical documentation. Of the hundreds of photographic images of the Lower East Side made by Riis, Byron, Hine, and others, few indeed depict synagogues. Once again, the religious life of the ghetto was thought to be of minor importance to its inhabitants, and was certainly considered unworthy of preservation by those who documented it. In these early constructions of Lower East Side memory, Judaism, and its concrete expression, the synagogue, were quite simply ignored.

Nevertheless, some hint of the existence of shuls can be found upon closer examination. Among the most frequently reproduced images of the Lower East Side are various views of the turn-of-the-century *Hazermark*, the Hester Street market between Essex and Norfolk Streets. These iconic photographs are to be found in many pictorial surveys of the Lower East Side, often including different angles of the same scene, as can be seen in Gerard Wolfe's walking tour guide to New York (1975).[12] Usually unremarked, however, is the presence of a synagogue—a three-story wooden structure with Gothic windows—in the center of the scene. This is verified by an extant close-up view (see fig. 5.10), in which the sign reads, "Beit Hakenesset D'Hevrah B'nai Yitchak, Anshe [illegible]." The shul might be related to the congregation later listed as B'nai Isaac Anshei Lechowitz, organized in 1892, and located at 93 Hester Street in 1919.[13] In any event, it was almost certainly a landsmanschaft shul, constructed as a tenement-style synagogue in the heart of the *Hazermark*.

Another photographic scene along these lines is Lewis Hine's 1912 portrait of a typical market street on the East Side (see fig. 5.11). Due to the rather monumental, though distant, synagogue located, once again, in the very center of the photograph, we can identify the scene

Fig. 5.9 The *Hazermark* on Hester Street, looking east from corner of Essex, 1899. Photographer unknown. Courtesy of the Museum of the City of New York, Print Archives.

Fig. 5.10 Closeup of 43-45 Hester Street, undated. The synagogue of Chevrah B'nai Yitzchak appears at right. Photographer unknown. Courtesy of the Museum of the City of New York, Print Archives.

Fig. 5.11 Rivington Street, looking east across Orchard Street. Photograph by Lewis Hine, 1912. Courtesy of Lewis W. Hine Collection, Milstein Division of United States History, Local History and Genealogy, The New York Public Library, Astor, Lenox and Tilden Foundations.

as Rivington Street, looking east across the intersection of Orchard Street. The synagogue is the First Roumanian-American Congregation, whose congregational origins remain in dispute, but whose physical presence is undeniable. As in our earlier examples, the sharply detailed foreground is given to the commercial life of the neighborhood, while the background contains a hazy view of a synagogue, an echo of the past. Whether or not Hine intended to make such a statement, the once central synagogue is now lost in the background, overwhelmed by the hustle and bustle of the new.

In the photographic legacy of the immigrant era, portraits of synagogues *per se* do appear, but only rarely. In the 1905 publication of *The Jewish Encyclopedia*, the article on New York was illustrated with many contemporary photographs, including two of Lower East Side synagogues: Beth Hamidrash Hagadol on Norfolk Street, a former Baptist church acquired by the pioneer Russian Jewish congregation in 1885

(fig. 5.12), and the Pike Street Synagogue of Congregation Sons of Israel Kalvarie, built in 1903 (fig. 5.13).[14] Representing the old world, Beth Hamidrash Hagadol had been the seat of Chief Rabbi Jacob Joseph. Pike Street, on the other hand, was intended as a more forward-looking young people's synagogue, and indeed, the Young Israel movement was founded on its premises in 1912. The tension between old and new is further highlighted by the architectural contrast between oriental pastiche on Norfolk Street and the Renaissance Revival on Pike.

The first sustained examination of Lower East Side synagogues only came about in 1937, as part of the WPA project to document New York

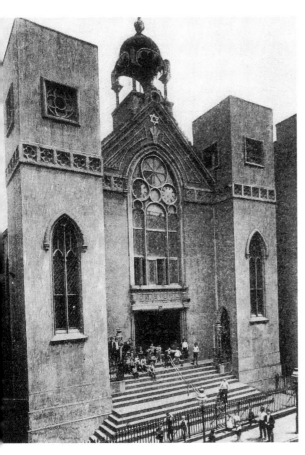
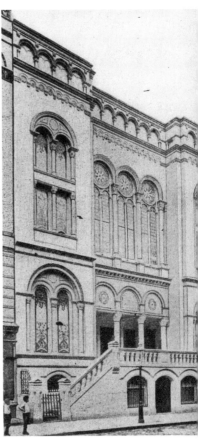

City life. It was a transitional time on the Lower East Side, and the photographic evidence reflects this era. The WPA photographers found a neighborhood still populated by Jews, but long past its heyday as the Jewish immigrant ghetto. As communal life dissipated, nostalgia began to creep in, and synagogues first came to represent a mythical past. Hence, the WPA group focused on the synagogues in a way earlier photographers had not. For example, their image of Beth Hamidrash Hagadol (fig. 5.14) shows the historic building sandwiched between adjoining tenements, one including a kosher butcher. The synagogue, in this perspective, was an integral part of a functioning Jewish neighborhood. Yet by the late 1930s both the Jewish population and the neighborhood, were in steep decline.

The WPA collection also included photographs of Kol Israel Anshe Poland and Beth Haknesseth Poel-Tzedek Anshe Ilya, both on Forsyth Street, and both, today, converted into churches. While Anshe Ilya (fig. 5.15), built in 1906 on the corner of Delancey Street, was still functioning as the well-known "Forsyth Street Synagogue" in 1937, Anshe Poland (fig. 5.16), built in 1892, had already been sold to a Greek Orthodox church, ten years earlier. Thus, both the glory and the decline of the Lower East Side were documented by the WPA historians.

During the following decade of the 1940s and into the post-War era, American Jews seemed to have acquired mass amnesia regarding the immigrant synagogue, as they were now busy constructing their modern and up-to-date synagogue-centers in the memory-free environment of suburbia. Even in publications that dealt with American Jewish life in general and with synagogue history in particular, the Lower East Side synagogues were virtually ignored. In the year of the American Jewish tercentennial, 1954, Bernard Postal and Lionel Koppman first published their popular *A Jewish Tourist's Guide to the U.S.*[15] Remarkably, in ten full pages delineating forty-three sites of interest on the Lower East Side, only one synagogue is listed—Beth Hamidrash Hagadol—which ostensibly earned the honor by being "the oldest Russian Orthodox synagogue in the country."[16] No synagogues

Fig. 5.12 Beth Hamidrash Hagadol, Norfolk Street, acquired 1885. "New York," in *The Jewish Encyclopedia* (New York: Funk and Wagnalls, 1905).

Fig. 5.13 Sons of Israel Kalvarie, Pike Street, built 1903. "New York," in *The Jewish Encyclopedia* (New York: Funk and Wagnalls, 1905).

Fig. 5.14 (*opposite*) Beth Hamidrash Hagadol, Norfolk Street, 1937. Unidentified WPA photographer. Collection of the New-York Historical Society.

Fig. 5.15 (*top*)Anshe Ilya, Forsyth Street, 1937. Unidentified WPA photographer. Collection of the New-York Historical Society.

Fig. 5.16 Anshe Poland, Forsyth Street, 1937. Unidentified WPA photographer. Collection of the New-York Historical Society.

are pictured, of course—the only institution that represents the East Side pictorially is the Forverts building. This common bias parallels Moses Rischin's map from 1962, and reflects many other works of the period as well.

A conspicuous lack of synagogues appears even where we might reasonably expect the opposite. Rachel Wischnitzer's 1955 publication, *Synagogue Architecture in the United States*, illustrates but a few structures located on the Lower East Side, including two former German-Jewish synagogues and two former church buildings.[17] The only illustration of a synagogue built by the East European immigrant community is the early watercolor of Eldridge Street. Even more surprisingly, such inattention to the immigrant synagogue has characterized surveys of Lower East Side history. Moses Rischin's *The Promised City* has been noted, but the same is true of Irving Howe's widely popular *World of Our Fathers*, published in 1976.[18] Howe's voluminous book is copiously illustrated, yet not a single depiction of a synagogue is to be found. Only the *Hazermark* photograph discussed earlier appears, making it the sole image of a synagogue to appear in that standard work of Jewish immigrant history, albeit unintended. Similarly, a more recent survey of the period, Gerald Sorin's *A Time for Building* (1992), also includes the *Hazermark* image, but in the tradition of Rischin and Howe, has no other illustrations of synagogues in the book.[19]

Disinterest in the synagogue thus characterized elite versions of Lower East Side history and prevailed through both print and photographic surveys, from Rischin (1962) to Howe (1976), and from Wischnitzer (1955) to Allon Schoener's 1966 exhibition at the Jewish Museum and the subsequent publication, *Portal to America: The Lower East Side* (1967).[20] Schoener, influenced no doubt by what he found in the many archives he visited, included but one synagogue, a 1911 photo of the Mishkan Israel Suwalki synagogue, formerly Beth Israel Bikur Cholim, Temple Emanu-El before that, and originally a Methodist church. The photo, taken just a few years before the building's demolition (circa 1914), reflects a Lower East Side already in decline.

Despite its secular bias, the publication of Schoener's book in 1967 heralded a new nostalgia that would refocus attention on the synagogue. Unlike *Portal to America*, the new popular history would come to praise the synagogue, not bury it. Taken about the same time as Schoener's exhibition and book are two unpublished snapshots by an anonymous photographer; both reveal a neighborhood in transition. One photograph (fig. 5.17) shows the Sineerer Shul on Madison Street, the home of Congregation Machzike Torah Anshe Senier V'Anshe Vilna. Built in 1851 as the Olive Branch Baptist Church, it was destroyed by fire in 1972. The second (see fig. 5.18) is the synagogue of the Polish Makower Congregation on Henry Street, established in 1893. Following the destruction in 1972 of Madison Street, the two congregations merged and became known as Congregation Senier and Wilno; this synagogue was itself destroyed in late 1975. Gerard Wolfe stressed the element of destruction, writing in 1978: "Only the burned-out shell remains of this once proud and active synagogue. . . . The destruction of this venerable shul shocked and outraged the commu-

Fig. 5.17 The Sineerer Shul, Madison Street, c. 1965. Unidentified photographer. Courtesy of the Educational Alliance.

Fig. 5.18 The Makower Shul, Henry
Street, c. 1965. Unidentified
photographer. Courtesy of the
Educational Alliance.

nity. Now marked for early demolition, the totally gutted synagogue
with its smashed stained glass windows, fire-scarred dome and Mogen
David, and ruined interior stands as a sad reminder of the ever-present
sickness of antisemitism."[21] To emphasize the point, he provided a be-
fore-and-after view of the building.

Beginning in the 1970s, therefore, new attention would be paid to
the synagogues of the Lower East Side. In a small but striking turn-
about, Postal and Koppman issued a new edition of their tourist's guide
in 1977, retitling it *American Jewish Landmarks*. In this edition, they

added five synagogues to their original listing of one. Wolfe's volume came out a year later, and the following years saw the publication of a series of pictorial surveys, such as Ronald Sanders's *The Lower East Side: A Guide to Its Jewish Past in 99 New Photographs* (1979) and Oscar Israelowitz's *Synagogues of New York City* (1982), both issued by Dover Publications.[22] Whereas Sanders stressed the deterioration of the synagogue, Israelowitz emphasized the former glory of the Jewish community. Compare, for instance, the former's interior view of the abandoned Anshe Slonim on Norfolk Street (originally built in 1851 for Ansche Chesed) with the latter's image of Sons of Israel Kalvarie on Pike Street. One is a lament for the destroyed, the other, a celebration of survival.

In subsequent years, the themes of destruction and survival are most often elicited in combination, as for example, at Eldridge Street. Urban historian Gerard Wolfe's "discovery" of the neglected synagogue in the early 1970s led to the restoration project headed by Roberta Brandes Gratz and its designation as a national landmark in 1980—marking its selection to serve the function of "synagogue museum" of the Lower East Side. As we might infer from contemporary photographs, the emphasis is now on the drama of encountering the past. Referring to Eldridge Street, architectural critic Paul Goldberger would write in 1989, "what distinguishes this project is the extent to which it stands as an affirmation of the belief on the part of lay people as well as architects that a religious building is an anchor in time, a symbol of continuity as well as a vessel of meaning in the city."[23] Today, therefore, the Jewish East Side is being increasingly remembered through the image of a single historic institution: the synagogue. Significantly, Eldridge Street is the only specifically Jewish tourist site operating in the area. Yet synagogues are the new repositories of Lower East Side memory.[24]

But is it an accurate accounting of history? The question counts for little, of course, for as we know, memory serves the needs of the present rather than the veracity of the past. As we have seen, representation of the immigrant synagogue has shifted between near-exclusion and over-emphasis. How may we explain this protean phenomenon? It is perhaps related to broader questions of American Jewish identity. The era of second-generation American Jewry (roughly 1920–50) was characterized by the rise of an ethnicity in which group identity was largely based upon the ties of historic peoplehood and common culture, and thus the synagogue understandably receded into the background. The following era (1950–80) saw the revival of an identity based on religious belief and affiliation (if not necessarily observance), and hence

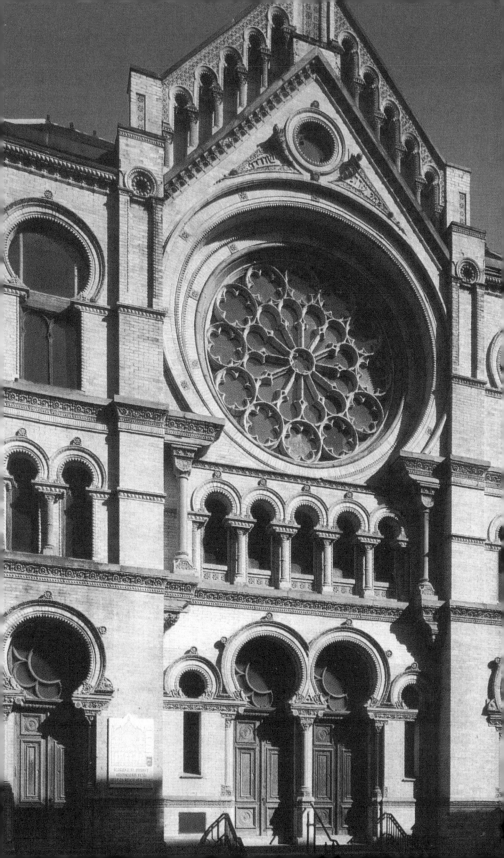

Fig. 5.19 Contemporary view of the Eldridge
Street Synagogue. Courtesy of the Eldridge
Street Project.

the synagogue became the very symbol of group existence. Today, as in the immigrant era itself, there seems to be greater awareness that Jewishness is a religious and an ethnic identity at once. Yet as long as confusion persists on this point, as long as Jews tend to emphasize one at the expense of the other, then the synagogue will remain on contested ground.

NOTES

1. For a more comprehensive history of the immigrant synagogue, see chapter 5 in David Kaufman, *Shul with a Pool: The "Synagogue-Center" in American Jewish History* (Hanover, N.H.: University Press of New England, 1999). On the issue of the centrality of the synagogue in Jewish life, see pp. 5–7.

2. Moses Rischin, *The Promised City: New York's Jews, 1870–1914* (Cambridge, Mass.: Harvard University Press, 1962). The map of the Lower East Side, found on p. 77, has been reprinted many times.

3. Ibid., p. 105.

4. A "landsmanschaft shul" is a small congregation formed by immigrants from the same hometown or region. The vast majority of immigrant synagogues began as such. For further discussion, see Kaufman, *Shul with a Pool.*

5. Eric Homberger, *The Historical Atlas of New York City: A Visual Celebration of Nearly 400 Years of New York City's History* (New York: Henry Holt and Company, 1994), p. 132.

6. Gerard R. Wolfe, *The Synagogues of New York's Lower East Side* (New York: Washington Mews Books, 1978), p. 31.

7. As estimated by *The Jewish Encyclopedia* (New York: Funk and Wagnalls Company, 1905), article on "New York," vol. 9, p. 284.

8. Kaufman, *Shul with a Pool,* p. 183.

9. Irving Howe and Kenneth Libo, *How We Lived: A Documentary History of Immigrant Jews in America, 1880–1930* (New York: Richard Marek Publishers, 1979), p. 92.

10. Lillian D. Wald, *The House on Henry Street* (New York: Holt, Rinehart and Winston, 1915), pp. 253–254.

Constructions of Memory

135

11. Hutchins Hapgood, *The Spirit of the Ghetto: Studies of the Jewish Quarter in New York* (New York: Funk and Wagnalls Company, 1902), pp. 21, 45, 73. Also note the illustration of a synagogue scene on p. 15, later used for the cover of the 1967 reprint by Harvard University Press.

12. Gerard R. Wolfe, *New York: A Guide to the Metropolis—Walking Tours of Architecture and History* (New York: McGraw-Hill Book Company, 1988), pp. 131, 147.

13. *The American Jewish Year Book* (Philadelphia: Jewish Publication Society of America, 1919), vol. 21, p. 460.

14. "New York," in *The Jewish Encyclopedia*, pp. 262, 264.

15. Bernard Postal and Lionel Koppman, *A Jewish Tourist's Guide to the U.S.* (Philadelphia: Jewish Publication Society of America, 1954).

16. Ibid., pp. 380–390, 388.

17. Rachel Wischnitzer, *Synagogue Architecture in the United States* (Philadelphia: Jewish Publication Society of America, 1955), pp. 48, 53, 55–56, 83.

18. Irving Howe, *World of Our Fathers: The Journey of the East European Jews to America and the Life They Found and Made* (New York: Harcourt Brace Jovanovich, 1976), illustration entitled "Peddlers and customers on Hester Street," found between pp. 140 and 141.

19. Gerald Sorin, *A Time for Building: The Third Migration, 1880–1920*, vol. 3 of *The Jewish People in America*, ed. Henry Feingold (Baltimore: Johns Hopkins University Press, 1992). Sorin's subsequent survey of American Jewish history reprints the Hazermark photo as its frontispiece and has Lewis Hines's photograph of Rivington Street gracing its cover. *Tradition Transformed: The Jewish Experience in America* (Baltimore: Johns Hopkins University Press, 1997).

20. Allon Schoener, ed., *Portal to America: The Lower East Side, 1870–1925* (New York: Holt, Rinehart and Winston, 1967), p. 156.

21. Wolfe, *The Synagogues of New York's Lower East Side*, pp. 118–121.

22. Postal and Koppman, *American Jewish Landmarks: A Travel Guide and History* (New York: Fleet Press Corporation, 1977); Ronald Sanders, *The Lower East Side: A Guide to Its Jewish Past in 99 New Photographs* (New York: Dover Publications, 1979). Oscar Israelowitz, *Synagogues of New York City* (New York: Dover Publications, 1982).

23. Paul Goldberger, "Why Design Can't Transform Cities," *New York Times*, June 25, 1989, Architecture/Design section, p. 30.

24. Some other contemporary examples: The most recent organization formed to promote the Jewish history of the neighborhood is the Lower East Side Conservancy, a group whose mission is to preserve the many aging synagogue buildings of the neighborhood. Their guided bus tours of the area shuttle visitors through a circuit of synagogues. In 1999, the Educational Alliance sponsored a photography show of synagogues, and the main exhibition at the Eldridge Street Synagogue was "Urban Diaspora," a survey of synagogue restoration projects around the country.

The One-Way Window:

Public Schools on the Lower East Side in the

Stephan F. Brumberg

Early Twentieth Century

At the beginning of the twentieth century, the schools of New York City set out to transform their immigrant students into the very models of modern American citizens. As Associate Superintendent John H. Haaran wrote in 1913,

> The school, as one of the instruments of civilization, must take its part in solving the problem that has been precipitated by the great immigration of people who differ from the great mass of our population not only in language, but in customs, political ideals, and to a considerable extent in religion.[1]

The Lower East Side was the quintessential target of educational transformers. As Ellwood P. Cubberley, the pre-eminent educational historian of the time, saw it,

> These people tend to settle in groups . . . and to set up here their national
> manners, customs, and observances. Our task is to break up these . . . settle-
> ments, to assimilate and amalgamate these people as a part of our American
> race.[2]

New York's schools created curricula and structured school life to promote the Americanization of its immigrant charges. First and fore-most, they promoted the English language, the carrier of the dominant American culture and the means whereby American lifeways and val-ues were to be communicated to students. In addition to the three "R"s, schools promoted an allegiance to a new fatherland and mother tongue, provided children with American forefathers and foremothers, mod-eled American lifeways, explicated the virtues of democratic govern-ment, and taught children how fortunate they were to be growing up in the United States, land of the free and home of the brave.

New York City's public schools were seen as the great bulwark against the immigrant invasion. The education system embarked on a race to see if "we" could change "them" before "we" were drowned in an alien cultural sea. The virtues to be protected are reflected in the following passage written in 1919 by Anning S. Prall, New York Board of Education President, in the aftermath of The Great War, and during the Red Scare that followed (a hot war in New York's schools):

> No city in the country has gone further than New York City in the direction
> of consciously motivated, systematic training for citizenship. . . . No city
> needs such training more, for this is no longer an American city, but rather
> a cosmopolitan city in process of being Americanized. [The public school
> must offset the influence of] the home with [its] alien traditions, alien aspi-
> rations, a foreign press, organizations subversive of law and order, with their
> public meetings and their street speakers, even competing Sunday and night
> schools which announce their aim to be—"to offset the vicious teaching of
> the public school."[3]

Window on the World

To help achieve their transformational goal, the public schools cre-ated a one-way window on the world. Schools encouraged children to look out to the larger American world, even as they looked right through the neighborhood of the Lower East Side and its cultural and linguistic community. The intellectual ferment of the East Side at the turn of the twentieth century was excluded; the art, music and litera-ture filtered out. The exclusive focus instead was on American lifeways, allegiances, history (and myths), aesthetics, and, of course, the English language. The goal of schools, and the teachers who staffed them, was to set their pupils on a path out of the ghettoized life of the Lower East Side, and direct them onto the great American Main Street.

In light of what the public schools were trying to do, what memories of school on the Lower East Side are recalled by individuals who were students there in the early part of the twentieth century? First we will listen to the recollections of five individuals who were pupils in the neighborhood eighty to one hundred years ago. Then we turn to a single event, the 1963 dedication of the new P.S. 20 on Essex and Stanton Streets, and to the canonization of one view of schools, immigrants, and the American experience.

Remembering Schooling on the Lower East Side

A character in Salman Rushdie's novel *Shame* expresses the dilemma of remembering, especially for migrants:

> As for me . . . I too, like all migrants, am a Fantasist. I build imaginary countries and try to impose them on the ones that exist. I too, face the problems of history: what to dump, how to hold on to what memory insists on relinquishing, how to deal with change.[4]

The five people who here speak to us were all immigrants to New York City and its East Side, where they attended public schools. They were extensively interviewed by the author, along with more than twenty other individuals who had attended schools in Europe and New York between 1893 and 1917, as part of a study of the turn-of-the-century encounter of Jewish immigrants and New York City's public schools.[5] Their recollections of schooling are complemented with school documents of the period, especially on the courses of study then in use in the New York schools.

These informants all moved on to lead distinct lives, embrace different values, follow different career paths, and, consequently, remember school differently. The differences in school recollections, however, were less than anticipated, and there was considerable overlap of memories and judgments. Like Rushdie's character, they shed parts of old lives, wrapped themselves in new ways (many of which had been learned at school), and now filter memories through personalities synthesized out of the experiences of the better part of a century of life.

When they were children, however, their public schools directed their gazes through the window and out to "America." At times, like Alice, the school literally passed them from the real world of the Lower East Side into the wonderland of America, or at least to uptown Manhattan.

Stephan F. Brumberg

> We were all expected to go down to St. Patrick's Cathedral and identify the
> flying buttresses, because when you study medieval history you study . . .
> architecture—you study everything except what they did to the Jews during
> the Crusades, and nothing about Jewish medieval history. . . . So I go from
> [the Lower East Side] to St. Patrick's Cathedral. I'd never been on Fifth
> Avenue in that area. And I go in, I'm scared. I didn't know what to do,
> whether I should put my hat on or off, terribly awesome. I looked around
> trying to find the flying buttresses and they turned out to be outside the
> Cathedral. This was an awesome experience.[6]

Like Morris Schappes, whose experience as a first-year high school
student was just recounted, our informants came from Jewish homes
and had little knowledge of the Christian world, or of "uptown"
America, but had certain fears and prejudices. Rather, they and their
classmates on the Lower East Side were not passive receptacles for the
receipt of school messages. They came with a child's store of knowledge, values, aspirations, allegiances, and biases—all of which filtered
what school was telling them. They, and their parents, represented
various tendencies that were reinforced or contradicted by school (socialism vs. capitalism, intellectualism vs. materialism vs. spiritualism,
nationalism vs. universalism, conversion to English vs. conservation of
Yiddish, etc.). Hence, the impact school had on them, and their recon-
structions of the past are very different.

American Lifeways

American culture was part of the fabric of the school: The culture
was reflected in its language, holidays, instructional content, rituals,
and especially its teachers. In dress, comportment, and interests, the
teachers modeled American manners and values. Mr. Fleischer, one of
the teachers at P.S. 147, is recalled by Harry Liebowitz:

> He was terrific. He was blonde, the athletic type and we had a bar across the
> entrance of the room of the classroom—placed there purposely and you'd go
> for chinning [P.S. 147 produced the fifth-, sixth-, and eighth-grade chin-
> ning champs of Manhattan in 1913 and 1914]. You had to chin a certain
> number of times—everybody—and he made us do it.[7]

Although probably Jewish, Mr. Fleischer is recalled by his student as
the very model of a sports-loving American. And sports were critical to
becoming American. A greenhorn was identified first by his speech,
and

> Second, he was not inclined to go out and play ball and stuff. We'd have
> games like pussycat. You'd take a broomstick, cut off one end of it, say about
> 6", and then you'd have the rest of the stick . . . and then you'd get up and
> you'd hit it. . . . The foreigners wouldn't play that.[8]

But not all recollections of teachers were so positive. Morris Schappes recalled a rather strict and severe teacher, nicknamed "Slaughterhouse."

> She was very tall, very lean, wore, ALWAYS, all the years I knew her, a long black dress up to [her chin]. She was the English teacher and to justify her name Slaughterhouse, once in answering a question or somehow she heard me utter in class the words "Jesus" or "Jesus Christ." I'm sure I didn't know what they meant. But she dragged me up to the board and banged my head against the board, and that was the last time I took the name of the Lord in vain. But, I got an education.[9]

Teachers communicated American aesthetics and proper womanly behavior, not just strict discipline. As Mary Frieman recalled her "American" teachers:

> I saw they were a different breed . . . the way they acted, dressed and so on . . . there was a certain thing—very retiring. See, my Jewish background is to be outgoing and to yell and scream and do everything. And I think the one big thing that I learned is to behave and to be retiring, not to be pushy. I think I learned that from my teachers. I think that's an American trait.[10]

Assuming an American identity also required the right clothes and shoes. And for some immigrants it wasn't until high school that fashion lessons were learned, at times with considerable pain. Morris Schappes had been admitted to Townsend Harris Hall, the most prestigious boy's school of its day, and arrived on the first day of classes in the company of two tenement district classmates.

> We were three boys in new knickers, long stockings, white shirts with tie, something special for high school and each of us had our lunch in a bag. Come into Townsend Harris Hall and we're the only boys in short pants and without jacket. Come into this upper West Side atmosphere and we felt utterly conspicuous and we had to go home and get long pants [a heavy financial burden to the families]. There were a few days we were wandering around in this Gentile school . . . [with] Gothic buildings . . . and I know it affected me very, very sharply. . . . I had been a street corner speaker at P. S. 64 [on the Lower East Side] but here I began to stammer and stutter.[11]

Learning American ways was not always simple. The literal-mindedness of a child, coupled with a child's wish to please a respected adult, could yield humorous incidents. Seven-year-old Rose Klein arrived in New York with her parents on December 11, 1913. Five days later she was enrolled in P.S. 161. During her first year in school she was asked to do an errand for her teacher.

> At lunch time [she] gave me a nickel and she said to go out please and buy her three bananas. Well, if the teacher said three bananas for five cents then

that's what it had to be, you know. Well, I went on Orchard Street, from pushcart to pushcart, they wouldn't sell me three bananas for a nickel—they'd only sell me six bananas for a nickel and my teacher said *three*! Finally, I got to one who sold me three bananas for a nickel and after I left he said, "here, take three more!"[12]

For the school, and for many students, American ways meant learning to garden. School authorities greatly feared that their immigrant students preferred the harsh precincts of the city to the "American" greenery of the countryside. The syllabus for "School Gardens" declaimed that

> The sordid panorama of our city streets pours its pernicious influence into the very soul of the rising generation during the most impressionable years, until the sense of beauty and naturalness is stunted and the garishness of city scenes is preferred to the gentle charm of nature's offering.[13]

With precious little space for school gardens on the Lower East Side, schools sprouted potted gardens on their rooftops. Gardening and songs celebrating "golden waves of grain" imparted the lesson that authentic America was the farm, not the pushcart markets.

But acquiring an American persona required more than manners, sports, proper commercial etiquette, and plunging your hands into American soil. A greenhorn label was attached to you if you were

> not speaking English. . . . I was embarrassed to speak Yiddish to my mother when we were outdoors, where people could hear me. I wouldn't feel that way now. Not speaking English, that was one thing. You tried to talk English all the time. We were very anxious to become American.[14]

And the public school was the place to learn American lifeways as you acquired the skills to compete in the American market place. As Ida Rosenbaum recalled:

> we all got an education because there was no other way out. I don't think it was choice. A Jewish girl couldn't get a job at Metropolitan Life or the Telephone Company, so she had to be a teacher. In that place there were fewer obstacles in her path. . . .You know, they kicked us upstairs. Why do we have so many doctors and lawyers? It was a complete drive to pull yourself up out of a mire and it had to be without money.[15]

Patriotism and Civics

The children of immigrants all recall efforts to instill in them patriotic feelings toward their new homeland. Flags and anthems and American heroes were staples of school life and learning. America's participation in World War I was recalled by all, although with different reactions. Dr. Harry Liebowitz recalled that "if you enlisted and worked on a farm to replace men who would go into the war, you would be forgiven [course credits to graduate from high school]."[16] He himself served on a tobacco farm in Connecticut and was granted a diploma from that state's Governor Trumble.

It was a natural response of immigrants to feel some patriotism toward America in response to the opportunities they perceived. Rose Klein recalled the difficulties Jews had encountered in Russia, where rigid school admissions quotas had been in force. She believed that one of the reasons her father emigrated was to provide his children with an education.

At times, however, the Americanizing messages conflicted with home understandings. Often the school view prevailed—at least in the short-run. Morris Schappes related that "in college . . . I learned economics. What did I learn in economics—about the marginal theory of value and so on, while my father would talk to me about class consciousness. . . . This contradicted everything I had learned. So there was no communication." Later, as he was exposed to the labor theory of value, to class consciousness, and to social struggles, he turned back to his father's viewpoint, "because he understood in an implicit way what I was just trying to figure out in an explicit, theoretical way."[17]

Patriotism was interpreted by each immigrant student in light of his or her own understandings of democracy, government, and the rights of the governed, some of which were learned in school civics lessons, and some at home. Ida Rosenbaum had been a committed socialist from childhood. She told a story of how her understanding of the right of free speech clashed with the school's assumptions of patriotic conformity. When President McKinley was assassinated in 1901, students at Wadleigh High School wore buttons to honor his passing. But, according to Ida,

> I don't think [McKinley] was the kind of man I'd like to honor by wearing a button and they said why, and I said my father is a socialist, and . . . when I consider that he put the miners' families out in the middle of the winter when they struck, I wasn't wearing a button. [She got into trouble when she was reported to the principal, who asked her,] "Do you think the school is a public platform for political discussion [referring both to her not wearing a button *and* to the response she gave to a fellow student]? I said, there was a girl who asked me why I didn't wear a button. She had a right to ask and I didn't have the right to answer?[18]

But the opportunity to learn was seen by all as a great American virtue. As Ida recalled, "we were both grateful and avid learners. We felt that Prometheus had come down and blown up the fire. And that made a big difference. We didn't accept it as simply as gentile children did because they . . . were not segregated, not kept out [as we had been in the Old World]."[19]

English Language

Most children of immigrants, even if born in New York, went off to school speaking Yiddish. Harry Liebowitz recalled that "when [I] went to school I didn't understand a great deal of the English spoken because the only language I knew was Yiddish."[20] English was learned in school, especially through reading. In fact, virtually every informant spoke of the importance of reading in their lives. We don't often realize just how important the pubic library was to the generation of Jewish immigrants who came at the turn of this century. The teaching of English was also a focus of the work in many of the settlement houses. Dr. Liebowitz recalled that at Henry Street, "they had people who came who graduated from the Ivy League colleges, and they'd come down to get their slum training, their social work so to speak, and Herbert Lehman [the future governor of New York]—he used to come down—and he would talk to us in good English, and they would correct us if we spoke poorly or incorrectly."[21]

Everyone wanted to learn English. Evaluating this phenomenon in retrospect, some now see the need for sustaining a child's mother tongue, but others are still vehemently opposed to the use of any language but English. Many, however, later became aware of what was lost by learning in an English-speaking world and coming home to Yiddish. Morris Schappes came to understand that

> the price I paid [for mastering English while allowing Yiddish to stagnate and atrophy] was very sharp alienation from my parents' culture, from Yiddish. At Townsend Harris . . . Yiddish was frowned upon—it would be damaging to your career. If you were preparing to be a teacher at City College, you not merely had to be sure that you didn't have a Jewish accent, but even that subtle thing, a Jewish intonation . . . Yiddish was no use at all except to speak to my parents.[22]

The English language itself became not only a conduit for Anglo-American culture, but of values, biases, and prejudices.

> In college I absorbed anti-semitism as a quite amenable part of reality. T. S. Eliot was a great poet, was an anti-semite—so he was a great poet, that was more important than he was anti-semitic . . . I would read Chaucer and Chaucer's anti-semitism I swallowed whole. It was part of the curriculum. I didn't question the curriculum. And so the price I paid was alienation from my parents [and their culture].[23]

Respondents, however, never completely rejected Yiddish, and as adults some returned to the language. Nearly all attended Yiddish theater, and some read its literature. But Yiddish had had no place in formal schooling. Ida Rosenbaum recalled that when she became a teacher, a mother sent a note in Yiddish. "I said I can read it, and [my fellow teachers] all said how did I dare admit to such a degradation, and I became the official interpreter."[24]

Adopting English was much more than a linguistic change: It effectively channeled most Jewish students away from Yiddish intellectual currents and into the American intellectual mainstream. It diminished the cultural and political world of their parents and replaced it with an American version. Morris Schappes relates that

> I was not listening to what my parents were saying. . . . Once my father came home with a book that he bought at the Workmen's Circle—a book by Mendel Beilis. He was here in this country lecturing, selling his book. He brought it home and I heard my mother read to him chapter by chapter, day after day. But I was doing other things. . . . It wasn't until twenty years [later] that I read it. My father had heard him attentively twenty years before, but we never talked about it. So, they would always hide from me any sense of disappointment, but I don't know—they must have been more aware of what I was doing to them than I was when I was doing it.[25]

Public school education had clearly influenced the children of the Lower East Side. However, each child was changed in distinct ways, and not always in the ways that were intended by the established school leaders. The intelligent, active learner ultimately held the upper hand over the school. He or she had the power to accept, reject, or reinterpret the messages the school transmitted. The school could construct a one-way window onto America, but could not control a student's vision. Participants rated public schooling as a positive and valuable shaping experience, but one in which the individual, too, played a part in determining who he or she would become. Ida Rosenbaum, speaking of the activism of her own son, claimed with pride that "My children inherited, just as I did from my father, a sense that you have to be part of the world that you live in, if you want it to get any better. You can't wait for the other fellow to do it for you. So. . . ."[26]

Canonizing the View of Lower East Side Schools

The variegated view of education on the Lower East Side—reflected in the reminiscences of the people interviewed—needs to be contrasted with another, more mythic, popularized version of public schools and immigrants. This latter view regards school as the benefi-

cent engine of change that Americanized the children of the tired, poor, yearning-to-breathe-free immigrant, and carried them into the American mainstream.

In 1963, the dedication of P.S. 20 on Essex and Stanton Streets was an event that perfectly summarized the prevalent mainstream view of immigrants who had come to the Lower East Side. New P.S. 20 ostensibly replaced old P.S. 20, which had opened in 1898, and which had been located nearby on Rivington Street, between Forsyth and Chrystie. P.S. 20 is one of the fabled schools of the Lower East Side. It numbers among its graduates George and Ira Gershwin, Paul Muni and Edward G. Robinson, Harry Golden and Irving Caesar, a score of prominent physicians, and last, but not least, Senator Jacob Javits and Charles H. Silver.

The new P.S. 20 was named, tellingly, for Anna Silver, mother of Charles H. Silver, who was a former president of the New York Board of Education and a leading philanthropist and humanitarian of his day.

In 1963, the P.S. 20 Alumni Association presented the new school with a mural by artist Lumin Winters, celebrating the Lower East Side

Fig. 6.1 Old Public School 20 (1898), located on Rivington Street between Forsyth and Chrystie Streets. Photographed in 1933. Courtesy of the New York City Board of Education.

Fig. 6.2 New Public School 20 (1963), located on Essex Street between Stanton and Houston Streets. Photographed in 1963. Courtesy of the New York City Board of Education.

148

(fig. 6.3). The dedication of the mural was part of the larger celebration ceremony marking the opening of P.S. 20 on February 14, 1963. A brief television news clip of the event has survived and as the following transcript of the reporter's comments makes clear, he has his Lower East Side mythology down pat.[27]

> This is New York's Lower East Side. We are here today, at Essex and Stanton, to dedicate [P.S. 20]. The Lower East Side cradled the community that was the new world. It was here that the immigrants came. It was to the old P.S. 20 that they brought their children, a haven in the promised land, where, under clotheslined tenement roofs, a new nation of immigrants and descendants of immigrants merged into a multicolored and multiracial pattern that is America.

The graduates of the old P.S. 20 helped build the mosaic of America. By implication, the new P.S. 20 was carrying on that tradition with its Hispanic and African American students shown in the news clip. The

reporter, who stands in front of the sign with Anna Silver's name displayed, continues:

Who was Anna Silver and why do we name this school in her honor? For many reasons. Anna Silver lived here on the Lower East Side for years and was very active in the schools and other community institutions. This concept of public responsibility was taken up by her son, Charles Silver . . . This beloved humanitarian [was a graduate of P.S. 20 in the class of 1900 and past president of the Board of Education]. In honoring the name of Anna Silver we honor all mothers of the Lower East Side whose concern for the education of their children helped to shape today's schools.

Fig. 6.3 Mural depicting the Lower East Side at the turn of the twentieth century. Presented to the school by the P.S. 20 Alumni Association, at the dedication of the new P.S. 20 building, 14 February 1963. Courtesy of the New York City Board of Education.

Charles Silver, who had lived a Horatio Alger story in his own right, was described as "a figure woven from the American legend of self-made success—an immigrant boy, brought up in the stress and privation of the Lower East Side, self-taught for the most part, sincerely believing in America as the land of equal opportunity and proving it not only for himself, but for the many he has helped along the way."[28] He was named "Man of the Twentieth Century" by the National Conference of Christians and Jews; he chaired the Alfred E. Smith Dinner (the year's major Catholic charities event) for thirty-five years; and he served on boards and committees as varied as the Grand Street Boys, Beth Israel Hospital, and Fordham University.

The reporter continues:

> People of humble origin who later became world famous found their inspiration here. Their names are history. They, and many others remembered what the school had meant for them by giving a magnificent mural depicting the panorama of life on the Lower East Side that now graces the lobby of the new school.[29]

The video shows a scene of the dedication ceremony's most prominent guest, his eminence Francis Cardinal Spellman, chatting with Charles Silver in front of the mural. The inter-religious nature of this "happening" is central to its meaning. Silver was a recognized leader of the American Jewish community. But he was also actively involved in civic and inter-religious affairs. Cardinal Spellman, a personal friend of Silver, put it aptly in published remarks of thanks to Silver for his years of work for the Alfred E. Smith Memorial Fund: "Charles Silver, proud of his Jewish blood, proud of his American citizenship, is also all things to all men in his charity. I offer praise and gratitude to this truly great humanitarian."[30] Subsequent scenes include shots of Senator Javits and other famous graduates: the comedy team Smith and Dale, humorist Harry Hirschfield, and songwriter Irving Caesar. School Superintendent Bernard Donovan was also on hand, along with an African American Protestant minister, who was a member of the Board of Education, and many invited guests.

Virtually all prominent groups in the city were represented at this coronation ceremony in which vows linking Jews to public schools were reaffirmed and the Jewish–public school marriage declared an unalloyed success. Airbrushed out were the more complex realities of positive and negative experiences, of losses as well as gains. Contradictions serve neither children nor myth-makers. The school's new mural was to confirm a myth and make it visible to future generations of schoolchildren; it was not part of an attempt to record history.

It is best to enter the mural from the inscriptions cemented into its margins. They indicate the lenses through which the visual elements should be read.

"Behold how good and how pleasant it is for Brethren to dwell together in unity."

"Give me your tired, your poor, your huddled masses yearning to breathe free."

"America is a nation of immigrants, descendants of immigrants."

Memory, with all its flaws, yields pictures that are visions and revisions of reality as actually experienced. The mural, however, was not built from recollections, but from beliefs. It was constructed from elements of a story whose narrative line is an ascent from poverty to wealth, from outsider to member, from cultural greenhorn to culture-maker. Much gain is depicted, but no sign of pain.

Peaceful coexistence has been achieved, say the mural makers. The ethnic separatism of the pre–World War I period has given way to an integrated community. Even religious antagonisms have been buried. Witness, for example, the Cardinal's presence at the dedication. Although the Church may not be a great supporter of public education, it can close ranks with its friends, especially Charles Silver, to "dwell together in unity."

In the mural, no mention is made that doors were closed in 1924, and that in 1963, at the time of the dedication, they still remained firmly shut. Nor is there the slightest hint that the European relatives of the turn-of-the-century Jewish immigrants celebrated in the mural were denied entry and perished in the Holocaust. This was, after all, a good-news mural.

In defining America as a nation of immigrants, the mural shows how Jewish immigrants were incorporated into the family of America. American lineage is traced not just from the *Mayflower*, but also from steerage. The display is replete with the iconography of a secular Madonna (Anna Silver, wrapped in robes, is portrayed near the mural's center), the Statue of Liberty, the friendly cop on the beat, the tenement with flying wash on the lines, ethnic street vendors, an American scientist and musician, the famous sons of P.S. 20 guiding the next generation of boys and girls portrayed as scouts and athletes. The very motto of the school (in the upper-right quadrant), "Per Aspera ad Astra," ("through aspiration to the stars"), had been realized by its graduates.

The mural teaches us that all Americans are immigrants (forgetting native peoples and descendants of slaves). Poverty is temporary and can be overcome in the land of opportunity. One can realistically aspire to the top rank of society.

The Lower East Side has thus become an iconographic point of origin, a launching pad into the good life, at least for those who made it. As Silver's biographer wrote:

> Sometimes, Charlie Silver walks again the streets where he lived and played near the darkened marquees of the once thriving Yiddish theatre he so dearly loved. He often visits the new school on the Lower East Side named for his beloved mother, Anna Silver, just a few blocks from the original P.S. 20 he attended many years ago. He recalls that sweet, early influence on his growth and development.[31]

In the late 1990s, students at P.S. 20 painted another large mural depicting the history of the Lower East Side (fig. 6.4). The new mural hangs in the school's auditorium. The school now enrolls mainly Hispanic students, with a small but growing number of Asians. Reading from left to right, their mural begins with the original Indian inhabitants of Manhattan Island, moves to Peter Minuit and the "purchase" of Manhattan, scenes of Dutch colonial New Amsterdam, farm settlements, and, on the far right, high-rise tenement New York. Conspicuous by its absence is the world of turn-of-the-century Jews. The past, we need to recall, depends on who is remembering.

In the early twentieth century, the public school invited its immigrant students to become Americans. Most accepted that invitation, and remade America in the process. But as we can see from contemporary student work, the public schools still invite their students to write themselves into America—an America which will ultimately become one of their own making.

NOTES

1. "Education of the Immigrant Child," in *Education of the Immigrant*, abstracts of papers read at a public conference under the auspices of the New York–New Jersey Committee of the North American Civic League for Immigrants, held in New York City, May 16 and 17, 1913 (*Bulletin* no. 51, Washington, D.C.: U.S. Bureau of Education, 1913), pp. 19–20. For a full discussion of the encounter of Jewish immigrants and New York's public schools at the turn of the century, see Stephan F. Brumberg, *Going to America, Going to School: The Jewish Immigrant Public School Encounter in Turn-of-the-Century New York City* (New York: Praeger, 1986).

2. Ellwood P. Cubberley, *Changing Conceptions of Education* (Boston: Houghton Mifflin Co., 1909), p. 15.

3. *Annual Report of the President of the Board of Education to the Mayor of the City of New York for the Year 1919* (New York: Board of Education, 1920), p. 23.

4. New York: Vintage Books, 1989, p. 92.

5. Brumberg, *Going to America*, pp. 124–125.

6. Interview with Morris U. Schappes, 11/14/83.

7. Interview with Dr. Harry Liebowitz, 10/18/83.

8. Ibid.

9. M. Schappes, 11/14/83.

10. Interview with Mary Frieman, 10/28/83.

11. M. Schappes, 11/14/83.

12. Interview with Rose Klein, 10/24/83.

13. Department of Education, the City of New York, "School Gardens for Public Schools of New York City," an elaboration of the Syllabus on Nature Study, as adopted by the Board of Superintendents, April 1917.

14. R. Klein, 10/24/83.

15. Interview with Ida Rosenbaum, 1/28/82.

16. H. Liebowitz, 10/18/83.

17. M. Schappes, 11/14/83.

18. I. Rosenbaum, 1/28/82.

Fig. 6.4 Mural of the history of the Lower East Side created by the students of P.S. 20 in 1997. Photograph by Stephan F. Brumberg.

19. Ibid.

20. H. Liebowitz, 10/18/83.

21. Ibid.

22. M. Schappes, 11/14/83.

23. Ibid.

24. I. Rosenbaum, 1/28/82.

25. M. Schappes, 11/14/83.

26. I. Rosenbaum, 1/28/82.

27. "P.S. 20 Silver Show," 3/63. Reel #1300, the Tape Archives of WNYC, the New York City Municipal Television Station, at the New York Municipal Archives.

28. Nathan, Theodore Reade, ed., *The City and Charles H. Silver: A Summary of the First Charles H. Silver Symposium on Urban Progress* (New York: National Conference Press, 1979) [National Conference of Christians and Jews], p. 1.

29. "P.S. 20 Silver Show," 3/63.

30. Nathan, *The City and Charles H. Silver,* pp. 8f.

31. Ibid., p. 8.

Re-creating Recreations

on the Lower East Side: Restaurants, Cabarets, Cafes, and Coffeehouses in the 1930s

Suzanne Wasserman

> History . . . creates this insidious longing to go backwards. It begets this bastard, but pampered child, nostalgia. How we yearn . . . to return to that time before history claimed us, before things went wrong. . . . How we pine for Paradise. For mother's milk—To draw back the curtain of events that has fallen between us and the Golden Age.
>
> Graham Swift, *Waterland,* 1983

In 1975 Sammy's Roumanian Steakhouse opened its doors at 157 Chrystie Street on the Lower East Side. For the past twenty-five years diners have feasted on garlic-stuffed karnatzlach, bread dribbled with schmaltz, and fried onions. Sammy's quarter century of success rests on its unique atmosphere as much as its gastronomic delights. With its white tablecloths and live bar-mitzvah-style band, Sammy's "is the place where you will find people recalling the good old days, many who are today's judges, doctors, politicians and journalists." Patrons can "join [in] the singing of old Yiddish songs . . . Just tear yourself away from the chopped liver and let go."[1] The appeal is in both the promise of feeling "at home," through reliving a communal past, as well as in the chance to let go and act "Orchard Street." Customers get to relive the poor immigrant past in an expensive restaurant on one of the East Side's most depressed streets. Intimate, festive, raucous, and expensive, the atmosphere in this contrived setting simultaneously celebrates a spurious collective past and conspicuous consumption.

Re-creations, like Sammy's, of a particular version of the Jewish immigrant past initially made their debuts on the Lower East Side beginning in the late 1920s, *not* in the 1970s. In the late 1920s, ex–East Siders began venturing back to the Lower East Side, many for the first time, searching for connections with their pasts. Eventually, the Lower East Side became a site of Jewish cultural pilgrimage even for those who had never lived there.

These pilgrimages encompassed myriad meanings: They could be a means to mark the passage of time, a way to fulfill real yearnings for a past perhaps remembered as more meaningful than the present, a means to deal with the ambivalence of assimilation, an avenue to locate oneself in a confusing and rapidly changing world, and/or a tool to justify and parade a rags-to-riches mentality.

Some ex–East Siders—mostly Eastern European Jews—began in the late 1920s to "clean-up" memories of their own past; these people retold the story of their lives on the East Side. The very nature of nostalgia rendered their memories highly selective. Ex–East Siders forgot and repressed some parts of the past and prettified others, remembering the past as quaint and colorful. Sentimental memories of shared values overpowered less agreeable memories. By the start of the Second World War, this retelling became increasingly sentimental and nostalgic, part of the pervasive, hegemonic tales of rags-to-riches and one readily accepted by non–East Siders and ex–East Siders alike.

In the late 1920s, some local merchants became annoyed that the Lower East Side remained an area that resisted acculturation. It retained the markers of poverty and ethnic culture. The neighborhood continued to house a predominantly poor population. Pushcarts and stooplines (displays in front of stores) remained despite attempts to remove them, public housing replaced plans for luxury apartment buildings, and Lower East Siders disregarded attacks on their leisure time activities and continued to frequent wine cellars and social clubs. Attempts during the 1930s to rid the East Side of its indigenous immigrant and ethnic nature largely failed.

But if the attempt to "de-ethnicize" the Lower East Side had succeeded, the emergence of a nostalgic tourist trade on the East Side would have been impossible. The sentimentalization of the Lower East Side required the persistence of at least some signs of a Jewish working-class community in order for ex–East Siders to return to visit what they felt they had left behind. It also required the passage of a certain amount of time and geographical distance. By the 1930s, many Jews had left the Lower East Side for other communities, but the East Side would become, at least for some, a symbol of cultural identification.

Although Lower East Side merchants fought to rid the East Side of its Old World customs and traditions, it became increasingly clear that the sight of haggling peddlers, the sound of Russian music and Yiddish songs, and the smell of pickles brought ex–East Siders and others back to the neighborhood.

The emerging tourist trade, promoted by some East Side merchants, created a new, safe and non-threatening arena and played on the longings of newly sentimental ex–East Siders. If visitors wanted to identify with the Old East Side, merchants could attempt to circumscribe and manage that experience. In fact, some ex–East Siders were not ready to return until that circumscription had occurred. The promotion of a nostalgic tourist trade celebrated ethnicity but in a sanitized, safe, and commodified form.

Obviously this was not simply a ploy concocted by East Side merchants. Former residents found that the image of being "back home" appealed to their own needs as ex–East Siders and newly assimilated American Jews. On the one hand, returning to the East Side to visit allowed them to reaffirm the classless vision of the American Dream. Like other Americans, they could view themselves as Horatio Algers, ascending the ladder from rags-to-riches in less than a generation. On the other hand, their return visits also bespoke the still tenuous position of some Jews in a non-Jewish world; the ability to visit "home" must have been a comfort as well. By the mid-1920s a commercial trade had emerged that re-enforced ex–East Siders' re-invention of the past.

Nineteenth-century sightseers had long been fascinated by touring the slums. Both progressive reformers and tourists had ventured to the East Side in order to view its exotic, alien, and deleterious conditions. Mike Gold remembered sightseeing buses rolling down his boyhood street: "a gang of kids chased it, and pelted rocks, garbage, dead cats and stale vegetables at the frightened sightseers. 'Liars, liars,' the kids

Suzanne Wasserman

yelled. 'Go back up-town.' What right had that man with the megaphone to tell lies about us?"[2]

Lillian Wald noted in her autobiography, *The House on Henry Street,* that she too felt that outsiders misrepresented the East Side by presenting only one side of the community. Writers focused exclusively upon the ugly side of life on the Lower East Side. She grew tired of this characterization at the community's expense, and she chastised thrill seekers, artists, superficial reformers and social scientists alike for portraying a one-dimensional picture of life on the East Side.[3]

Guide books of the 1920s continued to warn East Side visitors to stick to a safe, prescribed route. Upon leaving Grand Street, tourists should "hurry without much looking to the right or left until you reach East Broadway," warned tour guide Konrad Bercovici.[4] Although visitors continued to venture to the East Side to see how the "other half" lived, the focus for the bulk of visitors shifted away from searching for peeks at slum living and toward looking for familiar reminders of their own pasts. Symbolic "safe" memories of food, smells, home, and mother allowed some ex–East Siders to repress or forget other more threatening memories such as the difficult adjustments of immigration, terrible working conditions, tenements, disease, and poverty.

Before merchants began exploiting the Lower East Side's past, it was difficult for returning ex–East Siders to ignore the East Side's continued poverty; visits back to the East Side were

Fig. 7.1 *Corner Grocery Store*, Lower East
Side, 1947–1948. Photograph by Rebecca
Lepkoff. Courtesy of Rebecca Lepkoff.

marked by disappointment and a realization that the past was indeed lost forever. One ex–East Sider, Zalmen Yoffeh, clearly remembered the difficult living conditions, but these did not detract from his strong sense of sentimentality. "We were all happy on the East Side," he wrote, "back in a Jew's world."[5] He decided to return to the East Side to visit. The physical reality did not comport with his nostalgic longings. In fact, he resolved never to return, but instead "shed a sentimental tear for the old East Side. One will feel that there was something fine in the life he lived there, something distinctive, individual, something worth keeping, though inexplicable."[6] Writing memoirs like Yoffeh's seem to be one way ex–East Siders initially attempted to spell out that "something" that seemed missing from life away from the East Side.

The voices of journalists and other observers of East Side life during the 1930s reflected this new sentimentality. Even as the Lower East Side's future remained uncertain, these writers began to write eulogies to the passing of the East Side. Newspaper articles supposedly written to focus on the "new East Side" often lapsed into paeans to a romantic immigrant past.

A new vision of the East Side as unchanging, pre-modern and timeless arose, a vision that distorted the past and ultimately the present. Some articles noted with regret changes that reformers hoped would improve the East Side; these journalists focused instead upon that which would be or already was lost. The East Side, one journalist claimed, was "anchored irretrievably to its past"; thus, all improvements were, in fact, in vain. He wrote of his regrets about a passing world:

> What an amazing, incomprehensible world it was! . . . . foreign faces, queer clothes, queer objects in the shop windows and on the pushcarts. . . . To the slumming visitor this was indeed an exotic and incomprehensible world.[7]

Increasingly, memories of ex–Lower East Siders themselves moved farther and farther away from the recollection of shared values and experiences, both nurturing and disagreeable, and moved toward a view that would become a hegemonic perspective within the next generation. Sentimentalization of the past offered a selective view which shored up a conservative social ideology that espoused social mobility as a personal rather than a political phenomenon. The selective view became a substitute for a more somber and holistic memory of the past.

Founded in 1920, the Grand Street Boys' Association best exemplified this selective re-invention of the past. Ex–East Siders organized the Association in order to perpetuate the memory of the Lower East Side. Its stated purpose was social, benevolent, athletic and non-political. Its members were simply "brought together by their common love of the old East Side."[8] But Grand Street Boys promoted and perpetu-ated a very selective memory of the "old East Side."

Significantly, the organization was founded and headquartered on 55th Street. When one Grand Street Boy ran into a non-member friend outside the headquarters, the friend asked the Grand Streeter what he was doing in that area at night. "I'm a Grand Street boy," the first replied. Asked his friend, "Then what are you doing on 55th Street?" Instead of replying that ex–Grand Streeters gathered uptown to reminisce about the past, the member suggested that 55th Street be renamed "Upper Grand Street," in order to bring the Lower East Side uptown.[9] Grand Street Association members, for the most part, ex-tolled the past virtues of the Lower East Side from the seclusion of their uptown headquarters. In reality, however, it took the organization over fifteen years to make the collective two-mile trip to their boyhood neighborhood.

Members were required to be ex–East Siders, but they had to be successful, too. Famous Grand Street Boys included such celebrities as Al Smith, Jimmy Walker, David Sarnoff, and Eddie Cantor. Ex–East Sider judge and politician Jonah Goldstein, the third president of the Grand Street Boys, defined its members as individuals some of whom had, for instance, "once lived on East Broadway or Madison, went to school on Norfolk or Henry—, were [now] in business on Seventh Av-enue and lived on Central Park West."[10]

Far from being simply an organization to preserve the memory of the old East Side, the Grand Street Boys Association exemplified a rags-to-riches mythology that glorified Americanization. The organiza-tion portrayed the East Side as a temporary ghetto from which one could escape with hard work and a little luck. It looked upon those who still lived on the East Side as failures and embarrassments. As historian Deborah Dash Moore has written, this organization "fostered most in-sistently the moral and symbolic meaning of the Lower East Side as a source of the American Jewish self-made man."[11]

The life of Jonah Goldstein, judge and Democratic politician, exemplified qualities that the organization highly valued. Born in 1885, Goldstein was raised on Madison Street in a three-room tenement. There he associated with tough boys, but instead of turning to a life of crime he chose a life of "serviceable citizenship." He became the first club leader to emerge from the ranks of the Educational Alliance. As president of the Grand Street Boys, the Judge brought back "memories of 'the good old days' of Grand Street. He has so much of the 'old spirit,' so much energy, so much good fellowship," proclaimed his fellow club members.[12]

The song "Are You a Grand Street Boy?" written by member Morris Marks and published in the association's paper, further illuminated the organization's faith in a rags-to-riches ideology. The song recalled a father who when young had had a "heart full of joy, / With the dreams and the hopes of the East Side boy." Inevitably, he made it out of the ghetto and into the mainstream. Other members followed similar paths:

> You will find Grand Street Boys scattered all over town,
> Great deeds performing and winning renown,
> They're high in the clergy,
> In the bench and bar,
> Princes of commerce—both near and far,
> Though diff'rent directions—each now must take,
> Elsewhere their fortunes and homes must make,
> Ever the same Grand Street Boys they'll remain,
> Honored and happy to sing this refrain.[13]

Despite the advent of the Depression, Grand Street members continued to uphold their ideology of individual achievement. In 1939, member George Sokolsky bemoaned the advent of the welfare state and the growing cynicism that outsiders expressed toward the organization's philosophy. While delivering a speech in Milwaukee, Sokolsky was heckled by a member of the audience for claiming that anyone could make it through "equal opportunity." Sokolsky responded, saying: "Yet here we are. . . . For us who were willing to work . . . who dared the adventure of achievement and took the risks of failure—we know that there is equal opportunity."[14]

The organization's own historian, Alexander Rose, expressed the nostalgic and sentimental longings of its members for the East Side during the late 1920s and 1930s, admitting that their memories had softened over time:

> Tender memories and sweet recollections will always live in the hearts of the boys who came from the historic old East Side . . . It is a love for the place that witnessed our early struggles which has softened the memory of its hardships and has invested it with a particular charm . . . its former residents . . . are so much attached to it by the ties of love and affection.[15]

Not only did Rose remember the East Side sentimentally, but he also recalled it as a "world in itself."[16] Rose likened it to a village where Grand Street was "Main Street." In this world, there were no class conflicts, bitter labor disputes, prostitution, sweatshops, abandonment, or cold water tenements. Rather, East Siders were "contented with the neighborliness of [a] simple life."[17] Rose viewed the East Side with its "sympathetic heart" as a "bygone homeland."[18]

While these memories distorted the past, they also illuminated the present lives of club members. Although the men had become eminently successful, for some, feelings of frustration with assimilated life simmered close to the surface. The present seemed somehow emptier and more vapid compared to the past. Grand Street Boy President Jonah Goldstein expressed this sentiment explicitly: "There is more real social life in a cold water tenement than in a steam heated apartment. . . . Everybody knows everybody else's business in a tenement. They laugh with each other, they cry with each other. Life is real. . . ."[19] At the fifteenth annual dinner of the organization, one member recalled that we "all lived in squalid tenements but we lived on terms of accord. We made no distinctions between the Irish and the Germans and the Jews."[20] Goldstein and others saw life away from the East Side as spurious, disingenuous, and empty.

Yet Grand Streeters found actually visiting the East Side disturbing, for the East Side's problems remained immediate and real. This discomfort was the primary reason that Grand Streeters had no official contact with the Lower East Side until sixteen years after the organization was founded.

As physical distance grew and time passed for the one-time immigrant and his or her former East Side home, their memories softened, adjusted, and became more romanticized. Yoffeh and Goldstein, among others, could not bear to go back, but increasingly other ex–East Siders began to return on pilgrimages "home"—to walk the streets, smell the smells, to reminisce in old haunts, and to fantasize about the past. This was possible, in part, because the Lower East Side's ethnic character did not change as drastically and rapidly as some had hoped it would.

The complex and very real yearnings of former East Siders converged with the needs and desires of retail merchants on the East Side by the middle of the Great Depression. From 1917 on, the East Side's economy had spiraled downward. "The garment and needle trades, formerly the district's most important industry, are moving uptown or to outlying sections," explained journalist Loula Lasker.[21] A survey published by the Regional Plan of New York in 1928 made it clear that the East Side would have to depend on something other than manufacturing if it wanted to survive economically.[22]

But what could take the place of manufacturing? Lasker, in 1930, noted that "the largest business left is retail shopping."[23] But radical area depopulation, coupled with Depression conditions, meant that Lower East Side merchants would have to draw outsiders to their neighborhood, for the relatively poor local population alone could not sustain this kind of shift in the economy. In 1929, merchant William Freeman noted that "the steady decrease in population has made it impossible for most merchants to get enough trade from local residents."[24] Edwin Lahm, the vice president of the Citizen's Savings Bank on the East Side, wrote that merchants "must sell the Lower East Side to the shoppers of the city."[25] The "outsider must help the insider."[26]

Increasingly in the 1930s, East Side merchants came to realize that the neighborhood already had faithful consumers in those East Siders who had moved away. As early as 1927, one observer noted that ex–East Siders "are still loyal to the place of their rise and deliverance. It is their hometown, their Main Street. . . . These gaudy customers keep alive the old East Side."[27] "East Siders who have moved out and their friends and families still like to shop on the East Side," Joseph Platzker, editor of the East Side Chamber News, noted hopefully. "Most East Side customers come from other sections of the city and from the suburbs," he added.[28] The Lower East Side, no longer a center for production, would attempt to shift toward becoming a center of consumption.

Merchants hoped to capitalize on this faithfulness and began to emphasize the East Side's sentimental appeal. They understood that "for thousands the East Side meant poverty, hard work, long hours, ill health, inescapable dirt. But it meant something else" as well. "The new east side is not lacking in 'gemultlichkeit'" (a sense of feeling at home), the author continued.[29] Here was an articulation of that "something else" that Yoffeh had noted earlier. The idea of returning "home" might draw even reluctant ex–East Siders back.

East Side merchants encouraged those who insisted upon identifying with the East Side long after they had moved away. One merchant wrote:

> Migration from the East Side does not break the ties which have been formed by many years of residence there. The old timers cannot bear to stay away. They return on Saturdays and Sundays and other holidays to renew old friendships, sniff at old aromas, and wander up and down crowded and dirty streets that once were loved because they stood for home.[30]

Owners of night-life establishments began to exploit these sentiments, creating new cafes, cabarets, wine cellars and restaurants tailored specifically to ex–East Siders. One journalist noted that

> These night clubs are a very recent development; they are in fact, only about three years old . . . The restaurants of the region, like everything else, has changed to meet an altered patronage.[31]

These new patrons were the "newly rich . . . [those] who had their purses ample for the Ritz but their tastes remained in Delancey Street."[32] One restaurateur on Delancey Street fitted up a basement to imitate local wine cellars but charged a hefty cover to "keep out all but the more prosperous."[33]

Some establishments still catered to a local crowd, but other locales opened that hoped to attract former patrons back to the East Side:

> A few of the less conspicuous coffee houses subsist solely on the patronage of Hungarians, Poles, or Russians, but the more pretentious establishments, where the atmosphere is *synthetically achieved,* rely largely upon a trade of country cousins, visiting buyers and after-theatre parties from uptown and Brooklyn, Westchester and New Jersey. Taxicabs keep an all-night vigil before the cafes on the unrazed side of Allen Street and the Forsythe Street cabarets employ doormen.[34]

As this brand of tourism became increasingly popular, self-appointed aficionados as well as tourist guides advised visitors which places were safe to visit and which were not. Merchants, after all, could control the inside of their establishments more readily than the neighborhood streets. Guidebooks warned that the safest locales were located on main streets such as Second Avenue or Delancey Street. One could now go slumming in certain streets without feeling threatened or afraid. One writer warned visitors to avoid the "primitive" wine cellars of the Polish and Galician Jews east of Avenue A.[35]

As entrepreneurs realized that their establishments could appeal to an upscale, uptown crowd, they moved their wine cellars to "safer" streets. The wine cellar Moscowitz's moved uptown from Rivington Street to Second Avenue and became a restaurant.[36] When Moscowitz's moved, it tried to remain true to its roots. It still had singing and music, but only on the weekends.[37] Although the restaurant was no longer serving liquor because of Prohibition, customers could still "hear Roumanian music, haunting melodies; tripping dances, while you eat the highly spiced food waiting for Mr. Volstead's amendment to be forgotten."[38] Likewise, Greenberg's moved and became a legitimate restaurant. Opened originally in 1895 for "landsmen" from Roumania, it had catered to lonely immigrants who had no place else to go for entertainment and comradeship. By the late 1930s, Greenberg's had become a tourist destination.[39] At cabarets such as The Russian Bear on Second Avenue and 13th Street or the Russian Kretchma on East 14th Street, tourists watched elaborate floor shows complete with balalaika orchestras, flaming dagger dancers, and singers. [40]

Inside cabarets, one detailed description portrayed how customers were entertained with bawdy songs and titillating physical contact:

> In the evening the spirit of Roumania fills the air and the folk songs are gaily sung. . . . Sometimes songstresses, who also participate in card games with the customers, are employed in the restaurants. . . .The patrons sing folk

songs and also tunes from the Jewish American theatre, especially those pertaining to the Mother, the Home, with a half concealed hint of impropriety. The songstresses are adept at singing sentimental numbers. They are not professionals but are capable of veering from pathetic songs which bring tears to the eyes of the sensitive guests to the risque kind which incite male guests to caress them.[41]

Even the establishments south of Houston Street, which were often deemed unsafe and frequented by "natives,"[42] benefited from this new surge in tourism. For example, a wealthy patron from New Jersey took an investigator named Levy from the Committee of 14 (which investigated urban vice) to the Roumanian Restaurant at 64 Rivington Street. There Jennie the Factory and Sadie the Chink, two infamous Lower East Side madams, openly solicited johns for their prostitutes.[43] Sadie the Chink issued business cards for her place uptown as well as for her son, a dentist.[44] Once, when investigator Levy was in midtown, he asked a cabbie where he could go to "have a good time." The cabbie took him to a new Roumanian restaurant at 39 First Street. "It's a Jewish place. You don't mind that, do you?" he asked Levy.[45]

By far the most risqué place on the East Side, according to Levy, was Haimowitz' Oriental Roumanian Restaurant at 106 Forsythe Street. This restaurant, owned by Abie Haimowitz, was "frequented by a mixed crowd, mostly Jewish businessmen and also Gentiles."[46] Female entertainers sang songs in English, Yiddish

Fig. 7.2 First Avenue El, Allen Street, 1935. Note the Berkowitz Roumanian "Wine and Dine" Restaurant in the background. The sandwich board advertised "Tasty Food, Good Wines, and [not visible] Dancing." Photograph by Arnold Eagle. Courtesy of the estate of Arnold Eagle.

and Russian and also acted as hostesses.[47] They moved from table to table accepting tips, and often danced with male patrons. Liquor was served openly despite Prohibition. The doorman told Levy, "If you can't get fixed up here there is no other place downtown that you can be fixed up. Every girl steps out." Haimowitz, the owner, told Levy that "they all f___. The bigger a c___ you have the better they like it and you could f___ her in the a___."[48]

A survey in 1936 reported "the leading cabaret restaurants along Allen Street and Second Avenue are still attracting considerable patrons from among non-residents" despite the Depression.[49] By the end of the decade, the restaurants and cabarets of the East Side had become a million dollar industry.[50]

If the restaurants and cabarets were places where visitors could participate in raucous and even illegal behavior, cafes evoked other responses. The cafes and coffee houses created a different atmosphere. If one were "looking for real color and . . . dislike an atmosphere created for sucker tourists," wrote one observer, "drop in at the little coffee house at East Broadway and Division Street."[51] The attraction of a "home-like" environment drew many to the East Side cafes and coffee houses. Cafes had always been a prominent part of Lower East Side immigrant culture. They were the spots for the regular gatherings of Yiddish poets, actors, and intellectuals.[52]

The Cafe Royal at 12th Street and Second Avenue (in the heart of the Jewish theater district) was the prototype for all other East Side cafes. Its name appeared in almost every guide or description of the East Side in the '30s. Visitors often found it impossible to locate an empty seat in the evenings. "Winter nights all of 200 seats are eagerly occupied with many lurking in the aisles waiting to grab the first vacated seat," read one description. Even though the cafe was not small, guidebooks described the atmosphere as intimate. "Everybody there feels at home, sits around till all hours of the night enjoying the ceaseless drone of chatter and feeding the floating clouds of smoke," another guide book claimed.[53] Visitors included actors, actresses, musicians, dancers, radio personalities and even social directors of summer hotels. Fanny Hurst, David Sarnoff, Sholem Ash, Paul Muni, Moss Hart, and even Charlie Chaplin could be seen at the Royal on various occasions.[54]

Despite the fact that the Cafe Royal was a thriving establishment in the 1930s, visitors sometimes described it as a cultural remnant. Folklorist Nathan Ausubel likened activity within the Royal to a play. "It is all unreal, so utterly unreal, like some stage play—a pantomime of quaintly amusing ghosts . . . its stale smell of beer, the greasy, overworked waiters . . . look as if they had just stepped out of a continental musical comedy."[55]

Although Ausubel considered real people to be "quaint ghosts," it was actually nostalgic customers themselves who patronized the cafe in order to deal with their own ghosts. Successful businessmen, doctors, and lawyers returned to the cafe time and time again to reminisce about their youthful good old days of poverty, days they remembered as more meaningful then the present ones:

> They turned nostalgically to the days of their youth when they were endowed with ideas and sentiments but had nothing to eat except baygel [sic] and tea . . . nowadays they come down to the Cafe and listen to the delectable conversation of the hungry Yiddish poets . . . they begin to relive vicariously the unhappy days of their youth. Ah! and what a joy it is to relive the unhappy, distant past![56]

"Characters" at the Royal played their parts for audiences greedy for the atmosphere of the past.[57] The most famous "attraction" of all was Herman the Busboy. A sixty-year-old man with stooped shoulders, he was said to own a $5000 interest in the Yiddish Art Theatre across the street from the Royal, in addition to his other real estate interests. Herman often gave outsiders the worst seats in the house and was then uncivil to them. But many considered going to the Royal and letting locals abuse them to be part of the cultural experience.

Although non–East Siders considered "characters" such as Herman the Busboy entertainment, these "characters" in fact wielded power in their own milieu. East Siders like Herman were used by outsiders as entertainment as much as they, in turn, used tourists to their own ends. Herman demanded a five-cent tip from each of his some two hundred nightly customers.[58] On weekend nights, he took reservations by phone for twenty-five cents a seat; those without bookings had to stand. Tourists alone were charged a five-cent surcharge if they ordered only appetizers; this rule was not enforced for locals. These cafes did not exist for the "convenience of strangers who do not understand the conventions of the East Side cafes," one writer proclaimed. In fact, East Siders felt that outsiders were often "being more slummed against than slumming."[59]

For years within the Royal, a subculture existed that was totally inaccessible to outsiders. In the back room was a standing pinochle game that sometimes lasted up to fifteen hours a day. When the Royal opened some twenty years earlier, it apparently was a front for this card-playing, smoking, and betting. Rumor had it that one Yiddish actor was so addicted to pinochle that he turned over his hand to his dresser when he had to go on stage.[60]

Other haunts also became established stops on "noshtalgia" tours.[61] For example, Jewish visitors from as far away as California or Florida stopped at Yonah Schimmel's Knishery, according to Nathan Ausubel. They arrived in New York "bearing . . . the address of a recommended hotel and of Yoineh Shimmel's [*sic*] knish emporium:

> Ex–lower east Siders and their children and their children's children make periodic visits to Yoineh Shimmel's . . . they come from remote corners of the Bronx, from the lowlands of Brooklyn, and from the "high tone" exclusiveness of West End Avenue. They come with the hungry piety of pilgrims.[62]

By the late 1930s, merchants came to depend on the visits of ex–lower east Siders as much as ex–East Siders came to depend on these visits for a hit of *gemultlichkeit*. By 1937, Joseph Platzker announced that East Side merchants had succeeded in their mission:

> If the retailers in the Lower East Side would have to depend on local neighborhood trade for all their business, more than half of them would close in less than a month's time. For more than a decade many merchants have been cultivating the good will and patronage of thousands of families in other parts of the city as well as in the nearby states. The trading area for Lower East Side business now extends into New Jersey, Connecticut, Pennsylvania and Massachusetts—not forgetting Long Island and Westchester. Thus the decline in population has been more than offset by commuters and weekend excursionists.[63]

This tourist trade began to extend not only to those who had once lived on the East Side, but also to those who had never lived there yet now fantasized about the past:

> Numerous commuters from New Jersey, Connecticut, Pennsylvania and even upstate New York continue to make it a habit of taking weekend shopping trips to the Lower East Side—to the very shops where they or their parents or grandparents have shopped before.[64]

By the end of the decade, Grand Street Boys had an arena within which to relive their tempered memories. The time was ripe for their return to the Lower East Side, for a new context of tourism existed that allowed them to visit "home" more comfortably.

In 1936, after a sixteen-year absence, the Grand Street Boys decided to make their first official visit to their old home. Much was made of this upcoming event. A spring issue of their paper announced that a "Pilgrimage Back to Grand Street [was] set for May 17th." It promised "to be one of the biggest events of the year. . . . One day we give entirely to sentiment."[65]

Though the pilgrimage was a nostalgic journey to the past, it had a purpose, both implicit and explicit. Explicitly, the trip served to awaken "the appreciation of the members for the material things we have." Implicitly, it allowed these ex–East Siders to parade their successes before those still in the ghetto and to re-affirm their individualistic ideology. An editorial extolling the virtues of such a pilgrimage explained that both visitors and residents would benefit by a trip back: "We can all of us better appreciate what we have by seeing what little we had. And perhaps we can inspire a few of those youngsters and oldsters who still live there to fight and work for better things,"[66] as if East Siders had not always fought to ameliorate conditions.

Grand Streeters worried about returning. Many had not even been downtown in some twenty to thirty years.[67] They realized that their rosy memories might not match the reality of the East Side's streets. "Some of us like to remember the old days," continued the editorial:

> the pushcarts, and the clotheslines, and the gas lit railroad flats. Some of us like to forget. . . . "Back to Grand Street" might fittingly be not quite so gay a party as plans for the "Homecoming" indicate. But it is perhaps better that we be cheerful for this occasion . . . and try to make the present Grand Streeters forget their troubles for an afternoon at least . . . the Grand Street Boys go back to Grand Street, gayly, or perhaps a little sadly, or even reminiscently.[68]

East Siders turned out in full force to greet the returning visitors. The local settlements as well as the Drama, Art, and Music projects of the WPA held a huge "Pageant of the East Side" in Seward Park.[69] The *New York Herald Tribune* and the *New York Times* carried reports about the event. Five thousand local residents looked on as a thousand dancers and singers in national costumes marched by. Six floats from settlement houses presented the themes of Relief and Unemployment, Seward Park—Past and Present, Housing, Health, Social Security, and Peace.[70]

The pilgrimage became a yearly event. However, their trips were not connected to the message that contemporary East Siders hoped to impart, about ongoing struggles to fight slum conditions. Grand Streeters instead used trips back to the East Side to shore up their own world view. In 1937, eight hundred ex–East Siders gathered in Seward Park to swap tales and visit former East Side homes. They reminisced about fire escapes, gangs, and cellars. Promotion material for the second annual "Back to Grand Street" pilgrimage stated that ex–East Siders would visit "select" East Side restaurants "where members will recall the 'good times' of yesteryear."[71] Grand Streeters returned annually to the East Side, still claiming to "stir up old memories . . . and to try to bring back with us a little joy from the youth of yesteryear to the youngster of today."[72]

Unlike Konrad Bercovici's stern warnings fifteen years earlier about

171

where to go and where not to go, a 1939 *Fortune Magazine* article explained that "a walk through Orchard Street or Rivington Street on a
hot night, though perfectly safe, is still a walk through an exotic stink
hole." The article urged visitors to "tour New York's foreign villages."
In the same breath the author suggested that tourists go to listen to the
shofar on Yom Kippur in an East Side synagogue and then follow a Nazi
parade through Yorkville. [73]

Documentarians, journalists, slummers, and others came to view
the East Side as a safe venue for observing vestiges of a dying world.
Religious Jews on the East Side were increasingly described as "colorful," "a bit of living history . . . and a link with the past." Although
vanishing, they reminded one of "simpler ways of living and the complex of culture and tradition that surrounds less highly organized Societies."[74]

Lower East Siders themselves did their best to counteract a monolithic and simplistic view of their world. One documentarian studying
the Lower East Side asked an old woman how she made a living: "Pay
me and I'll tell you," she responded. Another woman, a challah seller,
refused to answer his inquiries and told him that his questions were
foolish.[75] When *New York Post* journalist Ruth McKenney asked a
young woman some questions for an article about the East Side, the girl
replied, "We get ten people a day here making surveys and writing stories and all that . . . my pop says to say nothin' to 'em."[76]

By the time of World War II, visitors found the East Side a less
threatening place, due at least in part to the roles played out by tourists
and merchants. Catering to tourists helped render the continued existence of tenement living more palatable. Although one still might not
understand why people lived there, it was now certainly a safer and
sentimental place to visit.

NOTES

1. Quotations found on an old Sammy's menu from the mid-1980s. In possession
of author.

2. Michael Gold, *Jews without Money* (New York: Avon, 1930), pp. 35–36.

3. Lillian Wald, *House on Henry Street* (New York: Dover, 1915), p. 249.

4. Konrad Bercovici, *Around the World in New York* (New York: Century, 1924),
p. 89.

5. Zalmen Yoffeh, "The Passing of the East Side," *Menorah Journal* (December
1929): 275.

6. Ibid.

7. Victor Bernstein, "A Changeless East Side Changes: Progress and Decay Are in the Melting Pot and the Two Vie for the Future of the Area," *New York Times Magazine*, April 25, 1937, pp. 14 and 24.

8. *WUXTRA!: Monthly Publication of the Grand Street Boys Association*, President's Message for 1946, 26th Annual Dinner, East Side files, Grand Street Boys' Association, Seward Park Library, New York (February 1938): 2. In 1946, President Goldstein included the preservation of a "close-knit communal feeling" as one of the main purposes of the Association.

9. *WUXTRA!* (January 1936): 2.

10. Ibid.

11. Deborah Dash Moore, "The Emergence of Ethnicity: New York Jews, 1920–1940" (Ph.D. dissertation, Columbia University, 1975), p. 90.

12. *WUXTRA!* (January 1936): 3.

13. Morris Marks, "Are You a Grand Street Boy?" *WUXTRA!* (September 1938): 2.

14. George Sokolsky, "The Grand Street Boys," *WUXTRA!* (February 1939): 2.

15. Alexander Rose, "Statelier Mansion," *East Side Chamber News* [ESCN] (October 1929): 10.

16. Ibid.

17. Alexander Rose, "Not So Very Long Ago," *ESCN* (October 1929): 21.

18. Ibid., p. 23.

19. *WUXTRA!* (February 1938): 2.

20. "Grand Street Boys Swap Bouquets at Fifteenth Dinner," *New York Herald Tribune*, February 1935, East Side files, Grand Street Boys Association, Seward Park Library, New York.

21. Loula Lasker, "Putting a White Collar on the East Side," *Survey Graphic* (March 1, 1931): 585.

22. Regional Plan Association, *Regional Survey of New York and its Environs* (New York: Russell Sage Foundation, 1928).

23. Lasker, "Putting a White Collar on the East Side," p. 585.

24. William Freeman, "Community Advertising for the East Side," *ESCN* (January 1929): 9.

25. Edwin Lahm, "A Banker's Bold Analysis: How to Put the Lower East Side Again on the Map?" *ESCN* (July 1929): 8.

26. William Freeman, "Impressions of the Third Annual Banquet," *ESCN* (February 1930): 14.

27. Zelda F. Popkin, "The Changing East Side," *American Mercury* (February 1927): 170.

28. Joseph Platzker, "Picturesque Division Street," *ESCN* (November 1928): 8.

29. R. L. Duffus, "The East Side Is Awakening to Its Glory of Olden Days," *New York Times Magazine*, May 3, 1931, pp. 21–22, and reprinted in *ESCN* (May 1931): 3.

30. Ibid., p. 21.

31. Popkin, "The Changing East Side," p. 171.

32. Ibid.

33. Ibid., p. 172.

34. Bertram Reinitz, "The East Side Looks into Its Future," *New York Times Magazine*, March 13, 1932, p. 22.

35. Bercovici, *Around the World in New York*, p. 88.

36. Gold, *Jews without Money*, pp. 80–81.

37. M. Goodwin, "East Side Restaurants," p. 6, in "Jews in New York," Box 3632, Federal Writers Project Papers (FWP), Municipal Archives, New York.

38. Bercovici, *Around the World in New York*, p. 88.

39. D. Krevistsky, "Night Clubs on the East Side," pp. 1–2, in Jewish Group, H. Berman-Editor, "Jews of New York," Restaurant file, Box 3632, FWP.

40. Philip Hurn, "World Tour of New York City," in Racial Group Survey, p. 6, Box 3711, New York Tours file, FWP.

41. "New York Roumanian Restaurants," Box 3632, FWP.

42. M. Glass, "East Side Cafes," *Saturday Evening Post* (May 9, 1932): 136.

43. Report of December 8, 1926, Box 35, Committee of 14 Papers, New York Public Library Rare Books and Manuscripts (NYPL). Name of investigator is changed.

44. Report of May 19, 1932, Box 22, Co of 14, NYPL.

45. Report of February 6, 1928, Box 35, Co of 14, NYPL.

46. Report of January 20, 1927, Box 35, Co of 14, NYPL.

47. Ibid.

48. Reports of April 1–8, 1927, Box 35, Co of 14, NYPL.

49. Joseph Platzker, "Million Dollar Industries on the Lower East Side—No. 1 Restaurants," *ESCN* (January 1936): 9.

50. Duffus, "The East Side Is Awakening to Its Glory of Olden Days," p. 22.

51. Hurn, "World Tour," p. 7.

52. Wald, *House on Henry Street*, p. 274.

53. Anonymous, "Cafe Royal," assigned on July 31, 1940, filed on August 9, 1940, Box 3617, FWP.

54. L. Shapiro, "Second Avenue: New York's Jewish Rialto," translated from the Yiddish by E. Venschleiser, p. 2, Box 3617, "Jews of New York," Theatres—First Draft file, and "East Side Restaurants," p. 5, Box 3632, FWP. See also Nahma Sandrow, "The Smell of Grease Paint—and Pickles," *New York Times*, September 25, 1988, p. H5.

55. Nathan Ausubel, "Hold Up the Sun! A Kaleidoscope of Jewish Life in New York," unpublished manuscript, 1935, FWP, chapter "Art with Tea and Lemon," pp. 270 and 279.

56. Ibid., 275.

57. Ibid., 282.

58. Glass, "East Side Cafes," pp. 10–11.

59. Ibid.

60. Ibid., p. 137, and Y. Sardatsky, "Cafe Royal," translated from the Yiddish by E. D. Coleman, p. 1, Box 3632, Jewish Group, Restaurant file, "Jews of New York," FWP.

61. Alan Dershowitz, "Lox on Both Their Houses," *New York Times*, August 9, 1988.

62. Ausubel, "King of Knishes," pp. 24–25.

63. Joseph Platzker, "Eighth Annual Report on Business and Store Activity in the Lower East Side," *ESCN* (August 1937): 1.

64. Joseph Platzker, "Community Planning Study For the Lower East Side," *ESCN* (September 1935): 1.

65. *WUXTRA!* (April 1936): 1–2, and Editorial, "Remember," p. 2.

66. "Remember," p. 2.

67. *New York Herald Tribune*, May 18, 1936, 30: 5–8.

68. "Remember," p. 2.

69. *WUXTRA!* (April 1936): 1.

70. *New York Herald Tribune*, May 18, 1936, 30: 5–8, and *New York Times*, May 18, 1936, 18: 1. See also "Back to Grand Street," Homecoming Festival of the Grand Street Boys Association Program—May 17, 1936, Seward Park Library files.

71. "Back to Grand Street," *WUXTRA!*, April 1937, and "Grand Street Boys Hear Melodies of Their Youth," *New York Herald Tribune*, May 16, 1937, Clipping in East Side files, Grand Street Boys, Seward Park.

72. *WUXTRA!* (May 1940): 2.

73. "The Melting Pot," Part I: "The People," Special New York Issue of *Fortune* magazine (July 1939): 72–77.

74. Helen Neville, "Religious Life," September 15, 1941, p. 2, Box 3632, Religious Life, First Draft file, FWP.

75. Jacob Ben Lightman, Comments on Photographs taken in 1932 Study, Box 5, Graduate School of Jewish Social Work, American Jewish Historical Society, New York.

76. Ruth McKenny, "They Might Starve Faster Indoors: Pushcart Peddlers Too Depressed to Care," *New York Post*, July 11, 1936, II, 3: 3–6.

Part 2.

Contemporary Recollections

Turfing the Slum: New York City's Tenement Museum and the Politics of Heritage

Jack Kugelmass

Laybush Scheinberg

A young man stands on a stage, dressed in a dark frumpy suit and a white shirt with a bow tie. Next to him is a small wooden table covered in white lace, a carafe of brown-colored wine, two Sabbath candles, and a challah. He is holding a remote control connected to a slide projector. When his audience of some twenty largely middle-aged couples with children, from a suburban synagogue, are all seated, he makes the following announcement:

> Now, before we begin let me tell you that the program is in two parts. The first part will be right in our theater where we are right now, and for the second part we'll be taking a walking tour of the neighborhood. So I'd like to take you back in time now to the turn of the century.

As he speaks, slides project onto the wall behind him.

Swelling to the bursting point with 700 persons per acre, as compared to the city-wide average of only 60, the Lower East Side seemed to sweat humanity at every window and door. Although Irish, Italian, Black and Chinese worked and resided in the area, the majority were Jews recently arriving from Eastern Europe. Now, Eastern Europe has lost a full third of its Jewish population to the United States, mostly to New York City. In Russia Jews could not rent or own land outside of cities, and their access to higher education and occupations was limited. Also, in 1881 the Russian pogroms began.

Now these were government-sponsored pogroms which wiped out entire Jewish villages. In Galicia, Austria-Hungary, where our particular story begins, thousands of Jews were starving to death every year. Government takeover of certain industries destroyed countless Jewish livelihoods. At times the refugees must have felt they had traded one misery for another. The physical and social conditions under which they labored on the Lower East Side attracted the attention of reformers who became legends in their own time. People like Lillian Wald, of the Henry Street Settlement, Emma Goldman, who organized the sweatshops, Baron de Hirsch, the charitable banker, Margaret Sanger, of Planned Parenthood, and Jacob Riis, the famous photographer. Together they documented the conditions and they fought for change.

The talk continues by describing the nature of tenement life, the social upheavals taking place in America at the time of mass migration, and related cultural and artistic movements. It then moves from the collective to the personal, from the ordinary to the exemplary: "Well, today we look at the Lower East Side through the eyes of the Scheinberg family," the speaker continues. Suddenly his speech is inflected with Yiddish:

So Shalom. I am Laybush. I was born in Galicia, now Poland, in 1910. The youngest of five children born to Henekh and Gite Scheinberg. So look, I want you should meet my family over here. You know we were living in America three years already when this picture was taken. We were living then on Eldridge Street. That's my mother, and that's my father. That guy there over in the corner is my brother Moishe. His American name is Morris.

The story proceeds by telling of Laybush Scheinberg's parents' life in the Old Country. His maternal grandparents were innkeepers, while his paternal grandfather was a Talmudic scholar and a Bobover Hasid. The couple owned a piece-goods store after they married. Laybush's mother was a business person whose brother went to America and lived on the Lower East Side. He sent a ship ticket to bring Laybush's father over, and Laybush's father eventually sent a ticket for the rest of the family. A few children remained behind temporarily and were cared for by local peasants—supervised, of course, by the grandparents who lived nearby. The narrator relates life aboard ship, the welcome at Ellis Island, the frequent moves into various apartments, sometimes due to fire, since immigrants resorted to benzene to rid themselves of lice (though later, the narrator concedes, the cause may have been for financial gains). The story concludes with a description of life on Eldridge Street, family life, tenement life, synagogue life, work in the family sweatshop, food, holiday celebrations, and local newspapers.

> But you know I haven't been back to the old neighborhood now in a very long time. And I figure, what the heck! I would take a look at some of the old places I used to hang out, where I went to school, all the things we used to do. You want to come along with me? That's good, because otherwise I'd be walking along the streets talking to myself, looking like a *meshugener*.

Living History

We know a good deal about Laybush and his rags-to-riches success story because one day shortly after the death of his brother, he visited the Lower East Side and walked into the family's former prayer house. Ruth Abram, a co-director at the time of the Eldridge Street restoration project, interviewed Scheinberg and later his sister and then wove the transcripts into a one-person performance piece. Performances such as this reflect the increasing movement toward (if not always sophistication of) living history museums nationally since the 1970s. This phenomenon is largely rural and/or pre-industrial in orientation, although there are some recent urban examples.[1] According to Jay Anderson, in 1970, a number of museum specialists, agricultural historians, geographers, folklorists, and farmers met at Old Sturbridge Village and created the Association for Living Historical Farms and Agricultural Museums (ALHFAM). This association eventually became an umbrella organization for the living-history movement. Originally based at the Smithonian, the organization publishes a bulletin and organizes conferences at living-history museums at various sites in North America. ALHFAM also encouraged various levels of government to become interested in living-history interpretation. In 1981, ALHFAM was opened to all living-history projects. Institutional members now include "villages, historic houses, forts, ships, urban neighborhoods, and archaeological sites."[2]

The hallmark of living history is the frequent confusion of its audience between performance and reality (at one Scheinberg performance, a Swiss couple turned to me and asked how "Mr. Scheinberg" could have had so many experiences yet look so young!), an indication that its goal of instilling "felt-truth" among its audience has been achieved.[3] Such confusion is frequently enhanced by meticulous attention to the accuracy of historical detail.[4] The net result is a striking ability to entertain, and this has considerable risks for those concerned with historical accuracy. Indeed, as Warren Leon and Margaret Piatt argue,

> By billing themselves as popular tourist destinations, institutions like Williamsburg have reached large audiences, but those audiences have included many visitors who neither want nor expect to learn disturbing information about the past. Such vacationers seek escape from their normal concerns and cares. Living-history museums, which charge higher admission prices and rely more on tourist dollars than other history museums, cannot afford to alienate this hard-won tourist audience.[5]

Fortunately, a possible tendency to pander is counterbalanced by other historical forces that continue to generate these museums. The living history movement anticipated the Bicentennial celebration and the vogue for bottom-up history.[6] The latter, in particular, contributed to making New York City's Tenement Museum a poignant response to Michael Wallace's warning that "If we wish to restore our social health, we had better go beyond Mickey Mouse history."[7] In addition, the restorations of the Statue of Liberty and Ellis Island have helped situate the Tenement Museum within a larger framework of lower Manhattan immigrant-history museums. Both indirect and direct benefits include a possible official affiliation[8] and a rise from 80,000 to an expected 250,000 visitors annually.[9]

Promoting Tolerance

Chartered in 1988, the Tenement Museum states that its mission is to "promote tolerance and historical perspective through the presentation and interpretation of the variety of urban immigrant and migrant experiences on Manhattan's Lower East Side, a gateway to America." An early brochure outlining the museum's future plans reveals that

> Once the tenement building is restored, the Museum will offer a "living history" experience in which visitors "meet" representatives of the many immigrant and migrant families who called the area and the building home in the 19th and early 20th centuries.

> Scholars, commissioned by the Museum, have worked steadily to trace the development of six immigrant communities on the 19th century Lower East Side: Free-African, Irish, Italian, Eastern European Jewish, German, and Chinese. In addition, research on the history of 97 Orchard Street has uncovered information on immigrants from over 25 nations. These research projects will form the foundation for a variety of Museum programs and publications.[10]

The museum is located at this address on Orchard Street, in the heart of the commercial section of what remains of the old Jewish East Side and of Kleindeutschland, which preceded it. It is a street that still attracts bargain-hungry shoppers. The building housing the museum was erected in 1863, intended by its owner, a German tailor, for working-class immigrants. Improvements were made in 1867 and 1905 according to the newly established housing laws. In 1929, when a new law required that each apartment have one toilet and improved ventilation, the landlord decided to use the building as a warehouse rather than comply. As a result, 97 Orchard Street is a relatively intact tenement, whose discovery is referred to by the museum's staff as nothing short of a miracle. Ruth Abram, the museum's director, relates:

Turfing the Slum

We found the building by accident. I had the idea years before of finding a tenement, but I had given up looking for a building of this sort, because in 1929 the housing law passed in New York resulted in the demolition or reconstruction and rehabilitation of tenements. And I had looked everywhere for one that wasn't touched. I couldn't find one. And so I decided simply to come here and use an office to tell the story of the immigrants who settled the city through drama, through walking tours, and not worry about having a building. And I responded to a sign in a window saying "Storefront for rent." And a woman I was working with, who's now a curator of the museum, walked in to respond to the sign and said, "This storefront would be just fine. We needed nothing more. But where are the toilets?" And then the landlord took her to the hall and she practically fell down, because she had been looking at enough of those photographs, and she felt she was standing on hallowed ground.[11]

"Hallowed ground" suggests that the value of the building has less to do with architectural than social significance. And on that score, one immediately sees the redemptive mission that underlies this museum. As one of its brochures points out, "When, even with the best intentions, we destroy every shred of physical evidence of a widely shared cultural memory, we suggest that neither the experience nor the people who shared it are worthy of inclusion in the historical record. The Tenement Museum refutes this point of view."

When the original research was begun (in the early 1990s), the Tenement Museum included a basement space for lectures and offices, and a main floor for offices and exhibitions, including a long-standing display on the history of peddling in lower Manhattan and a small performance space with a photography exhibition documenting tenement living conditions. The upper floors were not yet open to the public: They were intended for exhibition space, which would feature actors playing out the roles of various ethnic families who might have inhabited the building, artists in residence, personal reflections by museum visitors, and so on. On the main floor, the museum installed a large doll house approximately six feet long and four feet high called the Urban Log Cabin. The house is a scale model of the museum building with cutaways that expose each of its apartments. The left side represents the building in 1915; the right side shows how it appeared in 1870. The latter side includes German, Irish, and Polish families; the date selected—a decade before the beginning of Jewish mass migration to America—enables an ecumenical image of the area. The 1915 side, however, shows solely Jewish inhabitants. Inside each apartment are tiny figurines, some modeled after photographs of the actual people they represent. They show the building's families in their daily lives—working, playing, dining—with considerable cultural and personal detail provided. The log cabin has since been moved to a nearby storefront space, along with the museum's shop, and then to Ellis Island. Apartments on the second floor have been "interpreted," and they recreate fully furnished interiors, including the original wall paper and linoleum. In at least one case, actual family mementos are included—the latter from an Italian family who occupied the apartment during the Depression.[12] As the museum's official publication *Tenement Times* proclaims in its Fall 1994 issue:

> From clothes and coal scuttle to sewing machine and toolbox, the Tenement Museum's two "living environments" are now open to the public. It is a historic moment. Authentic re-creations of urban immigrant lives have never before been attempted. But now, at 97 Orchard Street, in the actual spaces in which they dwelled, the Tenement Museum reveals precisely how two families—one German Jewish, one Sicilian Catholic—lived during the early years in America.

Fig. 8.2 The Baldizzi apartment, inside the Tenement Museum. Photograph by Jack Kugelmass.

Turfing the Slum

185

Two other apartments—one of an Orthodox East European Jewish family (Rogarshevsky) and another of a Turkish family of Sephardic background (Confino)—have since been interpreted. Other apartments await further funding.

The *Tenement Times* provides extensive description of the two families' homes. Describing the Baldizzi's apartment, the publication relates:

> As Josephine remembers it, their apartment at 97 Orchard Street was dimly lit, barely furnished, and terribly cold. The cold had to have been memorable. Rosaria demanded that they take cold-water sponge baths each morning, and their weekly tepid baths (small amounts of hot water came from a heater attached to the stove) took place in the kitchen sink. Rosaria also insisted on enemas, which she administered in the chilly hall toilet.

> But hardship is relative. Rosaria decorated the apartments by draping fabrics everywhere: lacy curtains at the windows, coverlets on the beds, skirts across the shelving that Adolfo built into the walls.[13]

Nathalia Gumpertz's apartment is not quite so cheerful. After her husband abandoned her, Nathalia worked at home as a dressmaker:

> Nathalia's front room—the only one with natural light—was her workshop. If her customers had to wait for a fitting, they may well have sat in the kitchen, drinking coffee and cake served by the Gumpertz daughters.

The description also notes the upward mobility of the Gumpertz family—in part due to the lucrative nature of dressmaking but largely due to an inheritance from her legally dead father-in-law—and the family's eventual relocation to the German "suburb" of Yorkville.[14] Although neither the museum's installation nor the official publication makes much of this distinction, the striking contrasts between these two ethic social trajectories will be evident later in the essay.

Preserving Memory

If the Tenement Museum is about the preservation of cultural memory and, therefore, about the inclusion of individuals who might otherwise have been marginalized, then who precisely are the people whose experiences the museum intends to legitimize? The answer has much less to do with actual people who lived in 97 Orchard Street— some 10,000 people since it was built, most of them Jews, according to the research of the museum's consulting genealogist—than with the complex politics and agendas of the museum's creators.[15] Indeed, it strikes me that there are underlying tensions among the intentions of its developers, consultants, and audience. (Aside from school groups, a sizable proportion of visitors to the museum consists of synagogue groups, Jewish tourists, and shoppers drawn to the building and its public programs.)

In fact, the Tenement Museum's origins lie not solely in the redemptive mission of rescuing humble artifacts, but were shaped partly by the mission to preserve the most spectacular creation of the wealthier strata of East European Jewish immigrants—the Eldridge Street Synagogue, which is now listed as a national landmark. According to Roberta Brandes Gratz, who, together with Ruth Abram, spearheaded the synagogue preservation program in the early 1980s,

> the Eldridge Street Synagogue, was the first and grandest synagogue built on the Lower East Side by East European Orthodox Jews, and it belies historic impressions that all those immigrants—"your tired, your poor, your huddled masses"—were penniless.[16]

Gratz's remarks are from the epilogue to her book *The Living City*. Like the rest of the volume, the section from which this passage is quoted makes an eloquent plea for recycling landmarks and historical neighborhoods in order to preserve the vitality and complexity of urban life. The founder and president of the Eldridge Street Synagogue project, Gratz described herself to me during an interview as "coming out of the preservation world, not the Jewish world." The synagogue's importance, according to Gratz, lies in the fact that usually all that remains of the past are remnants that may not be the most significant physical manifestation of a culture. The importance of the synagogue stems from the aesthetic quality of the building and Gratz's assumption concerning its value to immigrants. As she explained,

> I was up in the balcony one day a couple of years ago at a time when the demolition of inner-city churches was a hot issue in the press—important religious institutions were in jeopardy, because [congregations] could not afford to maintain them in poor neighborhoods. It struck me that so many who came to Eldridge Street were poor and battered by life—crowding, miserable working conditions, with none of the leisure advantages of today. But they did have the refuge of this magnificent structure, within which they felt valued. It was one place for them of magnificence and obvious expense, whereas everything else in their life was short changed. So, more than anything else, the poor community benefited from the aesthetic as a place of refuge.[17]

Gratz's ability to initiate the preservation project in the 1980s was made possible because of her position on the board of the New York State Preservation League, an office that gave her considerable knowledge about government grants. However, the matter of preservation found little response, let alone initiative, from within the Jewish community. As she relates,

> Jews were not as quick to respond as the preservationists. Historical preservation never was a Jewish thing. It was a very Waspy and social thing, and to some extent elitist and aesthetically based, not socially conscious. Also, historical architecture is not a Jewish thing. Most Jews thought that if it was not in Jerusalem, what's the point of doing historical preservation. Ten years ago they were not even interested in those sites in Eastern Europe.

Gratz sees the significance of the project less in terms of its relevance to the cultural life of the New York Jewish community than in terms of Jewish acceptance and presence in the wider context of American society and national heritage:

> Eldridge Street is an important vessel the same way that Trinity Church, North Church in Boston, or any of the other important churches that we think of as significant markers of American history. We've never put a synagogue in that galaxy. Eldridge Street does that, and in a sense Eldridge Street is claiming for American Jews its rightful place in the thread of American history that is so ethnically based.

I'll have more to say about the meaning of these comments later. For now, suffice it to say that whereas Gratz's project relates to buildings rather than people, Ruth Abram, her former co-worker and now director of the Tenement Museum, describes the evolution of the museum as stemming from her Southern background and her family's involvement in the struggle for civil rights. But her first influence was much more personal, stemming from an understanding that she had of the difference between herself as a white person and her African American maid. In a published article that she herself wrote about the museum, Abram relates,

> I was a child, small enough so that to grasp my colored maid's hand, I had to stretch my arm upward. We boarded a bus, a new experience for me, as usually my mother was my chauffeur. Rosa May Maddox found a seat for me in the front and moved to the back. I was worried. What if she got off without me? I rushed back to sit with Rosa. She firmly brought me back to the front. My child's heart chafed against a society which, to my mind, would prevent an adult from protecting a child.[18]

When she turned thirteen, Abram was told by her friends that since she was a Jew she would no longer be welcome at their parties: "I did not understand how an identity in which I took pride could be a bane to others. The Museum grew quietly [in me]."[19] When her family moved north, Abram took to organizing rent strikes and was generally active in civil rights and poverty issues. Her involvement in the women's movement led to a discovery of "how powerful a tool history could be for those developing strategy for the present."[20] Another stage in the conceptualization of the museum occurred after an unpleasant personal experience in New York. After she had found a suitable synagogue and Jewish school for her children, Abram was informed by the rabbi that he could officiate neither at her children's bar mitzvahs nor at her funeral, since her mother had converted to Judaism only after Ruth was born:

> And the Museum's shape focused more clearly. I wanted a way to promote tolerance, to challenge stereotypes, to ask for a world where adults can protect children, where women's contributions are acknowledged, where differences are both acknowledged and appreciated and certainly not used as the basis for exclusion. I wanted a way to provide role models for those who might not have them in their homes or neighborhood—at least not just the ones they needed. I wanted a vehicle which would place history at the disposal of everyone in a respectful, non-rhetorical way and encourage discussion and debate.[21]

Abram then describes earning a master's degree in American history and developing a traveling exhibition on women's doctors from 1850 to 1920. This exhibit "raised the question: How does any group outside the dominant culture first gain and then retain hard won social, political and educational gains?"[22]

> I turned my attention to the Lower East Side. The Lower East Side is associated in the public's mind with immigrants. Most people link the area only with Jewish immigrants, when, in fact, Jews have had no longer a history in the area than immigrants from Ireland, Germany, Africa, China, Italy, and many other nations. My objective was now clear . . . the establishment of a tenement museum. The tenement building represented the common ground of immigrants from everywhere. Through it, one could discuss the history of immigration and immigrant life, the role of reformers, of government, the history of housing and our changing views as to what was an acceptable life style. But most of all, through a tenement museum, the general public, old and young alike, could be invited to consider this question: How will we be one nation and at the same time enjoy, appreciate and certainly not be afraid of the profound differences we bring to the table based on background.[23]

Providing that common ground has much to do with the ways in which immigrant history is written. Accordingly, the museum's consulting historians and researchers are quick to point to the numerous social problems that were an ever-present (though now scarcely remembered) part of the Jewish immigrant experience.[24] One example centered around family abandonment. With this in mind, Abram relates the accidental discovery of the Gumpertz case that was made by

Turfing the Slum

189

the museum's consulting genealogist who was pursuing research for a private client in the Surrogate Court:

> The records inevitably come mixed in with other unrelated records . . . she had to get through those unrelated records for her records, and she saw the name Gumpertz in one of the unrelated files and she said, "Where have I heard this name before?" Marsha has put together over 1,100 names of people who have lived here between 1863 and 1939. She opened the file, and it's dated 1883, and it says, "I, Nathalia Gumpertz, request at the court to declare my husband Julius legally dead. I live at 97 Orchard Street. In 1874 in October at 7:00 A.M. he left me and my four children to go to his job as a shoemaker on Division Street and he's never been seen since." And then came the building's landlord, Lucas Glockner: "I know the family, and Nathalia Gumpertz is telling the truth. I well remember the day that Julius disappeared." And then came the saloon keeper in the building, John Schneider, and he said, "I know this man. I helped to look for Julius. We looked everywhere. We questioned everyone who had anything to do with him." And then came her children, who said they barely remember their father. And so now we have the Gumpertz family, who you'll meet when you come back to the Tenement Museum.[25]

Indeed, Abram goes on to argue in favor of the importance of telling the true story of the immigrant experience by making the tales complex, complete with human foibles, cast against a backdrop of America with its dangers and delights:

> Such stories could provide today's settlers with the feeling of welcome which comes upon finding one's own reality captured. Such stories might safeguard those of us longer rooted [in this country] from a false sense of superiority of the "We did it, why can't they" variety.[26]

Abram's approach to immigrant history not only focuses on exposing the social problems that were common to all impoverished new arrivals, but it also underscores the lines of connections and the commonalities of class that undercut ethnic insularity. As she argues,

> My hope is that we'll look at this building as a common ground. This experience in the tenement is something that many different people have had in common, and we may have approached it differently or similarly. We are going to look at that here. In the history of the building itself, we start with Irish and German and English residents. We move to German residents, probably Catholic and Protestant, then German Jewish residents, then Eastern European Jewish residents, then Sephardic Jewish residents. All the while these people mixed. And then Italian, Chinese, Irish, and Jewish. So the building's own history has a rather remarkable mix of people, and one can talk about them in a serial way or together. And then we have, for instance, living next door, we found a freed slave. So we've decided to use the building to tell the story of the settlement of the Lower East Side by the

major groups that settled here and not to confine our interpretive work only to the people who actually lived here.

The Lower East Side is generally thought to have a Jewish story and that's it, partly because we're historically so short-minded. But even when people come around and finally realize there also is an Italian aspect, German aspect, they are just still floored that it has anything to do with blacks. The truth is that as early as 1820 the area is over twenty-percent freed slaves. And we're determined to tell this story. Jacob Riis writes a whole chapter on the coloreds in his *How the Other Half Lives,* which people also think of as a book about Jews. But he's associated with the Lower East Side. And blacks are very much associated with the tenement experience. German Jews were here starting in 1848. But not until the 1880s was the Lower East Side associated with Jewish cultural memory. Then it was called Kleindeutschland.[27]

Ethnic interdependence is another part of the museum's narrative, and the following "shabbes goy" anecdote is played to each group of visitors as they exit the Baldizzi kitchen. (A "shabbes goy" is a non-Jew who turns lights or the stove on or off on the Sabbath, when Jews are forbidden to do so.)

But we also decided that, for our first effort, we have two great stories—one given us by Josephine Baldizzi, whose apartment is there, whose family lived here during the Depression, and she lived across the airshaft from the Rogarshevsky family. The Rogarshevskys arrived as Rogarshevskys but left as Rosenthals. And I really have to laugh that that was the most they could ever dream to aspire to. I love that. But anyway, the Rogarshevsky/Rosenthals were very observant Jews, and Josephine remembers them fondly, and remembers lighting their lights on the Sabbath. And her family was very Catholic and Italian and being able to talk about the relationship between Jews and Italians in a tenement across the airshaft from each other. So I hope that most of us will be able to find out something, if not about our own type of family, then something about the settlement of the city and about American immigrant working-class life.

If we do it right, or do it the way I'd like to do it, I hope that first off, if we have any connections with history, we'll remember that we successful people are the descendants of people who were once viewed with some alarm, some concern, some consternation, some fear by the people who were already here. And I hope that that will make us pause and think about how we are feeling about the next group of people that are coming in. And then we may be able to make the leap and realize that they will have their generation that will stand in our shoes. And then we ought not to be so frightened.[28]

Sacred Turf

Given how sectarian cultural memory is, it should not be surprising that when groups do mingle, they will experience not so much a com-

Fig. 8.3 The Rogarshevsky apartment, inside
the Tenement Museum. Photograph
by Jack Kugelmass.

mon ground as a sense that their respective ties to the area constitute a contested vision of the past, present, and future. Although Abram is convinced that some of the museum's message reaches even the most sectarian of visitors, both she and her consultants acknowledge that museum visitors typically choose between Jewish, Italian, and Chinese programs, and that choice almost invariably reflects their pre-existing inclinations and affiliations.[29] Chinese visitors attending a Jewish walking tour of the Lower East Side are not pleased to hear Jewish voices lament the increasing Chinese influx and new ownership of old Jewish landmarks, such as the Forward Building, the Garden Cafeteria, and defunct synagogues. For their part, some Jews are not pleased to share a place of pilgrimage with newcomers or others for whom the Lower East Side never figured as prominently as an enduring Old World or as the paramount center for ethnic social and cultural life.[30] The museum itself has become a ground for contestation with at least one Jewish organization, which insists that Orthodox Jewish life be more fully represented in the programs and installations.[31] From a more secular perspective, a review in *Congress Monthly* in 1991 took issue with the museum's plan to devote each of its six upstairs rooms to interpreting the experiences of a different ethnic group. After comparing the mission of tolerance to the welcoming of strangers at the Passover seder—in itself a remarkable analogue—the reviewer comments,

> One need not be made happy by a museum. But one usually leaves feeling enhanced, enriched with new insights. Then why, on stepping out of the Lower East Side Tenement Museum into the sunlight of Orchard Street, I wondered, despite the fact that I admired the museum's mission, was I feeling disturbed, almost resentful?[32]

The author of the review notes that of the major encyclopedias, only the *Encyclopedia Judaica* has an entry for the Lower East Side, which she takes as an indication that "for all the varied populations the area sheltered, it was uniquely important to Jews." The review then suggests that in its desire to fulfill its mission to make native New Yorkers more tolerant of immigrants, to make Caucasians more tolerant of Hispanics, to make blacks more tolerant of Asians, the museum is redefining the term *Lower East Side*.[33] Other groups may complain about aspects of the museum's programming or its geographic nomenclature when referring to European localities of origin, particularly when the political provenance of those localities is contested by various states.[34] However, the idea that the very turf of the museum is somehow sacred, that it is mysteriously, and almost atavistically, connected to the very foundation of ethnic memory—an American Jewish version of Plymouth

Rock—is entirely unique to Jews. Take, for example, the following excerpt from a recent report on the Eldridge Street synagogue by the American Jewish writer Jonathan Rosen:[35]

> despite the requisite Hebrew school trip, many visits in later life and at least one walking tour, the Lower East Side has always been an emblem not only of topographical confusion (I don't do well where streets are named, not numbered), but also of a larger sort of confusion. I've never been sure what, if any, relationship the neighborhood has to me. (I understand this is a Jewish problem. I never find myself wondering what relationship SoHo or TriBeCa have to me.) But on the walk west along Canal to get to Eldridge, I pass streets whose very names—Essex and Orchard and even the once-sinister Allen, where the El and the prostitutes were—sing with a certain suggestion of meaning, even if I'm not quite sure what that meaning is.
>
> Nevertheless, I have what may be an American-born, suburban-bred resentment of the way writers have used the Lower East Side, and neighborhoods like it, as touchstones of Jewish authenticity—as if to be an immigrant was to be most fully Jewish, with all later generations merely representing the diminution of a primordial state. But the truth is, so many of the contradictions of Jewish life were carved in stone here that the Lower East Side has a sort of irresistible allegorical feel, so much so that when I wrote my novel *Eve's Apple*, I had my narrator, who is obsessed with immigrants, get lost as he roams the area—a dislocated, sentimental soul-seeking connection.

Literary scholars note that American Jewish culture acts like a region in much the way the West, New England, and the South have traditionally been in the American imaginary,[36] and its locus is New York City. But for Jews, that locus is much more focused; it lingers even *now* in the semi-mythic space of the Lower East Side. The collective memory fosters a strong sense of ownership, so it is not surprising to discover how programs that are clearly ecumenical in their orientation make little headway toward transcending ethnic boundaries. As Abram admits,

> I have taken people who are Jewish through the museum, and I introduce them through this imaginary tour to the Italians and the Chinese and the freed slaves and the Irish. And then at the end of the tour they tell me they never knew so much about Jews before this tour. Or if I do it with Italians and tell them about the Jews and the Chinese. . . . You see, I think it has to do with the fact that this experience is in the cultural memory. And so each group does feel it's theirs, and it doesn't matter if I talk about one group or the other.

Interestingly, Abram is not at all distressed by the idea of ownership, which she sees as less a result of turfing than of identification—the latter serving the needs of the institution by giving to it a committed audience:

> It's the same feeling I had when I went to Plymouth Plantation. Well, I'm a long way from the Mayflower, but when I got to Plymouth and met the Pilgrims, I felt like I wanted to find my great-great-grandparents. I was sure they're there, because this is America.[37]

Given the museum's stress on common ground, indeed, its political agenda of inclusiveness and tolerance, emotional identification based upon commonality may prove much more useful in promoting that agenda than the intellectual recognition of the differences of historical experiences.

Abram believes that commonality is typically apparent among New Yorkers. Guiding me through an unrestored upstairs three-room apartment, she insists,

> You can always tell a New York City person because they look at this and begin to decorate it. Anyone from out of town goes "Ahhhh. How could anyone live like that?" There was no water in the building at first, none at all. There was an outhouse in the back. There's a spigot in the back. And this is really pioneer living in the city. They called it the urban pioneers on the municipal frontier. [She points to a set of numbers scribbled on a wall.] It's left by a tailor in 1935.[38] Here he's left his inventory. The ILGWU said this had to be a sweatshop. The front room has a fire door leading to the neighbor's apartment. The windows are cut into the wall because of a 1901 law to improve ventilation. Ten, twelve or more people were living in these three rooms by the turn of the century, and privacy was an unattainable ideal, if it was an ideal at all. [Abram shows me a water pipe for the sink.] You could bathe a baby, but it's too small for adults, who went to the baths. Still, people remember beauty rather than misery. Linoleum on the floor is something they remember. Their mother's curtains [they remember], etc. I think, to a person, they will tell you that while it was extremely difficult living, I've not met one who felt they didn't lose something after leaving, and what they lost was that kind of community that's just not attainable in another setting.

> You know, living in their suburban boxes is just not the same. [She shows me where toilets were installed.] The airshaft to ventilate the toilets makes this the least desirable space to rent. There are lots of toilet stories. Josephine Esposito passed here and screamed. She said, she spent her childhood in here. And when we asked her why, she said, "My momma believed in enemas." And when we said that to Max Mason who was here as a child in the '20s, he said, "Well, mine did, too."

The Museum and the Public

In the lingo of living history, museums are time machines. But it seems to me that for most museums a better metaphor is found in the symbol of an elevator. Museums move their subjects up or down, often depending upon prevailing social currents and countercurrents or the political agendas of their founders and curators. For Gratz, the discovery and preservation of the Eldridge Street Synagogue enables Jews to assume their rightful place in the American pantheon by exhibiting a worthy (i.e., an aesthetically pleasing) religious institution integrally linked to the history of immigration. Seeing itself now as a nation of immigrants, America promotes its ethnic monuments, inserting immigrant experiences which would otherwise be absent from the nation's master narrative. Monuments enter the pantheon in large measure through their aesthetic virtuosity. One might say, therefore, that the Eldridge Street Synagogue elevates Jews and American Jewish history by asserting a new-found link between immigrant aesthetic concerns and the cultural values of America's elite.

Elevators do, of course, follow Newton's Law, and so it should not be surprising to find that exhibitions sometimes do the very opposite of what the Eldridge Street Synagogue is intended to do. Indeed, the Tenement Museum lowers its subject (assuming it to be primarily American Jews) and in so doing asserts the links between the Jewish working class and other immigrant groups, including those who have arrived most recently. Although one might make a similar case for a downward movement in the Holocaust Museum in Washington, the analogy is problematic. In part this is so because of the transvaluation of the Holocaust in recent decades into the quintessential experience of the twentieth century. Since the association with the museum's subject gives American Jews a new source of cultural capital, the net effect is to elevate Jews and the singularity of their experience. In part, the elevation is the *raison d'être* of the institution—an outgrowth of the interplay of national politics and Jewish bigwigs. And in part, the elevation is due to the fact that the institutions that will inevitably establish the common ground of genocide among Jews, African Americans, and American Indians are still in the planning stages. Until these institutions come into existence, the Holocaust Museum will reflect both the incommensurate qualities of Jewish history and the enormous wealth and power of American Jewry. Moreover, given the larger context of a national *Zeitgeist* that stresses cultural singularity and historical experience, in their search for common ground institutions such as the Tenement Museum seem like lonely flickering flames.

It stands very much to the Tenement Museum's credit, at a time when "Americans have become too afraid of each other" (as the intellectual historian David Hollinger suggests), that it attempts to mediate the particularism of its ethnic clientele with a cosmopolitanism necessary for some form of collective national identity.[39] Indeed, Hollinger argues that through simultaneous globalist and particularist pressures, states increasingly see themselves not as national communities but as "a multitude of constituencies united less by a sense of common destiny than by a will to use the state as an instrument of their particular agendas."[40] Yet without some ability to appeal to common destiny, state power could not be mobilized on behalf of the common good, whether for civil rights, for the building of the welfare state, or for adding to entitlements such as universal health care.

The salutary aspect of invoking Jewish poverty works particularly well if the paradigm of America as a nation of immigrants, with each newly arriving group working its way up the ladder of social achievement and economic success, prevails. Indeed, a belief in the past, present, and future probability of upward mobility underlies a sense of common destiny. Needless to say, this belief is very problematic with regard to African Americans, American Indians, and many Chicanos who are not immigrants. The idea of upward mobility does not apply in the same way to these groups as it does to Americans of European or Asian descent. Moreover, the very term *"common ground"* as used in Tenement Museum brochures, with its striking resonance with the 1980s presidential campaign slogan of Jesse Jackson, is also an ironic reminder of how little the Jewish immigrant experience resonates with that of Southern blacks who migrated northward to seek industrial employment during and after World War II. Moreover, the very speed of Jewish economic success in America is seen by some as proof that, Jewish claims notwithstanding, antisemitism is not a pervasive force in American life and that antisemitism certainly cannot be compared to the kind of racism that has long stood in the way of African American achievement.[41]

But good social history and good politics do not necessarily mesh. Therefore, the theme of common ground elides the unique history of individual groups while it does little to elucidate the complexity of ethnic interaction, particularly during the initial stages of integration into American society.[42] A variety of ethnic groups did live in the Lower East Side over the span of the past two centuries, but they were somewhat less co-territorial than their representation in the Tenement Museum would suggest,[43] and when they did interact, relations were as likely to be fraught with tension as they were cooperative.[44] The Tenement Museum is clearly more interested in the latter, and its representation of the past replicates a nostalgic trope stemming, in part, from the life stories it has collected that, in other respects, it seeks to subvert among the members of its audience. Invariably, social history takes a back seat to personal and political agendas, not to mention the practicalities of securing public grants for its installations or contracts with the department of education for school trips—the bread-and-butter of any small museum.

History and Heritage

If museums can be read as personal autobiographies,[45] they are collective autobiographies as well, that articulate, albeit unconsciously, discursive practices that situate and legitimize the institution.[46] History museums are particularly complex subjects. Like other museums, they define themselves in contradistinction to the exhibitionary complex within society—expositions, amusement parks, and department stores—by possessing and having a commitment to the "really real."[47] This is even more the case for living history museums, because their stock in trade is not merely authentic objects but also an authentic location.[48] Despite the rhetoric of authenticity, the competing needs of directors, patrons, audiences, and museum professionals can easily jettison the more sophisticated approaches to social history that may have been a part of the research agenda of resident scholars. At mega-installations, such as Colonial Williamsburg, for example, corporate and institutional needs have pushed social history to the back burner since the 1960s.[49] Still, one wonders whether or not good social history would have much of a chance of long-term survival at any living history museum, even small ones such as the Tenement Museum, if only because social historians bent on educating the public are poorly attuned to the impulses that draw visitors to these institutions.

The cultural geographer David Lowenthal's distinction between heritage and history offers particularly useful insights for understanding the difference between public and academic interests in living history museums. Heritage, according to David Lowenthal, is assumed to be "bad" history, its output "labeled as false, deceitful, sleazy, presentist, chauvinist, self-serving—as indeed it often is." But such labels are the result of a miscomprehension, since heritage merely "borrows from and enlivens historical study . . . [and] is not an inquiry into the past but a celebration of it."[50] "Celebration" played a prominent role in the formulation of nationalism during the nineteenth century among various emerging nation states in Europe, and it continues today to signal the supposedly innate character of a people and its legacy. Little wonder, then, that conflict is "endemic to heritage," and that "claims of owner-ship, uniqueness, and priority engender strife over every facet of collective legacies."[51]

Family and ethnic genealogy give most American Jews a legitimate and continuing connection to the Lower East Side and the past that its remaining landmarks connote. But it is the idea of uniqueness, of singularity, that has fixed the Lower East Side in Jewish memory and has given it a continuing connection to American Jewish life long after its most noted Jewish institutions have become nothing more than restaurants and discount stores. In widening and ecumenizing the immigrant experience within an important topos of Jewish memory, the Tenement Museum is unwittingly disturbing a site of Jewish *heritage*—a site that would probably have disappeared uncontested and largely (though not entirely) unnoticed, had the museum not attempted to preserve and interpret this building.[52]

So this very insistence upon common ground has the potential (museum officials do not feel that there is an insurmountable problem) to put the institution at odds, at least emotionally, with a major segment of its audience, American Jews, for whom the site and their experiences there are unique cultural patrimony.[53] And the potential for conflict is all the more acute given the fact that the museum takes its authority from history rather than ethnography. Were the latter the case, then Jews would have a very limited claim on exclusivity since they constitute a very small percentage of the area's current residents and only a minute percentage of those who still live in tenements. (Most Jews in the area live in the cooperative houses on Grand Street stretching from Essex Street to the East River.) But with regard to history, that claim has some weight. Moreover, the museum's subversion of a particular community's claim to exclusivity is part of its own strategy of ownership, of recasting local history and ownership into a larger, indeed, national context and subsuming it as patrimony or what James Clifford calls "the synthetic narrative of History."[54]

An American Jewish Allegory

But why such need to hold on to this turf? What meaning does it hold for the suburban Jewish visitor? Perhaps it is merely that the Lower East Side's institutions—its restaurants, museums, shops and the very sense of place it still conveys—constitute a veritable site of memory[55] whose architectural, graphic, and olfactory sensuality stands so much at odds with the aesthetic, social, and historical flatness of the suburban landscapes that have long been the locus of American Jewish life. Given the radical transformation of American Jewry, its rapid economic mobility, and the concomitant dispersal of its members to ever newer locations far from its institutions of origin, the need for an enduring site of origin is all the more acute.[56] The cause for nostalgia here is, of course, partly facilitated by the Lower East Side's "pastness" as an historical site, by the fact that until now the area has largely escaped gentrification and continues to sit there like a ruin allegorically[57] revealing a complex tale that oscillates between that of decay, the ephemeral nature of time, and the enormous distance traveled by its former residents on the road to success. The more distant the social and economic circumstances are from actual lives, the greater both the possibility of and, indeed, the need for nostalgia—an argument that applies as much to the physical location as it does to the immigrant experience. Moreover, the Lower East Side's location gives it an accessibility unlike almost any other former place of Jewish settlement in the New York area, such as Harlem, Brownsville, and Hunts Point, to name just a few. That, tied to the existence of its remaining stores selling Jewish ritual objects and collectibles, enables the area, according to Richard Rabinowitz, the Tenement Museum's planning consultant,

> to still sit there in the American Jewish collective memory as a place of memory. As with most communities, there is an impulse to go the earliest, the first of something. The impulse to go back to the Lower East Side has something to do with looking for the primitive experience of America of their great grandparents.[58]

This connection to grandparents is more than just a matter of individual family history. For Jews struggling with the huge distance that now exists between their social standing and their politics, the Lower East Side is a concrete reminder of a time when their language, politics, and even kinship networks were intricately connected to an organic community—a factor sometimes referred to as the culture of *yidishkeyt*. As Karen Bodkin notes,

> Perhaps Jews of my generation who have grown up white hold on to fragments and memories of that Jewishness as our ethnoracial identity precisely because it represents an alternative to the contradictions of whiteness. Yiddishkeit did not rest upon invidious comparison for its existential meaning, and it held out a different and more optimistic vision than that of modernity (even as it also participated in modernity). Instead of having to choose between individual fulfillment and communal belonging, it expected Jews to find fulfillment *through* responsibility to the Jewish community.[59]

As a site of memory, the lower East Side has particular *ideological* relevance because it stands almost as a point of mediation between the labor-based politics of the American Jewish past and, at least, the lure of fiscal and social-policy conservatism that some see (or would like to see) as a growing trend even among American Jews.[60] In an essay on the subject of Jewish liberalism during the Reagan administration, the literary critic Irving Howe argued that despite social attainment, the vicissitudes of history have taught Jews to be prepared for almost anything other than to be considered part of the dominant majority. Convinced that they will remain incompletely absorbed into American society, American Jews retain a commitment to liberalism even when it threatens immediate self-interest. They are, to use Milton Himmelfarb's aphorism, a group of people who earn like Episcopalians but vote like Puerto Ricans.[61]

According to Howe, this commitment to liberalism is based on two factors:

> The once powerful tradition of secular Jewish socialism, now fading but still felt and transposed into the images of liberalism; and by now, much more important, the premise, shared by many Jews for perhaps two centuries, that Jewish survival and interests are best served by an open society promoting social justice.[62]

But the continuing penchant for liberalism can also be seen as a nostalgic trope maintained, as the historian Stephen Whitfield suggests, because it helps American Jews differentiate themselves from the majority while still paying homage to the aspirations of their forebears.[63] Indeed, as Howe argues, the attachment to liberalism is a cornerstone of American Jewish identity and particularly so now as acculturation has left its mark on most. If American Jews were to deny their social responsibility toward exploited people and become complacent suburbanites,

> while fondly recalling the heroism of their socialist grandfathers . . . then a major and perhaps shattering change of self-perception would follow. Remove that thinning measure of social commitment and the problem of Jewish distinctiveness must become increasingly severe.[64]

Interestingly, Jewish distinctiveness is the very issue that both lures Jews to the Lower East Side and disconnects them from the experience of others—further evidence of the ever-present rift between history and heritage, the Tenement Museum's intentions notwithstanding. Indeed, Richard Rabinowitz maintains that Jews are attracted to the Lower East Side *because* it is teeming with poor people and yet is not as dangerous a neighborhood as other former areas of Jewish settlement such as Brownsville:

> It is almost a physicalization of family history that people are concerned with, and that has a lot to do with attitudes towards poverty and the whole

crisis in the last twenty or thirty years in American Jewish politics—the sense of commitment to liberal left-wing politics and the idea of social change that would lift a whole group up. And the tremendous ambivalence people feel about their own success and the other people left behind raises all kinds of questions, like "Why do Puerto Ricans and blacks have such trouble making it?" It's like the old song from *My Fair Lady*—"Why can't the blacks be like the Jews?"[65]

If historian Stephen Steinberg is correct, the answer to this question offers little comfort to newer immigrants. According to Steinberg, those who made the journey from tenements to solid working- and middle-class housing in New York's boroughs did so in no small measure because they brought with them skills that gave them a decided advantage in the country's *then* rapidly growing clothing and other light industries.[66] Evaluating the reasons for Jewish economic success in America, Steinberg concludes:

> If Jews set high goals, it is because they had a realistic chance of achieving them. If they worked hard, it is because they could see the fruits of their labor. If they were willing to forego the pleasures of the moment, it is because they could realistically plan for a better future, for their children if not for themselves. In short there was much in the everyday experience of Jewish immigrants to activate and sustain their highest aspirations. Without this reinforcement, their values would have been scaled down accordingly, and more successful outsiders would today be speculating about how much further Jews might have gone if only they had aimed higher.[67]

Initiated quickly into an emerging consumer culture and with a growing disposable income, the Jewish immigrant at the beginning of the twentieth century experienced an enormous rift in comparing the material possibilities of America and what he or she had experienced in the Old World.[68] Clearly that rift made Jews and others deeply committed to their adopted country. But in post-Fordist America—with global corporations ready to move jobs where labor is cheapest and increasingly committed to downsizing their work force, and with high-end jobs demanding ever more sophisticated skills and education—how much resonance is there in this Horatio Alger story with the daily lives of countless other recent immigrants?[69]

An Epic Culture

Laybush Scheinberg appears on stage at the Tenement Museum because he walked into the Eldridge Street Synagogue and gave his memoirs to the staff. And the fact that he did so, it seems to me, is not accidental. Jews have been writing memoirs *en masse* for more than a century. In fact, today there are countless other Laybush Scheinbergs, examples of a people determined to bridge the gap that exists between the life of their recent forebears and their own descendants—a response, in part, to the crisis of memory that is particularly acute among contemporary Jews, although by no means unique to them. So, memory here has little to do with the past or common ground. It has everything to do with the present, perhaps the future, and certainly the continuity of a people whose lives have been radically altered by more than a century of migration, with massive social, economic, and political change. At the same time, Jews experienced their most recent history through the linked paradigms of catastrophe and redemption. The problem that the Tenement Museum faces is that while it would like to see the immigrant experience as the common ground linking one group with another, the Laybush Scheinbergs do not see their lives as common but as singular and extraordinary, their own accomplishments as epic in significance. After all, theirs is a story that began in poverty, and frequently persecution, in the Old World. They lived through the disruption and the many trials of emigration and resettlement in a new country. Their experiences led to their ultimate redemption (Laybush became a doctor in America). And the belief that the New World offered redemption for European Jews is made all the more poignant by the terrible fate of countless friends and relatives who either refused to or were not permitted to make a similar journey.

Whatever its intention, the Tenement Museum is organically connected to American Jews and to what may remain the *uniqueness* of their immigrant experience. Given this fact, common ground may have to give way somewhat to the realities of audience expectations and the possibilities of funding for the interpretation of the building's remaining rooms and the running of its public programs. Jews will frequent this museum and will probably pay a significant part of the private contributions for its renovation. And they will do so in part because of a continuing commitment to liberal causes, but in part, too, because it is through the museum's recreation of the past that American Jews are able to continue some claim to a turf they abandoned except in memory some two generations ago.

NOTES

   Research for this essay was made possible in part through grants from the Lucius N. Littauer Foundation, the National Endowment for the Humanities, the Wisconsin Alumni Research Foundation of the University of Wisconsin-Madison and a summer

Turfing the Slum

travel grant from the College of Liberal Arts and Sciences at Arizona State University. Special thanks to Ruth Abram and her staff for a critical reading of this essay while it was still in manuscript, and to Ruth for all her help during my research. Copyright © 2000 Jack Kugelmass.

1. Warren Leon and Margaret Piatt, "Living History Museums," in Warren Leon and Roy Rosenzweig, eds., *History Museums in the United States* (Urbana: University of Illinois Press, 1989), p. 72.

2. Jay Anderson, *Time Machines: The World of Living History* (Nashville: American Association for State and Local History, 1984), p. 39. Anderson estimates that in 1978 there were approximately 800 living history museums in North America.

3. Ibid., p. 191.

4. See Anderson, *Time Machines*, pp. 191–192, on the critical appraisal of each other by "living historians." For an interesting report on the reconstruction of the Rogarshevsky room in the Tenement Museum, see Patricia Leigh Brown, "Mining a Family's Memories to Bring an Immigrants' Home to Life," *New York Times*, December 10, 1998, p. B11. Members of the family were tracked down through an ad in the *Forward* and *Modern Maturity* magazine. The curator made use of crime-scene photographs to get a more accurate sense of the interiors as they might have appeared on normal occasions. An interesting side note is that in restoring the apartment's wallpaper, the museum commissioned Scalamadré to silk screen the design which they now sell as "Rogarshevsky's Scroll" for $113 per roll. Upon seeing the walls of the restored apartment, a descendant remarked that it's "gorgeous. But it's perhaps too rich-looking for Grandma." What better proof could there be that "heritage is a 'value added' industry." Barbara Kirshenblatt-Gimblett, *Destination Culture: Tourism, Museums, and Heritage* (Berkeley: University of California Press, 1998), p. 150.

5. Leon and Piatt, "Living History Museums," p. 75.

6. Ibid., p. 68.

7. Michael Wallace, in Leon and Rosenzweig, *History Museums in the United States*, p. 179.

8. In 1997, New York Congressional delegates co-sponsored legislation to link the museum with the National Parks Service. The museum would remain independent but would benefit from Parks Service curators, engineers, and marketers and would be featured in brochures. Paula Span, "On History's Doorstep: N.Y. Museum Restores Tenement the Huddled Masses Called Their Home," *Washington Post*, August 5, 1997, p. B1.

9. The museum recognizes the need to integrate its activities with the needs of local businesses, many of which are experiencing a drop in customers through increased competition from other retailers. The museum works with members of the local Business Improvement District by issuing discount shopping and restaurant coupons to all ticket buyers. Also, in anticipation of expanding its audience, the museum is considering acquiring additional space, including the Essex Street Market built by Mayor LaGuardia, to house the pushcart vendors forced off the streets by anti-peddling legislation. *Tenement Times* 6, no. 1 (Fall 1996): 5.

10. Lower East Side Tenement Museum brochure (n.d.), p. 2. Not all of the museum's discoveries are the result of intense research. Information on the Baldizzi family, for example, came about much the way the Scheinberg story was gathered—a

knock on the door of the museum by Josephine Baldizzi Esposito, who wanted to see her childhood home. Span, "On History's Doorstep," p. B2.

11. Interview by author with Ruth Abram, March 30, 1992.

12. The Baldizzi material is thanks to Josephine Baldizzi, whose parents Adolfo and Rosaria were immigrants from Palermo. For extensive descriptions of the Baldizzi and Gumpertz families, see *Tenement Times* 5, no. 2 (Fall 1994): 1, 6, 7.

13. Ibid., pp. 6–7.

14. Ibid., pp. 1, 6.

15. Marsha Dennis has been examining public documents, including voting and marriage records, in order to trace the history of some of the building's tenants.

16. Roberta Brandes Gratz, *The Living City* (New York: Simon and Schuster, 1989), p. 389.

17. Interview by author with Roberta Brandes Gratz, 1992.

18. Ruth Abram, "A Museum Grew in Me," *The Workmen's Circle*, p. 10.

19. Ibid., p. 10.

20. Ibid., p. 11.

21. Ibid., pp. 11–12.

22. Ibid., p. 12.

23. Ibid., p. 12.

24. In the museum's publication *Tenement Times*, Ruth Abrams describes the data that the museum has been collecting:

> The files containing clues of rapid movement out of the East Side tenements also depict the moment when adults realize they will never even regain the status they enjoyed before emigrating. "My parents never learned English. That's why they couldn't get good jobs." And the genealogical searches which reveal orderly processes of immigration also uncover duplicity. "My parents snuck into the country through Canada; they were always afraid." And the evidence of hardy self-reliance is packed alongside wooden boxes stamped "HOME RELIEF." The numerous witnesses to the passionate hopes immigrant parents maintained for their children are offset by other first-hand accounts. "My parents never knew where we children were. They just couldn't imagine our lives." The records contain stories of failed ventures, of families and friends who refuse to help, of exploitative working conditions, of depression and suicide, of parents who stand in the way of children's education and of children turned bad.

Tenement Times 4, nos.1 and 2 (Winter, Spring, n.d.): 2.

25. Interview with Ruth Abram, March 30, 1992.

26. *Tenement Times*, p. 2.

27. Interview with Ruth Abram, March 30, 1992. Both to fund-raise and to educate, the Museum's public programs have pushed hard to replicate the immigrant experience of various groups: a German beer garden was held at the nearby Bowery Savings Bank (designed in 1894 by McKim, Mead, and White) complete with German food, music, and dance (*The Tenement Times* 2, no.1 [Winter 1991]: 7); an Italian musical cafe was created, complete with singing waiters; other programs are intended

to underline the similarity of the immigrant experience across ethnic lines. One such program, "Matchmaker, Matchmaker," made use of computer match-ups along with the presence of the actress who played the matchmaker in *Crossing Delancey*. The event took place at the recently renovated Asher Levy bath house and featured the Harlem Honeys and Bears, a senior citizens' synchronized swim group, as performers.

28. Nor is this utopian vision pure fantasy. The fact is that newer immigrants do learn about the humble origins of established groups, and particularly so for Latino and Asian American schoolchildren who visit the museum as part of school outings. Some have been heard to respond, "I didn't know there were ever poor Jews." Interview with Marsha Dennis, April 1, 1992.

29. More recent brochures indicate a change in public programs, such as walking tours that cater less to a single ethnic history.

30. Jack Kugelmass and Jeffrey Shandler, *Going Home: How American Jews Invent the Old Country* (New York: YIVO Institute, 1990).

31. Letter of November 29, 1996, from Joel Kaplan, Executive Director of United Jewish Council of the East Side, Inc., offering to assist the museum in a "proactive way, if and when you make the decision to commit the necessary resources to chronicle the predominant 'culture' of the Lower East Side—the orthodox Jewish community and its myriad of synagogues, shtiebels, charitable and 'self-help' organizations."

32. Estelle Gilson, "The Lower East Side Tenement Museum: A Ghetto with a Difference," *Congress Monthly* (January 1991): 11.

33. Ibid., p. 13.

34. See, for example, a letter dated January 20, 1998, to Ruth Abram from Athanasia Gregoriades, chair of the Issues Committee of the Hellenic-American Educators Association/United Federation of Teachers, protesting the identification of the town of Kastoria as belonging to Turkey in a performance of the Confino family, Sephardic immigrants who came to the United States in 1913. The author writes:

> We request that the script followed by the tour guide and the actress be changed to reflect correctly the geographic and ethnic identity of Kastoria. Kastoria is a Greek city and should be identified as such by the staff members. The fact that the city was occupied by the Turks, as was the whole of Greece, does not make it part of Turkey. Further, when we in America, today, speak about Texas and California, we do not in any way make reference to Mexico, even though at one time both Texas and California were part of Mexico.

35. Jonathan Rosen, "On Eldridge Street, Yesteryear's Shul," *New York Times*, October 2, 1998, p. B39.

36. Peter Schrag, *The Decline of the Wasp* (New York: Simon and Schuster, 1971), p. 108.

37. Interview with Ruth Abram, March 30, 1992.

38. Abram now thinks that the writing on the wall is a shopkeeper's inventory, and that the apartment was used as a warehouse after 1935.

39. David A. Hollinger, *Postethnic America: Beyond Multiculturalism* (New York: Basic Books, 1995), p. 146.

40. Ibid., p. 147.

41. See Cornel West's statement to that effect in Michael Lerner and Cornel West, *Jews and Blacks: A Dialogue on Race, Religion, and Culture in America* (New York: Plume, 1996), p. 136.

42. In conceptualizing America as an "immigrant culture," Francis X. Femminella considers the "emergent" nature of American immigrant cultures, each of whose impact upon American culture includes a "boundary crisis" when it encroaches upon the turf of an older group, and whose integration into American society may be violent and prolonged. Lawrence W. Levine, *The Opening of the American Mind: Canons, Culture, and History* (Boston: Beacon, 1996), pp. 139–140.

43. Even Jews tended to settle in subdistricts according to place of origin. In his classic study of the Lower East Side, Moses Rischin indicates that Hungarian Jews lived above Houston Street, Galicians to the south and to the west was the Rumanian quarter. "Levantines" who arrived after 1907 settled between Allen and Chrystie among the Rumanians. The remainder of the area, from Grand Street to Monroe, belonged to Russian Jews, which included those from Russian Poland, Lithuania, Byelorussia, and the Ukraine (pp. 77–78).

With regard to ethnic mixing, Rischin focuses much more on the issue of displacement with the arrival of newer immigrants: "The changes brought about by the great Jewish migration forced the district's middle-class Germans and Irish, living in predominantly two- and two-and-one-half story dwellings, to retreat to less crowded quarters." Moses Rischin, *The Promised City: New York Jews, 1870–1914* (New York: Harper Torchbooks, 1970), p. 79.

44. For an overview of ethnic antagonism among immigrant groups in the early-twentieth-century labor market, see Karen Bodkin, *How the Jews Became White Folks and What That Says about Race in America* (New Brunswick, N.J.: Rutgers University Press, 1998), pp. 53–76. Processes of exclusion that made some groups "white" while relegating other groups to non-craft industrial labor undoubtedly affected the fault lines of ethnic antagonism as well as mutual cooperation—a phenomenon whose specific ethnic parameters changed over time. The emergence of a large number of Jewish and Italian clothing factory workers and related unionization is undoubtedly a factor in Milton Himmelfarb's observation that

> most Jews like Italians. If there has not been actual friendship between the Jews and Italians, there has been peaceful coexistence, all the more to be prized because we can't always say as much about our relations with the Irish or Poles.
>
> A social scientist of Italian parentage once told me that when he was a boy in New York, he always thought of Jews and Italians as belonging together, as differing together from the real Americans, the Irish. The Irish were the real Americans because they had the important American and Americanizing jobs: they were the teachers, the principals, the police, the politicians. (For the Italians, they were also the bishops.) And the Irish were the real Americans, too, because they were the only ones we actually knew who came from families in which English was the language that had always been spoken at home.

"Are the Jews Still Liberal?" *Commentary* 43, no. 4 (April 1967): 69.

45. A side box in Ruth Abram's article "A Museum Grew in Me" in *The Workmen's Circle* quotes Ralph Waldo Emerson that "an institution is the elongated shadow of an individual."

46. Daniel Sherman and Irit Rogoff delineate four fundamental institutional practices of museums: (1) they base themselves upon a notion of and system for classifying objects which always takes place within discursive fields such as nation, community, or culture; (2) the context—epoch, artistic school, or style (a community of people or values)—that the objects are said to represent; (3) every museum defines its own public sphere and the audience that it seeks to serve; (4) how audiences respond to the material presented to them. Daniel J. Sherman and Irit Rogoff, eds., *Museum Culture: Histories, Discourses, Spectacles* (Minneapolis: University of Minnesota Press, 1994), pp. x–xi.

47. Tony Bennet, as cited in Richard Handler and Eric Gable, *The New History in an Old Museum: Creating the Past at Colonial Williamsburg* (Durham: Duke University Press, 1997), p. 222.

48. In an article titled "No Stone Unturned," *Tenement Times* 4, no. 12 (Winter/Spring n.d.): 2, the museum's official publication argues that visitors will be content with "the historical and structural accuracy of the Museum's 'urban log cabin.'" But

> not all of us at the Museum are reasonable or capable of being content. For example, we do not yet know whether the panels in the front door of the building were of glass or wood. We don't know whether the fire escapes are original to the building or were added later. And we don't know what the original entry stoop looked like.

The article then details various aspects of the restoration and the problematic nature of determining exact details such as the color of paint for a given year, or the wallpaper, the location of the privies, the water spigot, the condition of the street, the types of stores, etc.

49. Handler and Gable, *The New History in an Old Museum*.

50. David Lowenthal, *The Heritage Crusade and the Spoils of History* (Cambridge: Cambridge University Press, 1998), p. x.

51. Ibid., pp. 234–235. Jo Blatti makes a similar case regarding the tension between the interests of citizens and scholars' use of the past, a past which Blatti conceptualizes geographically for citizens as like a rolling field,

> populated by clumps of symbolism that are mythic, experiential, and nostalgic. It is often deeply, though perhaps implicitly, political terrain. Though many comparative judgments are made concerning then and now, few are made within or across the categories used by professional students of society. Further, it seems to me that the broadly public interest in history is for social utility. This interest may be as private and specific as family genealogy, as public and commercial as a downtown redevelopment plan based on historic structures. In either case, however, the effort is to locate oneself or community selectively in time and space. It is not to use history as an analytic system for understanding time and space as socially constructed concepts.

Jo Blatti, "Past Meets Present: Field Notes on Historical Sites, Programs, Professionalism, and Visitors," in Jo Blatti, ed., *Past Meets Present: Essays about Historic Interpretation and Public Audiences* (Washington, D.C.: Smithsonian Institution Press, 1987), pp. 7–8.

52. Clearly, one task of this museum is to find some way to balance its stated mission and the needs of a major segment of its audience. How can it do so? Perhaps by *not* producing a coherent integrative narrative but rather by exposing and exploring the multiple views apparent in history as recounted by museum professionals, scholars and multiple groups of citizens. See Blatti, "Past Meets Present," pp. 8–10.

53. While the museum's surveys count only 35% of its 80,000 visitors as having had any connection to the Lower East Side, that still constitutes a sizable proportion of its visitors. Personal correspondence with Katherine Snider, based on August 1999 survey.

54. James Clifford, *Routes: Travel and Translation in the Late Twentieth Century* (Cambridge, Mass.: Harvard University Press, 1997), p. 129.

55. It is interesting to note that even the museum's brochure includes a page whose banner reads: "To experience the whole Lower East Side, leave plenty of time for shopping and eating in the heart of the Lower East Side Historic Bargain District!"

56. Indeed, the historian Edward Shapiro ties this nostalgia, as evidenced by films such as *Hester Street, Crossing Delancey,* and *Lies My Father Told Me* (in this case a Montreal equivalent), to the appeal of the shtetl as evidenced by *Fiddler on the Roof,* and the book *Life Is with People,* all of which basically depict anti-suburbs and consider the process of Americanization "as a movement away from honesty and cultural authenticity" (p. 151). Shapiro continues,

> In *World of Our Fathers,* Irving Howe contrasted the moral and political passion of the immigrant communities with the spiritual vacuity of the suburbs. While admitting that vulgarity was not a monopoly of the suburbs, Howe surmised that "there may be some truth in the view often expressed by older Yiddishists and younger intellectuals that something about the vulgarity of the suburb was more troubling than the immigrant variety. (p. 152)

Edward S. Shapiro, *A Time for Healing: American Jewry since World War II* (Baltimore: Johns Hopkins University Press, 1992).

57. For a discussion of the connection between ruins and allegory, see Walter Benjamin, as cited in John McCole, *Walter Benjamin and the Antimonies of Tradition* (Ithaca, N.Y.: Cornell University Press, 1993), especially pp. 132–139.

58. Interview by author with Richard Rabinowitz.

59. Brodkin, *How Jews Became White Folks,* p. 186. For a sense of how the notion of an organic Jewish community connected to the Lower East Side continues even today, see Roberta Brandes Gratz's description:

> Although Chinese businesses predominate—most of them having opened in the four or five years I've been observing Eldridge Street— several strong vestiges of the century of Jewish dominance persist. A few doors away from each other on the north side of the Witty Brothers building, for example, are J. Levine & Company and Zion Tallis.
>
> The manager of the local Merchants Bank branch knows his accounts by

sight and calls them when they are overdrawn. A message can be left in a store on the block where, as well, help can be found in any emergency. A sense of neighborliness, or caring, persists, and memories and continuity prevail amidst the more obvious and constant change.

Roberta Brandes Gratz, *The Living City* (New York: Simon and Schuster, 1989), pp. 387–388.

60. For a description of the response to *Commentary*'s turn from a staunchly liberal to a leading conservative monthly, see Shapiro, *A Time for Healing*, pp. 221–223. Nor are all observers convinced that this turn to the Right has deep significance affecting large numbers of American Jews. According to journalist J. J. Goldberg, the inroads made by Republicans among Jewish voters during the Nixon and Reagan administrations came crashing down on September 12, 1991, when George Bush announced at a White House briefing that he was "up against some powerful political forces" in his request that Congress delay loan guarantees to Israel by 120 days in order not to anger Arab leaders shortly before a planned Israel-Arab peace conference. *Jewish Power: Inside the American Jewish Establishment* (Reading, Mass.: Addison-Wesley, 1996), p. xv. For a discussion of the deep rootedness of liberalism among American Jews during the 1960s and an interesting prelude to the rising tensions between Jews and African Americans, see James Yaffee, *The American Jews: Portrait of a Split Personality* (New York: Random House, 1968), pp. 239–265. Yaffee attributes the deep-rootedness of liberalism to its place in an American Jewish "lay religion." To a degree, Jewish liberalism stems from selfless motives apparent by the commitment to social welfare programs, despite the fact that "Jews on the whole, because of their affluence, get fewer benefits from social welfare than almost any other group" (pp. 246–247). Yaffee attributes such commitment to the core Jewish value of *zedakah*, or charity. But the second motive is hardy selfless and stems from the fact that liberalism is good for the Jews, while the Right has historically been linked with antisemitism. Moreover, fear of antisemitism propels Jewish commitment to civil rights, free speech and the separation of church and state.

61. Cited in Stephen J. Whitfield, *American Space, Jewish Time: Essays in Modern Culture and Politics* (Armonk, N.Y.: North Castle Books, 1996), p. 95. The journalist J. J. Goldberg writes,

Whatever gains Jewish conservatives may have made in recent years, the overall profile of the Jewish community—Jewish voters, Jewish officeholders, most Jewish social activism, and majority opinion on the Jewish street—remains overwhelmingly Democratic and liberal. Of the nine Jews in the U.S. Senate in 1995, eight were Democrats; of the twenty-four Jews in the House of Representatives, twenty were Democrats.

Within the world of liberal organizations like the ACLU and the People for the American Way, Jewish influence is so profound that non-Jews sometimes blur the distinction between them and the formal Jewish community.

Jewish Power, p. 46.

62. Irving Howe, *A Time for Compassion and Commitment: American Jews and Liberalism* (New York: Foundation for the Study of Independent Social Ideas, 1986), p. 8.

63. Whitfield, *American Space, Jewish Time*, p. 105.

64. Howe, *A Time for Compassion and Commitment*, p. 12. Indeed, so significant are social commitment and charity to Jewish institutional life that some scholars have come to see these, along with commitment to Israel, and preoccupation with Holocaust memorialization, as key components of a civic religion that gives American Jews the ability to involve themselves in Jewish communal life without a concomitant commitment to religious practice. See Gerald Sorin, *Tradition Transformed: The Jewish Experience in America* (Baltimore: Johns Hopkins University Press), pp. 242–244.

65. In a 1967 review of the Jewish Museum's exhibition on the Lower East Side, the literary critic Robert Alter remarks,

> The one disturbing thing I heard at the Jewish Museum was an exchange between two middle-aged men. Standing before a rear-view photograph of a row of tenements, they were moved to comment in tones of the deepest self-righteousness about the differences between the ghettos of past and present. That most of those people "pulled themselves up by their own bootstraps" was the not-unexpected conclusion. ("It is a cruel jest," Martin Luther King recently observed to a mixed audience in Atlanta, "to say to a bootless man, 'lift up by your own bootstraps.'")

Commentary 43, no. 1 (January 1967): 70.

66. Stephen Steinberg, *The Ethnic Myth: Race, Ethnicity, and Class in America* (Boston: Beacon Press, 1981), p. 99.

67. Ibid., p. 103.

68. For an interesting study on the place of consumerism in the immigrant's world, see Andrew R. Heinze, *Adapting to Abundance: Jewish Immigrants, Mass Consumption, and the Search for American Identity* (New York: Columbia University Press, 1990).

69. Indeed, how much more so, given the phenomenal wealth of American Jews which, measured by income, education and professional standing, puts the group at the very top of ethnic and religious groups in America (see Shapiro, *A Time for Healing*, pp. 94–124).

'Send a Salami to Your Boy in the Army':

Sites of Jewish Memory and Identity at Lower East Side Restaurants

Eve Jochnowitz

The Stories

Houston Street! Broadway of the East Side. In the Houston street wine cellars and hangouts writers, actors, poets, painters, and community leaders dreamed and dallied. On this very street that old Jewish delicacy, the knish, became an industry. On this street the first modern Yiddish theater was built. On this street in Little Hungary the late president Teddy Roosevelt ate goulash. Houston Street! . . .

We walk over the ruins, and every corner reminds us of other pictures and scenes. When the old houses were still standing we walked past without even giving them a thought, but now that the houses have been torn down it seems to us that with them a part of ourselves has been torn down as well. . . . [Here] we used to drink together with the police without bribing them.[1]

Amerike: dos land fun vunder, Jacob Kirschenbaum's colorful portrait of America's peoples and places for Jewish visitors, was printed in Warsaw in 1939 in anticipation of the waves of foreign tourists expected to come for the New York World's Fair. Although the book covered American history, major cities, and the Negro in America, it paid special attention to New York and the Lower East Side. While his book was meant to be a current guide to America for visitors from Poland, Kirschenbaum could not resist mixing descriptions of the Lower East Side as it was then with memories of the Lower East side as it *had* been, particularly when he came to the subject of eating. Houston Street, the north side of which had been recently demolished to make the street into a wide traffic artery, was the subject of special attention in a chapter called "By the Ruins of Houston Street."

> In the knish factory, that is, at Yonah Schimmel's on Houston Street, the ushers and poster-hangers from the Yiddish theaters used to gather. The theater people were the first to discover knishes, and there, in that small cafe, the ushers and poster-hangers used to discuss theater politics with the hangers-on from various theaters. The vaudeville actors also used to come to Yonah Schimmel's, because here you could eat knishes and drink sour milk for ten cents, and then, ten cents was a lot, not like now.

> Now the street is just a small link in the huge chain of streets; it has lost its glory and interest.[2]

Another Houston Street eatery, Katz's delicatessen, provides an intriguing case study for a look into the Jewish food-related memories of New York's Lower East Side. Its longevity and its changing role in the neighborhood have given it a sense of historical continuity. Iceland and Katz, as it was originally named, opened in 1914 on the east side of Ludlow Street, taking over a delicatessen restaurant that had been operating since 1888. (The site of the original Iceland and Katz restaurant is now a parking lot.) Chaim Iceland, brother of the Yiddish poet Reuben Iceland, sold his part of the business to concentrate on real estate. Katz's moved across to the west side of Ludlow Street in 1923 and then expanded north to Houston after World War II. Since the late 1970s, the menu has expanded to include some salads and coffee, in addition to the standard delicatessen fare of cured meats. However, the basic deli menu of corned beef, pastrami, tongue, salami, knobelwurst, and hot dogs has stayed the same since 1914.

Fig. 9.1 View of Katz's delicatessen and neighboring establishments on the south side of Houston Street. Photograph by Eve Jochnowitz.

As the Lower East Side has changed, Katz's has changed not in menu but in function—from a neighborhood restaurant to a destination restaurant and, furthermore, into a tourist attraction. Its setting has been used in countless movies (most notably the 1990 film *When Harry Met Sally*). It is a mandatory campaign stop for all New York politicians, and a place that attracts and nourishes memory—what Pierre Nora has called a site of memory.[3]

The Site

The short block between Orchard and Ludlow Streets on the south side of Houston reproduces New York's food world in miniature. Anchored by Katz's on Ludlow and Houston, the block, as of May 1998, is home as well to Hot Bagels and Appetizing, Chen's Chinese Restaurant, Tiaz Grocery, Rosario's Pizzeria, Punjab Palace, and Bereket Turkish Fast Food. Russ and Daughters appetizing store is just west of Orchard. The juxtaposition of the culinary creativity of New York's successive waves of immigration is itself thrumming with ethnographic relevance for students of the re-articulation of transplanted cuisines. Each ethnic restaurant negotiates its own path between gastric acculturation and what the historian David Lowenthal terms "creeping heritage."[4]

Before you enter Katz's, you might linger at the window, where reproductions of letters from Presidents Reagan, Carter, and Clinton and

Fig. 9.2 The entrance to Katz's on Ludlow Street. Photograph by Eve Jochnowitz.

215

from James Brady hang. Old bills from Katz's, labeled "Those were the days," show the lower prices of the past; signed photographs from Neil Armstrong, Don King, and cast members of *Fiddler on the Roof* are piled over and around one another, so that only portions of the mementos on the bottom layer are visible. The window display includes newspapers, magazines, and books that attest to Katz's importance and cultural significance; these include the volume *The Jews in America* and a magazine article in Japanese with photographs of the restaurant. News articles from American and British newspapers about Vice President Al Gore's "Deli Summit" with Russian prime minister Viktor Chernomyrdin announce another of Katz's functions—that of an international governing body. Through the windows, a visitor can see the stretch of the restaurant's spacious interior and the deli counter, which runs the entire length of the restaurant. Knishes and frankfurters, the items cooked on the grill, are closest to the window.

A man seated immediately to the right of the entrance hands every customer a small ticket. The Garden Cafeteria and other bygone cafeterias of the Lower East Side used this form of billing. Countermen with variously shaped punches punch in the codes for selected foods. Katz's offers both cafeteria-style service (at the longest deli counter in town) and waiter service. Three rows of tables run the long way down the cavernous interior. The row farthest from the counter is for table service. Waiters wearing black bowties and vests serve customers who sit along the left-hand wall.

Guidebooks recommend Katz's as a place in which to "soak up atmosphere,"[5] and, in keeping with Lowenthal's dictum that old things should look old,[6] Katz's decor has not changed since the restaurant has been at its current location (although many customers note that it is cleaner than it used to be). More tables are around the corner, where a second dining area occupies the shorter leg of an ell. A large sign that reads, "You have already passed it," directs clients back to the easy-to-miss restrooms. The walls here, and in the rest of the store, are lined with photographs of notables who have visited Katz's. Other signs, on posters, on paper placemats, and in neon, spell out Katz's motto since World War II, "Send a Salami to Your Boy in the Army."

The window and all of the right-hand wall as one enters are lined with hanging salamis and wursts. The characteristic smells of pickles, horseradish, and sizzling fat fill the air. The lively and busy sounds of cooking and conversation are ringing, but not harshly loud or raucous. "I *told* you you should have ordered the knobelwurst," one waiter scolds a dissatisfied customer, more roughly than he should, but not without kindness.

The daytime customers are almost entirely locals, mostly people dining alone. On evenings and weekends, a much better-dressed crowd of tourists and visitors takes over. Katz's is actually two places occupying one space: a neighborhood restaurant during the day and a destination restaurant by night. On weekends, especially during election seasons, office-seekers come to Katz's for what has become almost a required campaign appearance. When Al Gore and Viktor Chernomyrdin held their Deli Summit and photo-op at Katz's, owner Alan Dell reports, the secret service told him he could either close the restaurant or have all guests frisked before entering. Dell decided to keep Katz's open, reasoning that diners who did not want to submit to the pat-search could come back another time. Not only did all the customers agree to be searched, but no one even asked what was going on or seemed to think the requirement was at all strange. Was this perhaps the new procedure? No indignity will keep a *fresser* from his frank.

The Slogan

The command "Send a Salami to Your Boy in the Army" is plastered all over Katz's delicatessen and quoted in every article that mentions Katz's even tangentially. Along with Hebrew National's assertion that "We answer to an even higher authority," and Levy's assurance that "You don't have to be Jewish" to love their rye bread, Katz's admonition to remember and nourish a male relative serving his country with Jewish (if not kosher) food crosses from commerce to culture. All three slogans combine a basically positive approach to American Jewish identity with the teasing acknowledgment that there is something about the juxtaposition of American symbols with Jewishness that is essentially comical. All three slogans promote a Jewish food as the most accessible and comprehensible element of Jewishness. The nine words of Katz's slogan resonate so deeply because they contain within them all the signifiers relevant to the construction of American Jewish identity in the twentieth century.

Place

First of all, there is geography, signified here by dialect. If you're from the Lower East Side, Katz's famous motto rhymes. You hear these words, and you know you are in New York. New York in general, and the Lower East Side in particular, is a surrogate Holy Land for Jews dispersed to the far corners of the country. It is a new Old World, separated from Jews not in space but in time.[7] New York has become a new holy land even in the Holy Land itself. "New York Delis," as part of a phenomenon I call "creative anatopism," are familiar sights not only on the West Coast of the United States and in the Far East, but in Jerusalem and Tel Aviv as well. Jerusalem's New York Deli, where the menu promises H&H bagels, is just a short stroll from the Western Wall.[8]

Indeed, the farther from New York you travel, the more likely you are to encounter references to New York and specifically Jewish iconography in Jewish eating places. The West Coast chain Noah's Bagels tiles its shops to look like New York City subway stations, and an electric sign urges customers, using the Yiddish word for "homelike," to "have a heimish day." On the Lower East Side itself, however, restaurants are more likely to signify their Jewishness by maintaining their neutral decor.[9] When most of the restaurants in the neighborhood were Jewish or kosher, being a Jewish restaurant was the unmarked characteristic. When it was commonplace for Jews to eat in Jewish restaurants, there was no call to heap signifier upon signifier to be sure that no tourist will miss the point. On the contrary, the exterior walls of Ratner's Dairy Restaurant, Streit's Matzo, and the Schapiro winery, all Jewish food shrines of the Lower East Side, are decorated with the spray-painted murals of Antonio "Chico" Garcia, the artist best known for his work on memorial walls of the Lower East Side, an art-form unique to New York.[10]

Visiting the Lower East Side itself for sightseeing, shopping, and eating, for those who are able, is a pilgrimage. The Lower East Side was already a tourist destination for Jews from uptown and out of town at the beginning of the twentieth century, as Henrietta Szold noted (and lamented) in a letter to Louis Ginsburg in 1907:

> I became fully convinced of what I had always suspected—that the East Side is not half as inspiring or interesting as its devotees and condescending, slumming patrons would have it. There is squalor, to be sure, and to spare, but it is not picturesque squalor—and the misery of it![11]

Merchants of the Lower East Side struggled with a conflict between wishing to preserve local ways of giving visitors an authentic experience and cleaning up the neighborhood to make it more attractive to potential tourists.[12] Szold's comment that the squalor is not picturesque shows what a complicated task this was likely to be. While tourists at the current turn of the century came downtown in search of the dangerous and exotic, those who came after World War II were seeking safe reminders of their own pasts.[13] Both the decay of old age and the signs of antiquity are part of the patina that give a place the "look of age."[14]

Memory

   I went to Katz's delicatessen store on East Houston Street, and surprisingly, Mr. Katz knew me. I had delivered some packages for him many years ago. I remembered when the place opened. Two newly arrived immigrants established it, and they called it Iceland and Katz. Mr. Katz's nephew is the present owner. I never knew what happened to Mr. Iceland. I had a hot pastrami sandwich, pickle and a beer. . . .

   The next stop was the establishment of the late Yonah Schimmel, who invented the knish (a kind of pastry made of either potatoes or buckwheat groats—kasha—tenderly spiced and lovingly encased in a baked crust). I ate one of each—potato and kasha. Mr. Schimmel's large photograph with his beautiful black beard is still in the window, and I wondered how he would have felt if he had known that someday Yonah Schimmel's would be advertising "cocktail knishes." How do you like that? Little bitty things. . . .

   And finally the day's events were coming to a close with dinner on Second Avenue in the establishment of Moskowitz and Lupowitz. . . . The steaks and roast beef covered wooden planks about twenty-four inches square. And so this was a day on the Lower East Side, and, with a bit of imagination, I could "see" my parents and my friends, and I could smell the smells.[15]

For Two Cents Plain, Harry Golden's sentimental and humorous book of short sketches about Jewish life, makes many connections between Jewish eating and Jewish memory. The book's title refers to seltzer, called "two cents plain" in Jewish restaurant vernacular because a glass of plain seltzer cost two cents; the title also evokes the North American expression of the same vintage, "to put in one's two cents worth," meaning to comment briefly. In Golden's narration of his visit to a small section of the Lower East Side, food amplifies memories and points up which things have changed (little bitty knishes) and which have stayed the same. The ancient Babylonian Talmud specifically links foods to the power of memory:

   Five things restore one's learning. Wheat bread and much more so wheat itself, eating a roasted egg without salt, frequent consumption of olive oil, frequent indulgence in wine and spices and drinking water that remains from kneading. Some say, dipping one's finger in salt and eating it is also included.[16]

This passage recommends foods that might stimulate a student's memory of sacred texts. The memories evoked by the foods of the Lower East Side, by contrast, are of the neighborhood's imagined Jewish past.
   On the eve of World War II, the Lower East Side was home to fifty-

two delicatessens and countless other Jewish restaurants.[17] Those that remain are not necessarily the best or the most famous of the prewar era, but they function not merely as restaurants themselves but as markers for the establishments that are no more. Visitors to Katz's will sometimes remark that they remember when the restaurant was kosher, or that they remember when seltzer used to run in the water fountain. In fact, Katz's was never kosher, and the water fountain never had seltzer, but a fountain at another restaurant, Rappaport's, did. Such restaurants as Katz's, Sammy's Roumanian, Yonah Schimmel's, and Ratner's have absorbed the free-floating memories that were once attached to their neighbors. They stand in for restaurants that no longer exist and perhaps for some that never existed at all. All of these establishments consciously maintain their decor, and all sell some form of memorabilia in addition to food. When Harry Golden and Jacob Kirschenbaum were writing their memoirs about foods of the past on the Lower East Side, the secular shrines they described were simply restaurants that were continuing to provide their usual cuisines, although the "cocktail knishes" at Yonah Schimmel's may have been a small bow to the food fads of the 1950s. In this age of the artifact, it is necessary as well to provide T-shirts or some other lasting memento for the pilgrims to bring home.

The Army

Thirdly, there is the issue of Jewish military service. Strange as it may seem today, Jewish fitness for the military was one of the most hotly debated issues related to the emancipation of the Jews of Europe.[18] The question of military service was the stage on which Jewish fitness for citizenship was debated, just as military service has become an issue in the gay rights debate of our own day. In the United States, however, Jews have served in the armed forces from the beginning, and this service was at times a major component of Jewish Americanization. Service during World War II in particular transformed the generation of American Jewish males who experienced military service, as the historian Deborah Dash Moore has noted:

> As soldiers, Jews became normal Americans and men; like other normal American men, they returned to civilian life ready to struggle for their just desserts, including programs for liberal social change. Their common military experience helped spur Jewish political activism by changing their self perceptions.[19]

In the front windows of Katz's, one of the letters displayed alongside those from United States presidents is a V-mail letter dated 31 October 1966 from a Corporal Donald J. Murphy in Bien Hoa, Vietnam. Corporal Murphy had tasted a delicious Katz's salami received by one of his fellow pilots, and wrote to order one for himself. This faded bit of Vietnam memorabilia carries the message that the Jewish delicatessen could bring together Jews and gentiles in a new spirit of understanding and brotherhood. No annotation accompanies the letter, but passersby can easily enough imagine the Jewish pilot to whom the original salami was sent sharing his treasure with his ethnically diverse buddies.[20]

In the postwar era, when American Jewish organizations concerned themselves with spreading the message of peaceful co-existence, the Republican politician Samuel Persky responded to an homage to the Jewish delicatessen in *Commentary* with this only half-joking appeal:

> Who is to say that those much-feared "racial tensions" cannot be allayed if, instead of distributing educational pamphlets dedicated to the Truth About the Jew, we can so manage it that every rock and rill in this land of liberty be permeated by the gracious aroma of hot corned beef and pastrami?[21]

Religion

While Katz's has always been a Jewish delicatessen, it has never been kosher. For most of its history, Katz's, as well as many such restaurants, used to be called "kosher style," a term which came into fashion after World War II. This meant that while they did not have rabbinic supervision, they did not sell pork products. The term is no longer acceptable to the Rabbinic Council of America, and there is no one term for this kind of non-kosher Jewish restaurant.[22] Katz's agreed to remove a sign in the window with Hebrew letters, even though the letters only said "Katz's Delicatessen," because a rabbi who stopped in felt it might mislead customers into believing the restaurant is kosher.

While unapologetically *treyf* (unkosher), Katz's does make certain gestures toward kosher sensibilities. The deli serves tea in a glass, but a coffee or an egg cream arrives in a paper cup, so that the dairy beverage will not come into contact with meat crockery. Dell, the owner of Katz's, has no interest in making it a kosher restaurant, even if this feature would draw a larger pool of customers, because he believes that the kosher meat is just not as good. *Treyf* is better.

Gender and Sex

The subject of forbidden flesh brings us to gender and sexuality. Jewish sex, sexuality, and particularly forbidden or "unkosher" sexual unions are clearly very closely related in Jewish literature and liturgy to Jewish food.[23] The Lower East Side itself is the backdrop for Isaac

221

Rosenfeld's meditation on these connections. In "Adam and Eve on Delancey Street: Milchig and Fleishig Created He Them," Rosenfeld traces all of Jewish sexual pathology to the laws of kashrut. The article opens with the image of a crowd of Jews standing "in a sexual trance" several rows deep outside a kosher delicatessen on the East Side to watch, entranced, the slicing of beef fry, a kosher substitute for bacon:

> When the Lord forbade Adam and Eve to eat of the tree, He started some-thing which has persisted throughout our history: the attachment of all sorts of forbidden meanings to food in a system of taboos which, though meant to regulate diet, have also had as their function—perhaps the primary one—the regulation of sexual conduct.[24]

Rosenfeld goes on to argue that all anti-Semitism is rooted in gentile myths, all provoked by Jewish food, about Jewish superior sexuality.[25]

Other Lower East Side institutions have exploited the more posi-tive side of the suggestiveness of delicatessen in general and salami in particular. The Second Avenue Deli reverses the sexes of Katz's slogan in an ad that appeared shortly before Valentine's Day 1997, suggesting that a salami would be an ideal gift for St. Valentine's Day. "Say I ♥ you with 2nd Ave. Deli Salami: 2 pounds of kosher Lower East Side tradi-tion!" urged the ad copy.

Most notably, in Rob Reiner's film *When Harry Met Sally*, Billy Crystal's character, Harry (who is ambiguously Jewish), takes Sally (played by Meg Ryan), who is unambiguously not Jewish, to Katz's deli-catessen. Overwhelmed as she is by the environment vibrating with Jewish meaning, Sally's reaction is, as Rosenfeld might have predicted, to have an orgasm.[26] "I'll have what she's having," says Estelle Reiner, playing the part of another deli customer, but Estelle Reiner *cannot* have what she is having, not with a Jewish man, anyway. Not accord-ing to Rosenfeld.

The City of Refuge

The city offered up for consumption and communion in the Jewish eateries of the Lower East Side is a place where the tastes and smells of the present evoke the flavors and fragrances of a lost world. It is a city where Jews, traditionally so insecure in a hostile world, can take com-fort both in the physical gratification of eating and the reassurance of geographical rootedness. It is a place that reminds the exiles of their rights and privileges as Americans, where, paradoxically, rejection of religious strictures as well as their embrace can be an expression of Jew-ish identity. Even the minor discomforts of such restaurants contribute to the look and feel of age that make the sites historically intriguing.

Jacob Kirschenbaum captured the way in which a restaurant can conjure all of a city, a people, or an era when he wrote of yet another Lower East Side establishment, the Cafe Royale:

> Being in New York and not seeing the Cafe Royale is like being in Washington and not seeing the White House, or, as they used to say, like being in Vienna and not seeing the Kaiser. . . . Cafe Royale is the true "city of refuge" for writers, artists, and activists.[27]

The term "city of refuge" refers to passages about safe havens in the books of Numbers (35:9–15) and Deuteronomy (19:1–13). The biblical reference in this very secular guidebook highlights the textured braiding of food, language and faith in the discourse of Jewish memory.

NOTES

Grateful thanks to Esther Malke Leysorek Goodman, Alan Dell, and Rebecca Iceland Halperin for their valuable help.

THIS ESSAY IS DEDICATED TO ABE LEBEWOHL.

I did not restrain my heart from any joy, for
my heart rejoiced in all my labor.

—ECCLESIASTES 2

1. Jacob Kirschenbaum, *Amerike, dos land fun vunder* [America: The Land of Wonder] (Warsaw: Kh. Brzoza, 1939), pp. 117–118. My translation from the Yiddish. I am grateful to Jeffrey Shandler for bringing this book to my attention.

2. Ibid., pp. 122, 124.

3. Pierre Nora, "Between Memory and History: *Les Lieux de Memoire*," *Representations* 26 (Spring 1989): 7–19.

4. David Lowenthal, *The Past Is a Foreign Country* (Cambridge: Cambridge University Press, 1985), p. xv. Lowenthal uses the term "creeping heritage" to describe the changing roles of places that can no longer fill their original functions. See also Barbara Kirshenblatt-Gimblett, *Destination Culture: Tourism, Museums and Heritage* (Berkeley, Los Angeles, and London: University of California Press, 1998), on "A Second Life as Heritage," pp. 131–202, and Barbara Kirshenblatt-Gimblett, "Theorizing Heritage," *Ethnomusicology* 39, no. 3 (1995): 367–380.

5. Ed Levine, *New York Eats* (New York: St. Martin's Press, 1992), p. 168.

6. Lowenthal, *The Past Is a Foreign Country*, p. 149.

7. Jack Kugelmass and Jeffrey Shandler, *Going Home: How American Jews Invent the Old World* (New York: YIVO Institute, 1989), p. 22.

8. "H&H bagels" is a reference to a popular bagel shop on New York's Upper West Side. Anatopistic Jewish restaurants are doing business in all corners of the post–New York diaspora. A favorite example of mine is Hong Kong's "Cafe Beverley Hills: A New York Style Delicatessen."

9. See, e.g., Jack Kugelmass, "Green Bagels: An Essay on Food, Nostalgia, and the Carnivalesque," *YIVO Annual* 19 (1990): 78–79.

'Send a Salami to Your Boy in the Army'

10. See Martha Cooper and Joseph Sciorra, *RIP: Memorial Wall Art* (New York: Henry Holt, 1994).

11. Baila Round Shargel, *Lost Love: The Untold Story of Henrietta Szold* (Philadelphia: Jewish Publication Society, 1997), p. 69.

12. Jenna Weissman Joselit, "Telling Tales; or, How a Slum Became a Shrine," *Jewish Social Studies*, n.s. 2, no. 2 (1996): 57.

13. Suzanne Wasserman, "The Good Old Days of Poverty: the Battle over the Fate of New York City's Lower East Side" (Ph.D. dissertation, New York University, 1990), p. 323. "By the time of World War II, this distortion of the present, built on a reinvention of the past rendered the Lower East Side a less threatening place to the World. . . . While reformers, city officials, and developers failed to rid the community of its indigenous nature, ex-Lower East Siders, local merchants and tourists were able to rewrite the past and distort the present. Although one might not want to live there it was now a nice place to visit" (Wasserman, p. 386). Before the 1930s, improving the East Side meant de-Judaizing the East Side. After the end of World War II, gentrification meant re-Judaization.

14. Lowenthal, *The Past Is a Foreign Country*, p. 125.

15. Harry Golden, *For Two Cents Plain* (New York: Permabooks, 1959), pp. 58–64. I am grateful to Stan Iceland for bringing this book to my attention.

16. Babylonian Talmud, B. Hora'ot, 13b, cited and translated in Ivan Marcus, *Rituals of Childhood: Jewish Acculturation in Medieval Europe* (New Haven and London: Yale University Press, 1996), p. 57.

17. Jenna Weissman Joselit, "Telling Tales," p. 57.

18. Sander Gilman, *The Jew's Body* (New York and London: Routledge, 1991), p. 39.

19. Deborah Dash Moore, "Jewish GIs and the Creation of the Judeo-Christian Tradition," *Religion and American Culture* 8, no. 1 (Winter 1998): 47.

20. War propaganda played up the newly equal position of Jews in the service in messages aimed especially at the Jewish community. A war bond campaign advertisement read, "Out where the bullets are flying, our boys—our American boys—do not care if a wounded buddy is Protestant, Catholic or Jew, nor whether he is Negro or White." Quoted in Moore, "Jewish GIs and the Creation of the Judeo-Christian Tradition," p. 37.

21. Samuel Persky, letter to the editor, *Commentary* 2, no. 1 (July 1946): 67.

22. Ruth Glazer, "The Jewish Delicatessen: Evolution of an Institution," *Commentary* 1, no. 5 (March 1946): 60.

23. Daniel Boyarin, *Carnal Israel: Reading Sex in Talmudic Culture* (Berkeley: University of California Press, 1993), pp. 72–74; see also chapters 3 and 4 for a discussion of food and sex in the domestic sphere. Also see Chava Weissler, *Voices of the Matriarchs: Listening to the Prayers of Early Modern Jewish Women* (Boston: Beacon Press, 1998), on "Mitzvot Built into the Body," pp. 73–75.

24. Isaac Rosenfeld, *An Age of Enormity* (Cleveland and New York: World Publishing Company, 1962), p. 183. Rosenfeld's article "Adam and Eve on Delancey Street: Milchig and Fleishig Created He Them" first appeared in *Commentary* 8, no. 4 (October 1949): 385–387.

25. Rosenfeld, *An Age of Enormity*, p. 186. See Steven J. Zipperstein, "Commen-

tary and American Jewish Culture in the 1940s and 1950s," *Jewish Social Studies,* n.s. 3, no. 2 (Winter 1997): 18–27, for the fascinating story of this article and its consequences.

26. Within the context of the film, the explanation for Sally's outburst is that she is faking an orgasm for reasons necessary to the plot. This, however, is merely a pretext. Sally's response is built into the site.

27. Kirschenbaum, *Amerike, dos land fun vunder,* pp. 84–86.

Tripping down Memory Lane:

Walking Tours on the Jewish

Seth Kamil

Lower East Side

The Lower East Side is one of New York's most prized ethnic neighborhoods. This relatively small area attracts a vast array of visitors from
throughout the world and is regarded as a "must see" by the majority of
guidebooks. The Lower East Side also hosts the highest concentration
of walking tours of any ethnic neighborhood in New York City and,
quite possibly, the nation. While the neighborhood has been the first
area of settlement for numerous groups—German, Irish, Latino, to
name a few—the Lower East Side is perhaps most often understood as
synonymous with immigrant Jews. Yet whatever the background of the
tourists visiting the neighborhood, there is a sense that visiting the
Lower East Side is crucial to understanding New York City's past and
present. Tourists stroll through the district, some as individuals or small
groups with guidebooks and others on organized walking tours. These
tourists pass unharassed, and are even ignored by residents. This, too, is
the Lower East Side—a neighborhood that is both steeped in history
and equally modern, a part of New York that tolerates tourism.

Indeed, tourism has been a potent force within the Lower East Side for decades. It has led to the creation of numerous tourist initiatives, public events, and museums. The majority of Lower East Side tourists are American Jews. For many of them, a visit to the neighborhood is akin to going "home"—a home unseen for many years and clouded with nostalgia. In many ways, tourism itself has helped to maintain the vitality of the Jewish neighborhood, despite dramatic changes over the past years.

For more than a century, the Lower East Side has been the subject of both actual and vicarious tourism, the latter experienced through the reading of accounts of other visitors or through viewing images of the neighborhood. Charles Dickens commented on the Lower East Side as early as 1843, in his *American Notes*.[1] In the 1850s, American writers used ethnicity on the East Side as the foundation for literary exposés.[2] Many of these early works took the form of travelogues, told in the first person. The narrator, quite often the victim of a crime or mishap, would retell extraordinary sights and events encountered on the streets of the Lower East Side. Many of these tales involved conversations with petty criminals in illegal "dive" bars or colorful observations of the homeless or prostitutes on the city streets. Middle-class Americans could read both fictional and factual accounts of the urban immigrant masses. Beginning in the 1890s, Americans were exposed to the journalism of Hutchins Hapgood and Jacob Riis, as well as the stories of Abraham Cahan. Through the photographs of Riis and Lewis Hine, Americans could also picture the lives of East Siders. Much of this writing and photography was developed in the name of critical social reform and neighborhood improvement, a fact often overlooked by late-twentieth-century readers.

Guided tours of the Lower East Side were also available at the beginning of the twentieth century. The most famous guide was George Washington Charles "Chuck" Connors, who conducted tours of the Bowery district from approximately 1910 through 1914. Connors's tours focused on the "exotic" East Side: the Bowery burlesque theaters, Chinatown, and various other ethnic communities.[3] While it is not known if he actually led tours within the Jewish part of the district, he was clearly aware of what Riis had termed "Jewtown."

Today, most visitors come to the Lower East Side with some expectation of what they are about to experience. Many are disappointed with the contemporary neighborhood. Because so much literary, cinematic, and anecdotal imagery of the Lower East Side focuses on the brief period between 1880 and 1924, many people have forgotten about the past seventy years. The Lower East Side today is not a "teeming

227

ghetto." Children are not playing stickball in the street, nor are vendors peddling wares—at least not "traditional" East Side goods. The herring, underwear, and used pots of yore have been replaced by faux Rolex watches and "I ♥ NY" t-shirts. The pushcarts have been replaced by automobiles.

The journey "home" to the Lower East Side is supported and enhanced by the popular media. When tours pass Guss's Lower East Side Pickles on Essex Street,[4] participants often express surprise that it actually exists and wasn't part of a Hollywood set built in1988 for the film *Crossing Delancey*. They are quite shocked to learn that in 1975 the Lower East Side had undergone so much commercial development that the film *Hester Street* was actually shot in Greenwich Village, on Morton Street.

Further complicating popular imagery are familial stories. For many former residents, the Lower East Side ceased to evolve after their day of departure, remaining frozen in time within their memories. It is almost as if the neighborhood was meant to remain in stasis as each family departed.

∽

I began guiding others through the Lower East Side in 1990, after having lived in New York for little more than a year. My company, Big Onion Walking Tours, Inc., was established in the fall of 1991.[5] The company's roots are in the Lower East Side. One of the very first tours we offered was a walk through the Jewish Lower East Side on Christmas Day, 1991. This has grown into an annual tradition that regularly attracts several hundred people. Since then we have grown to offer more than twenty-five different tours, all focusing on New York's historic districts and ethnic neighborhoods. All of our guides have advanced degrees in American history or a related field, and most are active graduate students. We employ twenty different historian-guides who come from three local universities. We offer two different kinds of tours of the Jewish Lower East Side: First, we offer public "show-up" tours on a regular basis. Second, groups from around the world arrange private tours with us.

Our goal is to bring our academic studies onto city streets, where we delve into the many layers of the city's history and people—hence, our name: Big Onion Walking Tours. Although there is only scant evidence that *Big Onion* was a term for the Bowery District in the 1880s, we use the name as a metaphor for New York. Once one brushes off the layer of dirt, the history of the city peels away like the layers of an onion.

Fig. 10.1 Seth Kamil, director of Big Onion Walking
Tours, leading the annual Christmas Day Jewish East
Side Walking Tour, 1997. This tour is one of the most
popular offered by Big Onion and attracts several
hundred people each Christmas Day. Kamil is standing
in front of the Jewish War Veterans Memorial in
Straus Square. Photograph by Traci Kamil.

While some of my familial roots are in the Lower East Side, I am
two generations removed from the neighborhood. My parents, who
grew up in the outer boroughs of New York City, met in suburban Long
Island and elected to raise a family in Massachusetts. Only one of my
grandparents was an immigrant. This complicates my role as a tour
guide. Some visitors feel that the only way to "know" the area is to
have a resident (preferably one much older than I) as a guide. They
often assume that one must have personal experience living in the
neighborhood in order to understand it. However, my knowledge of
the neighborhood comes from reading, research, and personal observations. I have also absorbed the history and spirit of the Lower East Side

by spending a considerable amount of time in the area with its residents and business people. I have thus gained my knowledge and understanding as an "outsider." Despite the inherent skepticism of some tourists, being an outsider is, in fact, beneficial for a tour guide. While I am passionate about the history of the neighborhood, being somewhat removed from the experience limits my emotional attachment to an ever-changing environment. Although I am familiar with the area and many of its people, I am not a resident, nor do I make my livelihood exclusively in the neighborhood. I do not feel personally threatened by a new Asian grocery or Latino restaurant replacing a Jewish bookdealer.

∞

Nineteenth-century New York was much more of a walking city than it is today. Although mass transit was readily available in the post–Civil War era, the nature of urban travel was radically different from our current notions. The Lower East Side was, in many regards, a complete world unto itself. Residents would walk from home to school or work; they would walk to places within the neighborhood for shopping and recreation. Leaving the immediate district was more often a matter of choice than of necessity. A walking tour today explores the neighborhood without the protective walls of a bus or the comfort of watching a videotape at home.

Walking through the neighborhood allows tourists to experience the Jewish East Side on a number of levels. First, they are able to feel the closeness and complexity of the environment. Many are surprised at the moderate size and compactness of the Lower East Side. At the same time, they are awed by the great diversity of the Jewish immigrant experience that has taken place within this small area. Second, walking tours facilitate a non-linear understanding of history, enabling visitors to appreciate the diversity of the Jewish immigrant experience and its relationship to other immigrant cultures. Third, walking tours allow for the development of a broader understanding of the relationship between immigrant Jews and the larger urban environment.

Indeed, the Lower East Side of today remains a vibrant multi-ethnic district. There is still a strong Jewish residential presence in what is now a predominantly Asian and Latino neighborhood. However, there is no discernible Jewish commercial district. Along Essex Street, the heart of the East Side, kosher eateries, stores selling Jewish religious books and articles, Guss's Pickles, and a Jewish-owned accordion shop share space with a Caribbean botanica, a Chinese-language real estate office, and other ethnic businesses.

Both Jewish and American historians have written frequently about the *Jewish* East Side, in contrast to the *Lower* East Side. This is an important distinction. Though the neighborhood was often called "the ghetto," New York never established an actual ghetto that forced Jews to reside separately from others in a specific area. Yet most texts on the Lower East Side pay scant attention to the substantial number of non-Jews who lived in the neighborhood as well. At all times, the Lower East Side was home to many different immigrant peoples and ethnic institutions. The Jewish population of the area peaked in the early twentieth century. In 1892, approximately 75 percent of all Jews in Manhattan resided on the Lower East Side. By 1920, this number had declined to less than 25 percent.[6]

Moreover, the neighborhood's Jews were anything but homogeneous. As a tour guide, I will often emphasize that there was not one Jewish community on the Lower East Side; rather, there was (and still is) a series of overlapping communities within this one neighborhood. A walking tour enables visitors to see the relationship and, at times, mutual dependence of these divergent peoples. For example, Morris Hillquit had a law office on East Broadway in 1917, when he ran as the Socialist Party candidate for mayor of New York. Directly behind this office building stands St. Theresa's Roman Catho-

Fig. 10.2 Essex Street. The contemporary heart of the Lower East Side's Jewish shopping district. Photograph by Seth Kamil.

lic Church. How did the old Irish parishioners respond to the street speeches of their Jewish Socialist neighbor? The walking tour can use the urban environment to raise issues such as this.

Thus, one of the most important aims of a walking tour of the Lower East Side is to illustrate the complexities of the neighborhood for visitors. The tour guide's role is not only to provide facts, but also to facilitate interpretation and awareness. Tourists' questions of "who," "what," and "where" can be handled with straightforward answers, which are enhanced by the immediacy of the environment. Thus, hearing that the neighborhood boasted over seven hundred residents per acre in 1900 takes on added significance when a visitor stands on Hester Street and looks at its one-hundred-year-old tenements. In addition, I encourage tour guides to try to provide more open-ended answers to the questions "why" and to present facts that enable visitors to draw their own conclusions. At times, for example, guides might present multiple approaches to a single site, as in the case of the Educational Alliance on East Broadway. The Alliance can be discussed both as an example of a German Jewish philanthropic venture, as it was started in the 1890s to aid the new East European Jewish arrivals, or as an Americanizing force, striving to make the new immigrant Jews more acceptable to the American mainstream.

Tour guides can also place the crowded conditions and the tenements within a context of the history of housing in New York. Guides can explain to visitors that the current occupancy of some tenements remains at two to three people per room, six to nine people per 300-square-foot apartment. It is important to emphasize that while tenements were regarded as a necessary evil in the 1870s, they are still home to most Manhattanites who currently rent apartments. Today tenements are often associated with cheap housing, not immigrant overcrowding. In this way, a successful walking tour of the Lower East Side can not only explore the history of the immediate site but also place it in a broader context of urban and ethnic history.

Walking through the neighborhood reveals both the historic and

Fig. 10.3 The former Forward building. Built in 1912 by architect George A. Boehm, it was vacated by the *Jewish Daily Forward* in 1975. Until 1999, it was the site of the New York Ling Lang Church. In 1999, conversion of the building into luxury condominiums began. Photograph by Seth Kamil.

contemporary complexity of Lower East Side life. Consider, for example, the block surrounding the former site of Morris Hillquit's office on East Broadway. The site itself has been an empty lot for over a decade and is now slated for an eight- to twelve-story luxury apartment house. Not only was it adjacent to St. Theresa's Church (its parishioners, once Irish, are now Chinese and Vietnamese Catholics); it is also across the street from the former Garden Cafeteria (now the Wing Shoon restaurant), and down the block is the former Jewish Daily Forward building (now being converted from a Chinese church into luxury condominiums). Walk half a block in the other direction and one finds the yeshiva Mesifta Tifereth Jerusalem.

The Forward building epitomizes the dynamics of the neighborhood. This impressive building was erected in 1912 for the flourishing Yiddish newspaper. Yiddish letters spelling the word *Forverts* stand twelve stories above the street, directly below a large public clock. The

Tripping down Memory Lane

building became a New York City landmark in 1976, which preserved the physical structure but not its use. That year it was sold to become the New York Ling Lang Church. Along the entire side-length of the building the church painted a sign in Mandarin that says, "Jesus Christ is the light, the hope, and the way." In 1998, the building was sold to a developer, who is converting it into the Lower East Side's first luxury apartment house, complete with doorman and concierge service.

A common assumption made by tourists is that the immigrant Jews of the Lower East Side had a uniform experience, both in the Old Country and as new Americans. Walking tours allow for micro-history, an examination of specific sites and individual stories that complement the written macro-history, which often paints broad images and does not lend itself to relating the experiences of individuals. (Of course, micro-history can lead to contention with tour participants. Quite often, when relating my own family's story—Lower East Side, the Bronx, Long Island—someone will quip, "What's wrong with Brooklyn? Didn't Jews go to Brooklyn?") Relating examples of these micro-histories during a walking tour of the Lower East Side can reveal the diversity of the neighborhood's former Jewish residents, a diversity that was intensified by the density of the neighborhood. Thus, the journalist Lincoln Steffens once wrote: "[A]s the old men in black hats and long beards walk into the synagogue to pray on a Sabbath morning, they must walk around their own sons, sitting on the synagogue steps in shirt-sleeves and smoking cigarettes." The diversity of religious practice, political beliefs, occupations, and ties to local places of origin in Europe made the East Side a complex Jewish neighborhood in ways that are often now foreign to much of Jewish America. Thus, tour participants need to be reminded that the socialism of the *Forward* was an anti-Bolshevik socialism, or that the Triangle Shirtwaist Factory Fire of 1911 occurred on a Saturday, and that the Jewish women who perished in the blaze were hard-working immigrants who were willing to labor on the Sabbath.

⟨⟩

There is no single reason why Jews flock to the Lower East Side. Most of those who visit the neighborhood fall into three categories: first, those who come to relive experiences of their youth; second, those who bring a younger generation (on either a class or a family trip); and third, those who seek a piece of a learned past. This last group includes two basic subgroups: those who simply ask, "Where did I come from?" and those with a more academic motive. Quite often, each tour will bring together different people, each with a different reason for participating. And, of course, there are always some who are simply looking for an interesting walking tour.

The audience participating in a walking tour sets the entire tone for the experience. Engaged and lively participants make it possible to turn a walking tour into a dialogue about the neighborhood and the immigrant experience. Occasionally, though, the group dynamic is lethargic and passive, which can lead to a more routine touring experience.

The public "show-up" tours attract a wide array of visitors, sixty percent of whom are current residents of the greater New York metropolitan area. On average, thirty percent of these are current New York City residents. The majority of participants are between forty and sixty years old. However, in recent years we are seeing an increased number of twenty- to thirty-year-olds. Most, but not all, are of Jewish background. The number of men and women are about the same. Most of the clients on public tours are well educated, eager to learn about what they are seeing, and do not hesitate to ask questions or express opinions. For the guide as well as the participants, these tours can be invigorating, challenging, engaging, and at times contentious.

The private group tours attract a completely different kind of client. Most of these groups come from within New York City, and a significant portion of the remaining participants are from the New York metropolitan area. They are generally either high school students or adult groups traveling with a Jewish organization, such as a local synagogue or a chapter of Hadassah or B'nai B'rith. They share some common experiences, given that they have all come together from the same place. Many of these groups come for a three- to seven-day trip to experience Jewish New York, and their activities might include stops at Jewish museums, theatrical performances, or kosher restaurants, as well as visits to Ellis Island, the Lower East Side, and Hasidic neighborhoods in Brooklyn. Not all groups requesting Jewish East Side tours are Jews, however. An increasing number of tourists from Europe are coming to experience the East Side. Most of these are college students studying Jewish history. These tours focus more generally on the Americanization and acculturation process, as these tourists are less familiar with the immigrant experience.

One of the most interesting reasons people give for taking tours of the Lower East Side is their claim of searching for a history that was "previously denied" to them. Most of these people are looking for information about Jewish criminal activity or other forms of social deviance, such as Jewish gangsters, prostitution, or gang activity. Many are quite frank about wanting to know about aspects of Jewish history that they were not taught in school or that were not discussed around the dinner table. Quite often, those inquiring about Jewish crime express anger and disappointment at teachers and older family members for "denying" a part of their history. This can create an interesting dynamic among tourists, especially on a public walking tour. Not long ago, for example, a young man wanted to know everything possible about Jewish involvement in prostitution. After I responded to his question, we were both verbally attacked by another member of the tour, an older man, who stated that "Jews didn't do that." He continued with thinly veiled comments about antisemitism and what was "bad for the Jews." I responded with an academically sound and non-emotional explanation, stressing that prostitution should be seen as a form of economic activity rather than a moral issue, and illustrated the point by referring to Emma Goldman's experiences. My answer, of course, satisfied no one.[7]

In recent years, an increasing number of visitors on both public and private tours of the Jewish Lower East Side have demanded that their guide be Jewish. Such a demand is not limited to this particular tour; visitors request an African American guide for a tour of Harlem and a homosexual guide for a gay and lesbian tour of Greenwich Village. Like other communities and institutions throughout America, Jews are claiming ownership of "their" history. For example, in 1999, a Florida confirmation class requested a neighborhood tour and went so far as to inquire into the Jewish "sect" of our guide. They refused to entertain the notion that a non-Jew could lead the tour. (They canceled the booking before I could ask which "sect" they were looking for.) Conversely, some groups are pleased to know that a non-Jew is well versed in the history of the Jewish Lower East Side. Big Onion's primary concern is that a guide know the history of the neighborhood and the community under discussion.

Tour guides will also contend with the assumption of many visitors that the Lower East Side was once a beautiful, clean, and pleasant Jewish community, and that some Jews have made a conscious effort to keep the neighborhood that way. In 1997, a woman, who was part of a group from a Jewish community center in suburban New York and who had never lived on the East Side, became distressed half-way through a two-hour walking tour. She finally exclaimed: "When we lived here the streets were wonderful, you never had to lock your door, you knew all of your neighbors—it was like family. Everyone spoke Yiddish. It was wonderful. Why can't these immigrants learn English already? I can't believe how they ruined our East Side!" Quite often comments such as these are followed up with a question: "How can we save the neighborhood?"

How ought a guide respond to such comments as these? One might simply suggest that if the visitor were to move the family to the Lower East Side, there would then be more Jewish residents in the area. While such a glib answer might well alienate the visitor, it would also high-light the assumption that the tourist wants the neighborhood's "past" to be maintained, but not by having to make a personal commitment to living in a tenement there.

Another approach would be to explain that the Lower East Side is a living entity that is constantly changing. While most of the Jewish-ness of the area is in the past, viewing the contemporary ethnic resi-dents can provide a better understanding of the Jewish immigrant past. Comparing the migration, acculturation, and Americanization of the contemporary Latino and Asian residents to the Jewish immigrant ex-perience demonstrates both strong similarities among these groups as well as the uniqueness of each. (Equally compelling is a comparative discussion of American nativism. Using sites on the tour to recall the anti-Catholic violence of the 1840s and the anti-Chinese laws of the 1880s dispels notions of the Jews as uniquely persecuted within Ameri-can history.)

෨

The Jewish East Side of today is dependent upon tourist dollars. Sunday is the most profitable day of the week for local shopkeepers; the district's prime tourist day, it is also when suburban Jews drive into the neighborhood from surrounding communities. But it is the daily shop-pers, the Latino and Asian residents, who now sustain the economy of the neighborhood. Many successful Jewish shops now hire Spanish- or Cantonese-speaking assistants. Orchard Street, once the heart of the Jewish commercial district, now conducts a significant amount of local business on Saturday.

The economic fabric of the neighborhood is also changing with increased gentrification, which is taking two forms. First, new Asian immigrants are moving into the Lower East Side. The area west of Allen Street is now known as "the New Chinatown." Second, there is new "uptown" money streaming in, opening restaurants, boutiques, and bars on Ludlow Street and the surrounding blocks. The most obvious sign of this trend for visitors is Lansky's Lounge, a martini bar that opened in the back room of Ratner's Dairy Restaurant in 1998. This feature allows Ratner's to serve two communities: tourists by day and the bar scene by night. Ironically, most of the neighborhood's older Jewish residents are on a strict fixed income and cannot afford to eat at Ratner's.

Changes in housing offer some of the best illustrations of how the

Fig. 10.4 While many of the Jewish shops on the
Lower East Side are being replaced by Asian
immigrant businesses, this is an example of the
opposite. The former Rendez Vous Cafe was
replaced by a kosher bagelry in 1996.
Photograph by Seth Kamil.

neighborhood has evolved. Most of the available housing is in tenements, largely erected between 1870 and 1910. These buildings were
meant to be inhabited for thirty or forty years, not over one hundred.
Throughout the late nineteenth century, social reformers and architects proposed alternative forms of housing.[8] Despite these plans, the
tenements have remained. Following the depopulation of the Lower
East Side in the 1930s, and again during the fiscal crisis and near bankruptcy of New York City in the 1970s, numerous tenements were abandoned or burned for insurance-policy income. Currently, the Lower
East Side is experiencing its strongest economy since the 1920s. This

boom is primarily fueled by new immigrants, with similar hopes and ambitions as the Jewish immigrants of the last century. Since 1995, nearly 70 percent of the abandoned tenements below Delancey Street have been renovated into viable housing. Many of the garment sweatshops are now being sold to new investors. In late 1998, a single floor of a nineteenth-century factory cost as much as $2,000,000. Most of this purchasing and renovating is being done by new Asian immigrants.

∞

One of the most difficult issues that the Lower East Side tour guide confronts is the blurring of history and nostalgia. Historian Suzanne Wasserman notes that for some first- and second-generation immigrants, nostalgia served alternatively as "a tool of accommodation and justification as well as one of resistance and opposition."[9] For the immigrant generation, nostalgia was a mechanism for contending with the anxiety of acculturation and urban life, while it enabled their children to alleviate guilt over becoming successful Americans. But how does nostalgia for the Lower East Side figure in the consciousness of today's third-, fourth-, and fifth-generation American Jews? Many no longer have any direct contact with the immigrant generation, and this factor has transformed the tourist audience dramatically. It is increasingly difficult for young American Jews to relate to the Lower East Side immigrant experience. Their older relatives' memories of bygone days date back to the 1930s or later, dwelling on the second area of settlement and early suburbanization. These memories focus heavily on the Holocaust, the Cold War, and postwar assimilation and consumption. The notion of a thriving, contentious, immigrant Jewish environment tests their powers of imagination. Some visitors laugh openly when the guide tells them how Rabbi Moses Weinberger wrote in 1887 that America was *treyf* (unclean or not kosher) and Poland was a good Jewish home,[10] and they scoff at the notion of a Jewish anarchist or that in the 1890s intermarriage meant a wedding between a Jew from Vilna and one from Lvov.

The relevance of the Lower East Side changes with the advance of a new American Jewish generation. Less often a place where one goes to see where one's immigrant grandparents grew up, it has become a mythological place of wonder about Jewish life before the Holocaust. Having moved beyond the realm of nostalgia, the Lower East Side has become for younger generations their Old Country.

The Jewish Lower East Side is following the pattern of many other ethnic neighborhoods of the Ellis Island generation of immigration. The neighborhood is experiencing a slow and steady decline. The days

240

of a mass Jewish population are gone; most of the shops once owned by
Jews are changing hands. How will this transformation affect Jewish
tourism on the Lower East Side? As the Jewish presence in the neighborhood continues to diminish, and as young American Jews lose contact with the immigrant generation, Jewish interest in the Lower East
Side will eventually decline. Perhaps the next generation of tour guides
will be organizing trips to the Long Island suburb of Levittown, so that
American Jews can understand where *their* grandparents came from.

NOTES

1. See Charles Dickens, *American Notes* (New York: Modern Library, 1996).
2. For example, see John D. Vose, Esq., *Seven Nights in Gotham* (New York:
Bunnell and Price, 1852). Vose focuses on the Irish and German populations and on
what later became the Italian Lower East Side.
3. See Chuck Connors, *Bowery Life* (New York: R. K. Fox, 1904).
4. The official name of this business is the Essex Street Pickle Corp. It is located
at 35 Essex St.
5. For more information about Big Onion Walking Tours, see the following Web
site: www.bigonion.com
6. Moses Rischin, *The Promised City: New York's Jews, 1870–1914* (Cambridge,
Mass.: Harvard University Press, 1962), p. 93.
7. Goldman, a Polish Jewish immigrant, attempted prostitution on 14th Street
and later advocated unionization of the trade.
8. For an excellent discussion of this topic, see Richard Plunz, *A History of Housing in New York City* (New York: Columbia University Press, 1990).
9. Suzanne R. Wasserman, "The Good Old Days of Poverty: The Battle over the
Fate of New York City's Lower East Side during the Depression" (Ph.D. dissertation,
New York University, 1990), p. 8.
10. See Jonathan Sarna, *People Walk on Their Heads: Moses Weinberger's "Jews and
Judaism in New York"* (New York: Holmes and Meier, 1981).

The Lower East Side in the

Memory of New York Jewish Intellectuals:

Joseph Dorman

A Filmmaker's Experience

The New York Jewish Intellectuals—famously radical in their youth, notoriously conservative or centrist with age—have been accused of political amnesia.[1] Their later political views, so the charge goes, have obscured and distorted their memories of their early left-wing ideals. While there may be some truth to this statement, autobiographical revision being all too human, it seems equally plausible that memories of their youth have played a critical role in informing their changing political beliefs. Paraphrasing Freud, the political child is father to the political man. It was with this in mind that, in the course of making the film *Arguing the World*,[2] I asked Irving Howe, Nathan Glazer, Daniel Bell, and Irving Kristol to remember their childhoods in New York's Jewish immigrant neighborhoods, among these the Lower East Side.

The documentary traces the threads of these childhood influences as they weave their way through the four protagonists' Marxist student days at New York's City College, their entanglements in the controversies of the McCarthy era, their conflict with the New Left in the 1960s, and their fight over a resurgent conservatism in the 1980s and 1990s. By this time, the four had left their Marxist radicalism far behind, and their political beliefs had scattered across the political spectrum. Howe had become a democratic socialist, Kristol a godfather of the neoconservative movement, and Bell and Glazer voices of the center left and right, respectively.

While *Arguing the World* is an intellectual biography of these four men, it is a document about twentieth-century Jewish-American life as well, most notably in its depiction of Jewish immigrant life. Daniel Bell once wrote that to be a Jew is to be part of a community woven by memory,[3] and in this sense the film is an act of social memory. Remarking on *World of Our Fathers*, his 1976 social history of the East European Jewish experience in New York, Irving Howe distinguished between the image of the Lower East Side that has been nostalgically preserved in Jewish memory and the neighborhood as revealed by historical analysis.[4] Of course, he was also aware that such historical interest could itself be a product of nostalgia. For the Bronx-born Howe, the Lower East Side became an iconic neighborhood on which he could focus his own intellectual interest in, and emotional longing for, the world of his youth. As the son of a Midwestern Jewish family, my own attempt to recapture the neighborhood on film is laced with a desire to understand both the era and ethos in which my parents, children of immigrants themselves, were raised.

Like all films based on human memory, *Arguing the World* is a refraction of history, even if it is one supported by a great deal of research. It is my protagonists' relationship to their Depression-era communities that I ask the audience to observe; four older men's memories of their child's-eye view of this world. Their recollections embrace both the hardships as well as the defiance of youth: "I was called 'the *vilde*,'" Bell proudly remembers of his own early childhood with his widowed mother and brother. "I was 'the wild one.' My grandparents didn't want to have me in the house there, you see? So I would roam the streets and come back."[5]

A documentary's ability to evoke the past comes through its mix of these powerful verbal recollections with equally potent images. Film's potential for deception lies in its tendency to dramatize rather than analyze; movies produce myths more often than they debunk them. The director Oliver Stone, widely criticized for his distortion of the historical record in his 1991 dramatic feature *JFK*, claimed that he hoped to provide a countermyth to the accepted history of the President's assassination. In doing so, he turned to the grammar and vocabulary of the documentary idiom to lend a historical credibility to his own idiosyncratic and highly contested view of Kennedy's murder. In recreating the Kennedy assassination, Stone masterfully edited actual archival film with newly created images digitally dressed up to appear as archival film. This ability to use counterfeit historical images gives filmmakers like Stone a powerful tool unavailable to historians or the authors of historical novels.

We documentarians, of course, must also come to terms with the medium's ability to manipulate. And while it would be both impossible and undesirable to make a documentary without a point of view, the medium's sly simulation of the real can mask a filmmaker's own personal agenda. A documentary filmmaker's visual syntax—his or her use of image as metaphor through the process of editing—makes the documentary medium and its conjuring of the past less literal than poetic in its compression of meaning through image. In the twenties, the great Russian director Dziga Vertov (né Denis Kaufman), one of the founders of documentary filmmaking, boasted of his ability to give a higher reality to mundane images of life through the art of editing. In recent years, the use of re-creations both in historical documentaries as well as in network newsmagazine programs further complicates the issue. As each documentary filmmaker attempts to reach beyond a mere recounting of facts, the potential for distortion, as opposed to interpretation, increases.

Historical filmmakers such as Marcel Ophuls and Claude Lanzmann have shown the power of documentary to recount history with the emotional immediacy only film can convey while at the same time pointing up very different methods of filmmaking. In *The Sorrow and the Pity* (1972), his complex portrait of Vichy France, Ophuls makes brilliant use of filmic metaphor, employing archival images of French singer and icon Maurice Chevalier as he entertains a Nazi audience to illustrate the French nation's ambiguous and morally compromised relationship to the German occupation. In contrast, in Lanzmann's celebrated documentary *Shoah* (1985), the filmmaker notably avoided the use of archival footage to tell his story, using only contemporary footage to communicate the story his subjects relate. The very absence of historical images itself becomes a metaphor, an indication of an erasure, the film implies, partly due to the erosion of memory over time, but equally the result of the willed physical destruction of that past and the continuing emotional denial of its unimaginable devastation by victims and oppressors alike. All of which is to say that any documentarian is aware of the impossibility of capturing reality on film and therefore is also aware of the importance of producing an artistic vision that remains faithful to the truth as he or she sees it.

Arguing the World covers a contentious history, one in which what happened—in the form of both facts and interpretation—has been fought over by the Left and the Right in this country for many years. Political belief gives one, after all, a world-view. Disputes continue over the guilt or innocence of Alger Hiss long after his death, despite the appearance of new documents in the wake of the Cold War that all but confirm his role as a Soviet spy. The controversy over the awarding of a lifetime achievement Academy Award to film director Elia Kazan—a cooperating witness before the HCUAA in the 1950s—points up the still furious debate over McCarthyism and its legacy, which continues to rage in certain circles.

Therefore, *Arguing the World* attempts to portray controversial events through multiple perspectives in order to allow for the complexity of narrative created by having four subjects. The city of New York, which figures as a powerful symbolic presence as well as a geographic locus, serves, in part, as a unifying element in the film. Still, the film is ultimately an exploration of the interaction of personality, history, and ideology in the shaping of individual meaning. In one sense, the four men's memories of the Depression-era Jewish neighborhoods in which they were raised convey a common world of claustrophobic poverty set against a culture of ecstatic political idealism, a world that nurtured in each young man a precocious political awareness. But in remembering their youths, these men also reveal stark differences of perception, shaped by personal temperament as well as family history. When their stories are interwoven with archival photographs and film footage, another set of reflections on the past is added to create a textured and, at times, contradictory portrait of a bygone era.

In *Arguing the World,* the depiction of Depression-era Jewish life, drawn from the early childhood memories of the film's protagonists, is an impressionistic portrait of the Jewish communities in the Lower East Side, the Bronx, and Brooklyn. In viewing Jewish life almost exclusively through the lens of radicalism, and through the political conversions of my subjects, the film is clearly selective in its portrayal; one might just as easily have conjured up a Jewish world of passionate religious observance, or plumbed more deeply into the family life of the four men, but the fact is that the film is not a traditional four-person biography; rather, it is an attempt to capture the ideational lives of

these four thinkers, to capture an American Jewish process of searching and understanding the world through passionate argument.

For *Arguing the World* I drew on a number of image sources to portray the world that these men remember: newsreel footage and news
photos to illustrate the historical events through which they lived, archival film and photo images, my subject's personal photographs, and
newly shot footage of the men revisiting their old neighborhoods.[6] I
was interested in using these images to recreate the feel and texture of
these men's lives, in visually rendering their stories of poverty and political awakening without sentimentalizing their existence.

As it turned out, the archival film and photographic record is rich
with images. In the case of the Jewish immigrant community, it is also,
with few exceptions, an "unofficial" record. Professional newsreels of
the period almost completely ignore Jewish life. Instead, the amateur
documentarian and the politically inspired filmmaker provide witness
to this world. With their eye on the quotidian, these photographers
produced a portrait of Jewish street life as it happened, with both its
dull regularity and its bursts of passion. As social documentarians, their
work is anti-romantic, a counterpoint to the myths of nostalgia. At the
same time, the material did contain one striking, yet revealing, historical limitation.

Of my four protagonists, only Bell actually grew up on the Lower
East Side. Kristol grew up in Brooklyn, and Glazer and Howe in the
East Bronx. But I quickly learned that visually depicting Jewish immigrant life in New York meant relying largely on images of the Lower
East Side. The extant footage and photographs from the period document this neighborhood almost exclusively. The Lower East Side had
already been enshrined as *the* symbol of Jewish life in New York.

There were some exceptions. The early documentarian Jay Leyda,
a protégé of the great Russian director Sergei Eisenstein, made a film
called *Bronx Morning* (1931). Self-consciously avant-garde, often photographed at extreme angles with an eye to odd details and abstract
compositions, it is an atmospheric hymn to the borough's Jewish neighborhoods and to the drama of street life.

Because much of the Jewish community resided in overcrowded
tenements, life was lived on the streets. Re-creating this life was critical to telling my story. The world of the streets was particularly important to Jewish children during the Depression, many of whom were of
necessity loosed, as Daniel Bell had been, from the supervision of overworked parents. On revisiting the Lower East Side with me in 1994,
Bell eyed the abandoned buildings and now-vacant lots that scar the
area and was struck by the difference between life then and now, be-

tween the dense street life of his childhood and the relative quiet of today:

> [Today] it's all mixed, it's all kind of crazy-quilt patterns. Nor-
> mally, you would have had a whole series of blocks, solid fa-
> cades. With all trees in front. And you would have pushcarts
> all along the street. It would be lined with people coming
> along, and they'd be buying from the pushcarts. . . . In the
> wintertime, you lived in the staircases. It was cold outside, and
> therefore, everybody would congregate on the staircases, par-
> ticularly kids. There were a lot of kids there, . . . so we lived
> inside. . . . And then outside, there's a stoop, three steps or
> four steps, and in the summertime . . . older people would sit
> on the stoop, the kids would run around on the streets. . . . It
> would be crowded.[7]

Bell, whose mother worked "nine, ten, twelve hours
a day" as a dressmaker during the busy season, remembers that the streets, dominated by horse-drawn wag-
ons, "would be full of shit, literally, so that you'd get
those smells. . . . Urine. Defecation. Garbage." But that
they were also a place of endless adventure:

> We used to go to the west side fruit markets, which were under
> what is today the West Side Highway. And at . . . twelve
> o'clock at night the trucks would come rolling in with pota-
> toes, lettuce, and tomatoes. And we'd make grabs. Some-
> body'd walk by and knock over a crate. The crate would break.
> We'd grab and run back.[8]

Among the richest images captured on film from
the period are portraits of children, like Bell, who spent
so much of their formative years on the streets of the
Lower East Side. At the National Center for Jewish
Film I discovered footage taken in the 1930s by an
anonymous wealthy businessman interested in recording the daily life of the Lower East Side children. His
film captures them in settlement house playgrounds and
sledding down snow-covered streets. The politically
conscious photographers of the Film and Photo League
set about documenting life on the Lower East Side, much as Walker
Evans had photographed the South during these same years. Jerome
Liebling captured a group of children aloft in an abandoned building,
triumphantly smiling down at his camera; Maurice Huberland found a
pair of boys, faces pressed next to each other, stopping to light a ciga-
rette on the street (fig. 11.1).

Fig. 11.1 Smoking on the sidewalks of New York,
c. 1940. Photograph by Maurice Huberland.
Courtesy of the Collection of Riverside Films.

Joseph Dorman

Even when Hollywood ventured to the Lower East Side, it could not help but discover its street children. In one archive, I came upon a stunning tracking shot of a Lower East Side street, part of a series of stock New York exteriors filmed for Warner Brothers sometime during the 1930s. It records the Lower East Side at its most iconic, a busy home to pushcart peddlers. Yet as the cameraman dollies down the street, two intrepid young boys suddenly appear, chasing the camera with their restless eyes, giving the familiar image a new and unexpected sense of life.

I was also able to draw on the personal photographs of my four subjects to deepen and modify their memories, cutting these images together with my four protagonists' verbal recollections to reveal their complex relationships to their own childhood poverty, then and now. Irving Howe recalls the bankruptcy of his parents' grocery store, which plunged his family into financial ruin:

> The transition was very difficult and perplexing, and painful. It was like having everything fall out from under you. . . . For many years I didn't have a room of my own. . . . The pain of this was overwhelming. . . . The thought of a career or future was not something which one could live by. The expectation that one's parents could bring in enough money next week by which to live was very small.[9]

This recollection was intercut with a photo of Howe as a young boy posing for the camera in child's suit, a violin tucked under his chin (fig. 11.2). While the memory and the photo each provide a fragment of the story, together they produce a portrait of a world of terrible poverty leavened by cultural aspiration—a reaching out toward the world—that would ultimately be echoed in Howe's gravitation toward the socialist vision.

Tenement life, its indignities as well as its forced intimacies, was ever present in these men's memories, though reflected differently by their distinct sensibilities. Of his own childhood, Irving Kristol remembers sleeping "in the hallway, on the balcony" and that "everybody was doing that. When poverty is near universal, you don't experience it as poverty,"[10] he explained, in his typically offhand way. A man who tends to underplay his own emotions, Kristol expressed a bemused sense of his own impoverishment. Kristol remembers that, despite accepted bonds of love and loyalty, "Being close to your parents wasn't really regarded as being all that important. Your parents were your parents and that's all there was to it."[11] Kristol, whose mother died when he was sixteen, shopped for his family on the way home from school and played punchball in the streets.

Through the succession of tenements in which he and his family

Fig. 11.2 Portrait of a young Irving Howe, c. 1930. Courtesy of Nicholas Howe.

249

lived, Daniel Bell remembered the cold of the indoor toilets in winter: "The thing I always wanted was sweaters. And I think one of the things I have now, I have a large room of sweaters in the house. I don't need them all, mind you. But if it's a nice sweater, I have to get it."[12]

For Nathan Glazer, a trip back to the Bronx neighborhood of his youth brought out the sociologist and urban critic and, ultimately, memories of the child he had once been. It was impossible to enter a tenement on our visit to his old neighborhood, but Glazer agreed to visit the Lower East Side Tenement Museum. Here again, this neighborhood has been used to enshrine the experience of the entire Jewish immigrant community. In this particular case, what has been preserved is a turn-of-the-century existence that nevertheless carries strong associations with life as Glazer's family lived it some thirty years later. Though the footage of this visit never appears in the film, a memory triggered on this occasion (used only in a voice-over) became integral to the film's portrayal of Glazer's youth. Discovering a Singer sewing machine at the museum brought back memories of his father and of a suit that he had made for young Nathan. (Clearly an important possession, a tintype still exists of Glazer wearing the suit, and we were able to use this image in the film.) As a sewing-machine operator, Glazer's father would also regularly turn (i.e., reverse) collars for him. "I throw out perfectly good shirts today," he told me, "because who's going to turn a collar anymore?" Surveying the almost empty bedroom in which we were filming, he noted that in his own family of seven children

> I always slept with someone. In fact, I'm trying to remember at what point did I start sleeping alone. . . . First, there was a war, which took three brothers away. There was marriage, which took a sister or two away. . . . By about my mid-teens I might have had a bed of my own.[13]

Embedded within the experience of life on the Lower East Side, in the Bronx, and in Brooklyn lay the history of generations of East European ancestors, as Irving Howe recalls:

> Historical consciousness was part of immigrant Jewish life. . . . The immigrant Jews brought with them legends and stories that had happened there, so you absorbed this kind of historical consciousness at the kitchen table, literally at the kitchen table.[14]

At the YIVO Institute for Jewish Research I found a series of evocatively grainy film images, portraits of the Lower East Side and its inhabitants by an unknown photographer who managed to capture archetypal elements of an Old World existence that persisted in immigrant communities: a beggar sewing his clothes on the street, a toothless older woman wrapped in her shawl, a bearded patriarch. Shot at silent-film speed, the footage has an otherworldly quality; it plays across the screen almost as a ghostly embodiment of Howe's memories.

Though all four men were shaped by their youth, it was clear that Bell and Howe had a different relationship to their childhood than either Glazer or Kristol, a difference that is reflected in their various political allegiances. Significantly, Yiddish provided a critical link to their childhood for both Howe and Bell. During his lifetime, Howe was professionally involved with the Yiddish language and was dedicated to promoting past Yiddish authors of the Old and New Worlds through the several anthologies of literary translations that he co-edited. Bell has maintained strong personal ties to the language; Yiddish, as he often reminded me, was the language in which he learned to speak and in which for many years he dreamed. In his conversation and letters he made constant recourse to Yiddish and was continually disappointed at my own meager knowledge of the language. Knowing Yiddish, understanding its world-view, provided both men with an ongoing connection to their childhood, which was so much defined by it.

Bell and Howe also seem to have experienced a more crushing poverty than either Glazer or Kristol; at least that is how they remember it. The death of Bell's father left only his mother to support their family, while the Depression forced Howe's parents into the terribly acute financial devastation mentioned above. Perhaps, then, it was the traumatic nature of their childhood that has kept this period—and its world—alive for them. Not coincidentally, I think, both Bell and Howe discovered socialism early on, at the ages of thirteen and fourteen respectively. Amidst the poverty and the shabbiness of Depression-era Jewish life in New York, and within the confines of its narrowed existence, socialism promised limitless possibility. "The world was a drab, dreadful world," Bell remembers. "It was a problem getting something to eat. So you're trying to say, in effect, 'No, there's a way out.' Socialism gave us answers to this world."[15] For Howe, "the socialist view, the radical view, seemed to bring to young people a total understanding. It wasn't fragmentary. It seemed to suggest a conceptual frame by which one could *structure* and give meaning to these very difficult experiences."[16]

Howe was deeply affected by a successful garment workers' strike, in which his parents participated. The conclusion to the strike relieved his family of the worst of its poverty. Both Bell and Howe joined the Young People's Socialist League and found their way into a new life dominated by the febrile intensity of Marxist politics. It was a world of open-air arguments and street-corner speakers, as Irving Howe vividly remembers:

One would begin talking about the terrible conditions of life, unemployment, . . . the threat of war, the problem of fascism, . . . and from there you went on. There was no great requirement that you be entirely coherent or that you have an organized structure. Those of my friends who spoke well, and some were quite brilliant at this, were able to achieve an emotional tie with the audience, were able to strike some chord in the feelings of the workers and the people who would gather around a street corner meeting.[17]

This world was also captured by the photographs of Arnold Eagle, yet another member of the Film and Photo League. During the thirties, Eagle produced a series of photographs of Union Square crowds, where knots of men and women are gathered in endless conversation. Showing hands in the crowd raised in wild motion as each speaker in turn preached political salvation, these images evoke the world that Howe and Bell once knew.

The discovery of socialism for Bell and Howe, and their "conversion" to the socialist cause, became a defining moment in their impoverished lives. Bell's ideological journey could even be mapped across the eroded contours of the Lower East Side. In the midst of filming, I pointed out to him an abandoned and boarded-up synagogue. He stopped, looked down the street, and explained:

You found a *shul*, and right over there is where the Socialist Party headquarters used to be, and that framed my life, the *shul* and the Socialist Party. When I had my bar mitzvah, there was a *melamed* who taught me my *haftorah*, and I said to him, "I've found the truth. I don't believe in God. I'll put on *tefillin* once, in memory of my dead father, but that's all. I'm joining the Young People's Socialist League." So, he looked at me, and he said, "*Yingl*—kid—you've found the truth. You don't believe in God." He says, "Tell me, you think God cares?"[18]

Two Lower East Side buildings—both an intimate part of Bell's history, both now condemned shells—and yet they evoke two separate responses. The old synagogue, a faded part of a still-living and vibrant tradition, remains in Bell's memory as a symbol of his discarded religious orthodoxy. The former Socialist Party headquarters, once home to an expired political party, invokes a passionate memory of a passion-

Fig. 11.3 Daniel Bell revisits the streets of
his childhood on the Lower East Side,
1994. From *Arguing the World*. Courtesy of
Riverside Films.

ate political. Bell, who otherwise calls himself a cultural conservative and political liberal, remains, in his own words, a socialist in economics. Until his death, Howe, too, remained a socialist. This is, of course, in marked contrast to the neoconservative Kristol, who has long since journeyed beyond the radicalism gleaned from the New York neighborhoods of his childhood and youth. But even the centrist Glazer—whose father was a faithful socialist and a reader of the *Jewish Daily Forward*—mused aloud to me that he didn't understand how Bell and Howe could continue to believe in socialism, when to him there seemed little left of socialism in their political beliefs.

Unlike their friends, Glazer and Kristol remember their childhood with fewer stings, despite the steady hardships that they, too, faced. Surely this is partly because of their own individual temperaments and perhaps, in part, the result of the Great Depression's less devastating effect on their families. Significantly, though, their different memories of childhood poverty have, over time, informed very different political visions. While it is overly simplistic to equate Kristol's and Glazer's political views (as of course it is equally problematic to lump together the very different politics of Howe and Bell), it is true that they have both severed any emotional attachment to the radicalism of their youth. Each considers this radicalism as a formative phase of his life, but only that. In contrast, the socialist vision has remained for Howe and Bell as a living presence, something intrinsic to who they are in the world.

As I interviewed Bell over the years, I found that his commitment to socialism grew stronger, not weaker. For both Bell and Howe, it seems clear, socialism remained an ideal of social justice that they clung to, even as they matured and came to understand the impossibility of realizing the socialist dream. It remained for both men, even into their later years, an idealized vision of what life *should* be, rather than any set of concrete policy formulations.

One of Bell's most powerful, and revealing, statements in the film is a memory of first discovering socialism:

> Coming out of an immigrant world, in which one's parents were preoccupied with making a living, preoccupied with day-to-day existence, who are not illiterate, but not basically cultured, and suddenly the world opens up, and this is what the socialist movement did for me. It suddenly shows there's a world of ideas, a world of experience, a world of imagination, so that, well, eagerly, you know, one becomes almost greedy in reaching for this.[19]

This revelation came in the final moments of my final interview with him, some six years after our first meeting. Bell was seventy-seven years old at the time. It was clear that socialism and its ideals, which had first opened the door beyond the Lower East Side for him, had been transformed over time into a distillation of the world in which he had grown up. "Socialism," Irving Howe and his friend Lewis Coser once wrote, paraphrasing Tolstoy, "is the name of our desire."[20]

But just as early experience can shape later political beliefs, those beliefs can also reinforce childhood memories, perhaps even become a selecting conduit for remembrance. For Kristol, who has studied Jewish theology over the course of his life and who has become ever more convinced of the importance of religious belief, it is the religious traditions of his youth that have, over time, provided a connecting thread between his childhood and his mature conservative philosophy:

> [I] came out of [an] Orthodox Jewish background. The rabbinic tradition in Judaism is very good on social justice because it is very explicit on social justice. Whereas the prophetic tradition, which is very eloquent and beautiful to read, is often vague. Which is one of the reasons socialists have always liked the prophets more than the Rabbis. Of course, you can talk about brave new worlds without getting very specific. The rabbinic tradition, when you talk about helping the poor, . . . will tell you what you must do to help the poor, and how: what your obligations are. . . . [The] tradition doesn't mention rights. It mentions obligations. But the obligations can be the obverse of many of what we call rights.[21]

Given his life-long interest in ethnicity, the city, and the urban poor, Glazer, I suspect, continues to ponder questions vitally related to his youth in New York. In our travels to the South Bronx, Harlem, and the Lower East Side, Glazer, more than the others, demonstrated an intense curiosity about the streets and life of these now Caribbean, black, and Chinese neighborhoods, continually comparing his own past with the lives led by their present-day inhabitants.

It is, perhaps, then, a question of how these four men have individually come to terms with their past and of how that past—now held fast in collective Jewish memory as the world of the Lower East Side—has continued to live on in each of them. Each of the four, in his own way, remains deeply marked by his youth. Clearly for Bell and Howe this neighborhood embodies, in part, the essence of the socialist politics that forever changed their lives. But for Bell the neighborhood also remains his childhood home, its streets—their sights, sounds, and smells—embedded in his memory. For Irving Howe, the Lower East Side became a symbolic home to which he laid claim through an act of passionate historical scholarship. Irving Kristol has found in it a world of theological searching, once discarded and now intellectually reclaimed. And in Nathan Glazer's sociological excursions into ethnicity, one cannot help but see a latter-day incarnation of the curious child once staring in open-eyed wonder at the urban Jewish landscape around him—rich, chaotic and boisterous—which would provide his entrée into the wider world of America.

NOTES

1. Allan Wald, *The New York Intellectuals: The Rise and Decline of the Anti-Stalinist Left from the 1930s to the 1980s* (Chapel Hill: University of North Carolina Press, 1987), pp. 3–24. The introductory chapter lays out Wald's theory of political amnesia among the New York Intellectual group.

2. *Arguing the World* (New York: First Run/Icarus Films, 1997) had its theatrical premiere in January 1998 at the Film Forum theater in New York. The film, which was made possible by a grant from the National Endowment for the Humanities, aired on American public television in the spring of 1999.

3. Daniel Bell, "Reflections on Jewish Identity," in *The Winding Passage* (Cambridge, Mass.: Abt Associates, 1980), pp. 314–323.

4. Television interview with Irving Howe by Herbert Kaplow, *Directions: Lower East Side, Search for a Dream* (ABC/Jewish Theological Seminary), aired 16 May 1976. National Jewish Archive of Broadcasting, The Jewish Museum, New York, item no. T832.

5. Interview by the author with Daniel Bell, Lower East Side, May 1994.

6. In the case of Irving Howe this was impossible, because he had died in May 1993, before this phase of production had begun.

7. Interview by the author with Daniel Bell, Lower East Side, May 1994.

8. Interview by the author with Daniel Bell, Lower East Side, 1991.

9. Interview by the author with Irving Howe, Manhattan, 1989.

10. Interview by the author with Irving Kristol, Brooklyn, July 1994.

11. Interview by the author with Irving Kristol, Brooklyn, July 1994.

12. Interview by the author with Daniel Bell, Lower East Side, May 1994.

13. Interview by the author with Daniel Glazer, Lower East Side Tenement Museum, June 1994.

14. Interview by the author with Irving Howe, Manhattan, 1989.

15. Interview by the author with Daniel Bell, Lower East Side, May 1994.

16. Interview by the author with Irving Howe, Manhattan, 1989.

17. Interview by the author with Irving Howe, Manhattan, 1989.

18. A *shul* is a synagogue; a *melamed* is a Hebrew teacher; the *haftorah* is a selection from the Prophets read after the weekly portion of the Torah; and *tefillin* are phylacteries. Interview by the author with Daniel Bell, Lower East Side, May 1994.

19. Interview by the author with Daniel Bell, Cambridge, Massachusetts, March 1995.

20. Lewis Coser and Irving Howe, "Images of Socialism, 1954," in *Legacy of Dissent: Forty Years of Writing from Dissent Magazine* (New York: Harcourt Brace Jovanovich, 1993), p. 29.

21. Interview by the author with Irving Kristol, Washington, D.C., March 1995.

Performing Memory: "The Matzoh Factory" on the Lower East Side

Aviva Weintraub

The Lower East Side of New York occupies a central place in American Jewish memory culture. This neighborhood has entered the collective memory through various media, including memoirs, films, photographic exhibitions, and performance art. Because performance art is often based on personal experience, it is a particularly rich vehicle for invoking and exploring memories and memory.

Performance became accepted as a medium of artistic expression in its own right in the 1970s. At that time, conceptual art—which insisted on an art of ideas over product, and on art that could not be bought and sold—was in its heyday, and performance was often a demonstration or an execution of those ideas.[1] Performance art is not as slick and as glossily produced as mainstream theater; also, it can be open-ended: not every moment is precisely choreographed. Performance art is often presented in non-conventional theater spaces such as cafes and museum galleries, and even urban streets and sidewalks, bridges, and farms. It defies easy definition, though RoseLee Goldberg's gloss of performance art as "live art by artists" speaks to its essential character.[2]

Since the 1980s, performance art has become increasingly text-based. The borders of what is considered performance art have always been fluid enough to include, for instance, the monologues of Spalding Gray, Allan Kaprow's open-ended happenings, the multi-media work of Laurie Anderson, and the conceptual pieces of Yoko Ono, to name just a few.[3] In the 1990s, performance art often served to explore personal identity issues and the acknowledgment of the concurrent existence of different identities within the individual: identities based on ethnicity, gender, profession, family circumstances, sexual orientation, and so on. Performance art has a "pared-down" quality: Embellishments such as costumes and sets are usually kept to a bare minimum. This allows for a focus on the text and the evocation of emotions.

In May 1996 a performance called *The Matzoh Factory* took place on the Lower East Side, at a venue called The Synagogue Space. *The Matzoh Factory* is a site-specific solo performance piece, conceived, written, and performed by Abe Wald. The piece is autobiographical and explores Wald's memories of his childhood and its impact on his adult life. Because the piece was presented as site-specific, the history of The Synagogue Space is essential to a study of the performance itself.

The Synagogue Space

The Synagogue Space for Visual and Performing Arts was situated in the site that was home to Congregation Masas Benjamin Anshe Podhajce, at 108 East First Street, between First Avenue and Avenue A on the Lower East Side. This congregation had been organized in 1895 by immigrants from the town of Podhajce in southern Galicia. The three-story building, which probably dates to the 1880s, was bought by the congregation in 1926 and was expanded and restructured to serve as a synagogue, with a study on the first floor, a sanctuary on the second, and the women's section on the third.

In the 1920s the building was shared with another congregation, also from Podhajce (Congregation Rodeph Shalom Independent Podhajce) and by the early 1980s was being used by yet another congregation, Kochob Jacob Anshe Kamenitz, of Kamenitz, Lithuania. The building was not in use from 1985 to 1990, when it became home to Congregation Beth Yitzchok. In 1995 three artists—Jeffrey Bock, Timothy Fryberger, and Rocky Kenworthy—rented the building from

Fig. 12.1 Entrance to the Podhajcer
synagogue, located at 108 East First Street,
home of the Synagogue Space for the
Visual and Performing Arts from 1995 to
1997. Photograph by Jack Kugelmass.

Congregation Beth Yitzchok and founded The Synagogue Space for
the Visual and Performing Arts.

The building has thus housed layers of memory, even in its original
function as a stand-in for a piece of the *alte haym* ("old home," meaning

Jewish Eastern Europe). At first, it was a gathering place for immigrant *landslayt* (compatriots) from Podhajce in their new home. While for a number of years the actual community in Podhajce still existed simultaneously with the Podhajce-in-exile in New York, today neither exists. In The Synagogue Space's brochure, which details the chronological development of the building, the two histories—of New York and Galicia—are interwoven and somewhat conflated, as the early history of the synagogue in New York segues into the deportation of the Jews of Podhajce to the death camp at Belzec. The brochure continues,

> The Congregation of the People of Podhajce no longer exists, either. The once-thriving Jewish community of the Lower East Side has shrunk significantly, due to the far more benign forces of demographic shift and economic mobility. Left in the wake are dozens of small synagogues, many of which have been demolished or converted into apartment buildings. While it is not violent pogroms which have driven the former congregants from the neighborhood, but rather economic success, the sight of a formerly vibrant synagogue left to crumble into disrepair is no less lamentable. Part of the mission chosen by the directors of The Synagogue Space is to preserve the aesthetic integrity of the building, and to foster an appreciation of its history.[4]

The founders of the artistic space liken a neglected building to a neglected tradition. They locate a commitment to Judaism in their commitment to a tangible house of worship. Even while acknowledging the reason for the neglect, they still find that the sight of an abandoned synagogue resonates mournfulness. Collective memory—real and imagined—allows for this conflation of events: An abandoned synagogue on the Lower East Side may function as a visual analogue to an abandoned synagogue in Europe, where the reason for its emptiness is far darker. Though in New York the image is symbolic, the artists have embraced this symbolic substitution. By allowing the synagogue itself to stand for the history of its congregation, they allow the liquidation of the actual Podhajce to echo in the abandonment of the virtual Podhajce in New York. Their work at reclaiming the synagogue's history can also be seen as a symbolic redemption of European synagogues that were destroyed or used for profane purposes during and after the war. The Lower East Side, with its history and strong associations with immigrant Jewish communities, is a particularly potent place for such a gesture.

The directors of The Synagogue Space saw the preservation and restoration of the building and the fostering of an appreciation of its history as part of their mission. Not wanting only to occupy the space as tenants, they referred to the former function of the building in delineating a set of guiding principles for their own program. For instance, they wrote:

A synagogue is called a *Bet Knesset* in Hebrew, which literally means "House of Gathering." Synagogues have served many purposes in Jewish communities for well over a millennium, providing far more than simply a building in which to pray. Traditionally, synagogues have been centers of learning, where culture and history are passed down through generations; places of beauty, from the meticulous calligraphy of the torah scrolls to the expressive architecture of the sanctuary; places of entertainment, including the engaging narratives of the bible and the ancient melodies of the *chazzan* [cantor]; and places of social importance, where the entire community gathers to honor its celebrations and its mournings. In a somewhat different fashion, The Synagogue Space will continue to serve these needs of the community.[5]

This description goes on to detail activities in each of those four categories: *Learning* is achieved through artists' and arts administration workshops, which particularly target the young people of the neighborhood; *beauty*, through art exhibitions and restoration of the space, whose interior walls had included hand-painted images; *entertainment*, through presenting performing arts of all disciplines, a film festival, and providing independent filmmakers with a location for shooting; and *social importance*, through serving a diverse constituency of all ages and backgrounds, "where individuals concerned by an irreverence for the past will see clear evidence of our respect for the cultural legacy represented by the building."[6]

To provide a narrative of continuity, the founders of The Synagogue Space distilled what they saw as the essential elements of a synagogue (learning, beauty, entertainment, social importance), and presented the current activities as applications of those principles. One could argue that this is enabled only through eliding the element of religion or rendering it into universal values. Most but not all of the programs had some connection to Jewish, and often Yiddish, culture. The programming presented at The Synagogue Space tended to be innovative, cutting-edge material by young artists whose work was not familiar to most mainstream audiences.

While a decision was made to retain the word *synagogue* in the new name Synagogue Space, it was also clear that "you don't have to be Jewish" to perform or to visit there. The name Synagogue Space retains the association with the origins of the building as a synagogue, but modified its function with the word *space*.[7] Space itself connotes openness, perhaps emptiness—a territory on which to map the multiplicity of uses envisioned by the artists.

The building could be used differently according to each performance or art exhibition. The main performance space was in the large room that had served as the sanctuary when the building had functioned as a synagogue. Elements of that incarnation remained, both in the architecture and the furnishings, which included the *bimah*, the raised platform from which prayers were led and the Torah was read. The seating in the theater space consisted of moveable wooden pews, left over from synagogue days. The choice made by the founding artists to keep such architectural details allowed for a visible manifestation of the layers of the building's history. Rather than opting for either the black box of the conventional theater or the white cube of the art gallery, they allowed for a presence of the archaeological layers of the space.

The Matzoh Factory

Abe Wald, who wrote and performed *The Matzoh Factory*, has been working in the medium of autobiographical solo performance since the mid-1970s. His areas of study and influence include movement and dance, experimental theater and film, Eastern body disciplines such as yoga and karate, and body–mind therapies such as Trager Body–Mind Integration. In addition to being a writer and performance artist, Wald is a practicing psychotherapist specializing in body-oriented therapy.

He has studied with such pioneers of experimental theater, dance, and film as Spalding Gray, Andre Gregory, Meredith Monk, and Ken Jacobs. Wald has performed with Alex Rubin's Primal Theater Workshop, danced with Bill T. Jones, and appeared at such New York performance spaces as Theater for the New City, La Mama Experimental Theater Club, and Dance Theater Workshop.

In the late 1980s, Wald moved to Boulder, Colorado, where he worked, studied, and performed at the Naropa Institute, a Buddhist-influenced school founded by Allen Ginsberg and others in the previous decade. At Naropa, Wald developed a solo improvisational performance process that incorporates movement, language, character, sound, and autobiographical material. This technique is implemented in *The Matzoh Factory*, which incorporates visual and audio elements, including tape recordings of family conversations and oral histories, music, factory sounds, telephone answering machine messages, and Wald's stress-reduction therapy sessions. Visual media include slide projections of family photographs from his childhood and old family film footage. These elements are interwoven throughout the performed text. Wald writes, "The structure of the performance is episodic, appropriating elements from experimental theater, dance and avant-garde cinema. . . . The effect is not a linear narrative progression, but a cumulative experience."[8] Like the process of memory, this constructed whole makes up a dream-like and, at times, nightmarish montage.

Wald plays all the characters in the piece, often assuming more than one role in a conversation. His character shifts are accomplished in full view of the audience with no major costume changes but through the re-orienting and shaping of his body and face. His most striking metamorphoses occur when he portrays himself as a child interacting with his doting mother and high-strung father.

The performance takes place in and around the former sanctuary of the synagogue. The use of this space is crucial to the piece itself; in fact, the space should be considered one of its performative elements. The audience is at first seated in chairs which face the doors they have passed through to enter the room. This space becomes the Wald family home, with the women's section of the synagogue, located on a balcony overlooking the main sanctuary, functioning as the second story. The corridor leading into the sanctuary is recast as an outdoor courtyard, where the child Abe plays basketball. Between acts, the audience is asked to leave the space. Upon re-entering, they find that the room has been re-oriented: chairs now face in the opposite direction, and the *bimah*, which was formerly behind the audience, is now at the center of the room, where it is used as a lectern and also as a backdrop for further parts of the story.[9]

This performance piece is constructed from various elements, but the result is more than the sum of its parts. The "glue" that hold the piece together, that transforms it into something larger, is memory, which operates on several levels. In the performer's words, *The Matzoh Factory* "reflects Abe's long personal and professional struggle to find a form from which to express, construct and reconstruct the self of the artist caught in the impossible history of growing up as a child of Holocaust survivors."[10] Wald views the performance as being very much about its formal elements.

The technique that he uses, which includes moments of improvisation, employs memory as a constantly renewable source of material. This literally means that he mines his memory at the moment of performance; the audience is witness to the processing of his past. At times, he appears to be channeling the voice of his former self far more than acting. Thus, the moment of the performance represents an archaeology of memory. To his personal memory is added a stratum of collective memory by virtue of the location of this performance. Abe's body remembers and recovers his own past (his child body) and his ancestral past (through his parents' bodies). This takes place within the body of a building, The Synagogue Space, which, through its architecture and decor, resonates with its own history. Abe's body, through his presence and his performance, activates the space.

Museum Theater

The walls of the room are covered with an assemblage of objects that have played a part in Abe's family history: prayer shawls, violins, mathematical symbols, letters from the Hebrew and German alphabets, and old factory motors and fans. More an installation than a stage set, the walls evoke an abandoned attic in a family home, or a museum (perhaps a neglected museum) of religious and mechanical arts.

An additional layer of images and memory is added with slides projected onto these walls. The projections include photographs of Abe's father returning home to Cluj, Hungary, after his release from a concentration camp in 1945. One image shows him at the matzoh factory that he had designed and built in Cluj before the war; in another, he stands in front of the matzoh factory ovens, these carrying the added burden of parallels with familiar images of the sinister ovens of the death camps that he has survived. A further layer of performance is added with the playing of an audiotape of factory sounds. Here the Lower East Side is reintroduced, as the tape was actually recorded in a matzoh factory on Rivington Street.

Evoking the process of memory, the archaeological layers move from the outside in and back again: the walls of the Lower East Side synagogue, on which are displayed factory elements, over which are projected photo images of the matzoh factory in Hungary, and which is overlaid with sounds of a matzoh factory on the Lower East Side.

Patina

The interior walls of the sanctuary/theater are the most concentrated site of memory. The original synagogue walls, with their painted images of the signs of the Zodiac and the Hebrew months invoking the passage and marking of time, can still be seen. A marble tablet on one of the walls lists the names of deceased members of the congregation. Inscriptions outside the sanctuary list the congregation's officers and contributors to the synagogue, and the front gate says, in Yiddish, "Contributed by the Podhajce Ladies Auxiliary." Thus, the history of the congregation is literally inscribed on the walls of the synagogue. The marble *yizkor* (remembrance) tablet is the locus of the most direct inscription of memory: names of the dead. These elements are not covered or modified during the performance; they remain as reminders of past inhabitants of the space.

Beneath the synagogue's ornate lighting sconces, Wald has installed a bricolage of factory equipment, mathematical symbols, Hebrew and German letters, musical instruments and prayer shawls—all elements from his childhood home and family history. Abe remembers his father:

> He constantly worked on his electrical inventions and mathematical computations. You could always find him typing, reading, writing, thinking, and jotting down equations all the time. . . . In my parents' bedroom was all his electronic equipment. There were wires, oscilloscopes, tools, switches, circuits, and papers flying all over the place with mathematical equations written on them. You could also find his violins and music notes everywhere.[11]

The blending of machinery and text, and the proximity of the Hebrew alphabet to the motors and fans lends those objects a feeling of ancientness beyond the simple fact of their current obsolescence.

The passage of time has endowed these mechanical objects, which were "state of the art" during Abe's childhood, with the veneer of patina. Patina, as evidence of history and the passage of time, lends a certain authority to an object.[12] What adheres to objects referring to the Holocaust is the patina of tragedy; it alludes to a past that Abe, as the child of survivors, finds is always present. He writes that his performance "speaks of the very real inheritance that unconsciously determines the psychic life of the child, and subsequently the adult, who struggles to make sense out of his experience. The adult is witnessed in a process of attempting to grab hold of the elusive past in order to claim his identity in the present."[13] By re-creating the atmosphere of his childhood home, in a space and, indeed, even a neighborhood imbued with patina, Wald constructs the perfect environment in which to access his memories.

Memory Theater

The theater in which *The Matzoh Factory* is performed functions for Wald as a memory palace. There is precedence for the mapping of knowledge or ideas onto architectural space in the history of the theater and of the memorative arts. The orators of antiquity had devised a system for memorization which involved choosing mental images for each paragraph of text to be memorized. According to art historian Richard Bernheimer, these images "could be selected among likenesses of the things to be remembered or . . . be related to them allegorically or in some other indirect way. Then . . . the orator walked slowly through a familiar building . . . and placed the images . . . upon its salient parts. . . . [The delivery of the speech] consisted of a second, this time fictitious, walk through the same architectural environment, during which 'one asked from every chosen place that which had been entrusted to it' and thus recalled in proper sequence what one had intended to say."[14]

In the sixteenth century, writer and inventor Giulio Camillo set about building a structure in which to practice this art of memory, called a memory theater, or *theatrum mundi*. *Mundi* because the space was meant to be comprehensive and reflective of the universe. Camillo's memory theater had a wooden framework within which the entire structure of the world—according to divine plan—was displayed. He drew his inspiration from classical, Christian, Talmudic, and Kabbalistic texts. The walls of the theater contained images of planetary gods as well as scenes from classical mythology. Camillo's memory building was to "represent the order of eternal truth; in it the universe [would] be remembered through organic association of all its parts with their underlying eternal order."[15] His "theatre [was] a system of memory places."[16]

In the historic memory theaters, under the images of the planets, "there were drawers, or boxes, or coffers of some kind containing masses of papers, and on these papers were speeches, based on the works of Cicero, relating to the subjects recalled by these images."[17] Similarly, Abe Wald's performance, and his use of the space in which it takes place, resonates with the notion of "a memory organically geared to the universe."[18]

In a memory theater, the "spectator mounted the stairs and contemplated the images, posters, and boxes of manuscripts that crowded around the individual doors, each a little world of its own."[19] While Wald's performance did not involve the little cabinets and coffers of the historical memory theaters, the multimedia elements of the piece performed this purpose, each projection and sound snippet like the opening of a secret drawer.

An extension of the model of the memory theater can be seen in the framework of the Internet, where each information pathway contains embedded layers of information. A year after the *Matzoh Factory* performance, The Synagogue Space ceased operations.[20] But a presence for the space and its history lives on in virtual form on the World Wide Web. Its home page states, "The Synagogue Space was a not-for-profit art space and performance space situated in a former synagogue on New York's Lower East Side. The project is now defunct, but there is much information on the neighborhood to be found on this site."[21] Like a memory theater, the web site provides layers of history, including that of the synagogue and its congregation, the community of Podhajce, and information about the Lower East Side, including local art spaces and local synagogues. The palimpsest effect evident in The

Synagogue Space is also found in the descriptions of other Lower East Side art spaces. For instance, the listing for the Orensanz Foundation at 172 Norfolk Street says, "Founded by Spanish-Jewish sculptor Angel Orensanz, the Orensanz Foundation is situated in the oldest synagogue building in New York City (1850s). The gothic structure, designed after the cathedral in Cologne, Germany, is used for art exhibitions, film shoots, and performances." In fact, a benefit for *The Matzoh Factory* was held there, and its flyer described the venue as "a most haunting location."

All layers—the Lower East Side past and present, the synagogue and The Synagogue Space, Podhajce real and diasporic—exist simultaneously in virtual space. Indeed, the World Wide Web, it would seem, is our age's wardrobe of secret drawers, a postmodern *theatrum mundi.*

Philosopher Gaston Bachelard reminds us that "wardrobes with their shelves, desks with their drawers, and chests with their false bottoms are veritable organs of the secret psychological life . . . a model of intimacy,"[22] and that "small boxes such as chests and caskets . . . are evident witnesses of the need for secrecy, of an intuitive sense of hiding places."[23] A walk through a memory theater allows for the retelling or uttering of the secrets of the past, while it also quietly alludes to what is hidden below the surface. A memory theater is the perfect site for what Bachelard calls "topoanalysis," the psychological study of the sites of our intimate lives.[24]

The function of the memory theater has changed, however. It exists not for oratory purposes but to uncover hidden or forgotten memories. Psychoanalysis and the talking cure have replaced oration; Freud has replaced Cicero. Secret spaces are opened to access the past, and the past is mined for keys to the present. *The Matzoh Factory* served simultaneously as therapy and theater for the performer and perhaps the audience.[25] Its location in an evocative building in a history-laden neighborhood allowed for a wide range of associations. The performance of a multi-layered personal narrative transformed a space that could become a museum of its own obsolescence into an activated theater of memory.

NOTES

1. RoseLee Goldberg, *Performance Art: From Futurism to the Present* (New York: Harry N. Abrams, 1988), p. 7.

2. Ibid., p. 9.

3. For an overview of the genre, see Robyn Brentano and Olivia Georgia, *Outside the Frame: Performance and the Object—A Survey History of Performance Art in the USA since 1950* (Cleveland: Cleveland Center for Contemporary Art, 1994).

4. *The Synagogue Space*, brochure and web site: www.panix.com/~ilduce/

5. Ibid.

6. Ibid.

7. For New Yorkers, the name Synagogue Space may resonate with another performing arts venue, Symphony Space (on the Upper West Side). The word *space* might be associated with one of the leading downtown venues for performance art, P.S. 122: the former Public School 122, now Performance Space 122.

8. Abe Wald, *The Matzoh Factory*, typescript (promotional material).

9. In fact, it is used as a pulpit for the re-enactment of a short excerpt of a speech by Louis Farrakhan. Beyond the obvious irony, I do not think Wald was trying to make a specific point here in using the *bimah*. Wald says the *bimah* was simply there, in the space, and in retrospect he felt that, at times, "the space read too much into the piece" (Wald, telephone interview with author, 31 August 1999).

10. Wald, biographical resume, typescript.

11. Wald, "Story about Dad," typescript (promotional material).

12. For a discussion of patina, see Grant McCracken, *Culture and Consumption* (Bloomington: Indiana University Press, 1988), pp. 31–32.

13. Wald, *The Matzoh Factory*.

14. Richard Bernheimer, "Theatrum Mundi," *Art Bulletin* 38, no. 4 (December 1956): 228–229. Latin poet Simonides of Ceos (556–468 B.C.E.) is credited as the "inventor" of the art of memory because of his recollection of guests at a dinner based on their spatial arrangement at the banquet table. This story is told by Cicero in his *De oratore*. Aristotle also developed the connection between thought and mental images in his *De anima* and *De memoria et reminiscentia*, positing that it is impossible to think without a mental picture (Francis A. Yates, *The Art of Memory* [Chicago: University of Chicago Press, 1966], pp. 1–2, 32).

15. Yates, *The Art of Memory*, p. 138.

16. Ibid., p. 144.

17. Ibid., p. 144.

18. Ibid., pp. 144–145.

19. Bernheimer, "Theatrum Mundi," p. 231.

20. At present (August 1999) the building appears to be unoccupied.

21. *The Synagogue Space*.

22. Gaston Bachelard, *The Poetics of Space* (Boston: Beacon Press, 1994), p. 78.

23. Ibid., p. 81.

24. Ibid., p. 8.

25. At the end of the performance, Wald invites the audience to "feel free to hang out, stick around if you want to talk, want to share any thoughts."

Translating Abraham Cahan,

Teaching the Lower East Side:

Mario Maffi

Memory is hunger.

—Ernest
Hemingway

A View from Italy

I would like to begin this brief essay of mine—an outsider's view of the Lower East Side—with an act of remembrance, which I believe is appropriate to the theme and meaning of this volume.

I first came to know the Lower East Side of New York and its long, impressive history, in November 1975, during what was also "my first time in the United States." This "discovery" of mine was indeed the outcome of three different experiences combined together. While in New York, I went to see a revealing exhibition of Jacob Riis's photos at the International Center of Photography. Then, in a small bookstore in the heart of Pennsylvania, I discovered and immediately devoured Abraham Cahan's novels *Yekl* and *The Imported Bridegroom*. Finally, back in New York, I visited a friend who happened to live on East 9th Street off Avenue B, just in front of the huge Christodora Building, which was abandoned at the time, and of the equally huge public school, which was still in use. (Later I would learn that the former, today a notorious symbol of gentrification in the area, had been built on the site of a settlement house where a teenage George Gershwin had first played his compositions, while the latter was soon to house Charas-El Bohio, one of the most vital multiethnic institutions on the Lower East Side).[1]

What struck me—in that first encounter in which I *saw, read,* and *experienced* the Lower East Side—was the continuous, fascinating interaction of languages and cultures, the close contiguity of bodies and ways, the key role played by the street and other public places in molding and remolding everyday life and expressions, the unrelenting history of struggle and resistance, creation and organization that have always distinctively marked the neighborhood. And all this in a territory which surely was a separate one, but which at the same time entertained a strong and fruitful relationship with the city as a whole, and with the whole of American culture as I was then beginning to study and understand it.[2]

From the start, the neighborhood was to me a veritable crossroads—of things past and present, cultural and social, existential and political; a crossroads of received knowledge and actual discovery, of subtle suggestions and astonishing confirmations. This is perhaps the strongest image I still hold and treasure of the Lower East Side: that of a crossroads. To be sure, it is (and always functioned as) much more than simply an image. In the following twenty years or so, during which I kept coming back to it, both actually and metaphorically, the "Lower East Side as a crossroads" implied for me the growing awareness that the neighborhood also functioned as a vital paradigm through which I could study and understand, interpret and teach American culture and society.

Let me try to explain what this meant to an outsider such as myself, who came from a place so imbued with "Americana," so reactive to all things American, that even today it is really difficult to sever actualities from stereotypes and prejudices. It meant, for instance, that, against the deep-rooted notion of "America" as a clear-cut, well-defined, monolithic, and one-dimensional social and cultural *milieu,* whose roots invariably led back to seventeenth-century New England, now stood the perception of a much more complex (and still current) phenomenon of change, development, and hybridization, which went well beyond that circumscribed physical and cultural territory. It meant that, against the commonplace of an American culture devoid of a past and forever living in the present, now stood the experience of a thick, closely knit texture of history and of a red thread running through it: that of memory. It also meant that, against the widespread conception of urban wilderness, *anomie*, and desperation, now stood the discovery (within past and present harsh realities) of a thriving, communal street culture, made up of different contributions, ever contradictory, ever evolving, ever reinventing itself, which kept influencing what lay beyond the neighborhood borders. Finally, it meant that, against the ideological construction of the melting-pot myth with its abstractly ideological, one-way-process pattern, now stood the knowledge of Americanization as a clash, as a dynamic of dramatically contrasting fields of energy, as an exquisitely dialectical process which involved both America and the immigrant.

This is what the Lower East Side as a crossroads meant to me, as I came to know it in that November of twenty-five years ago, in Jacob Riis's photos, in Abraham Cahan's words, and in actual experience.

∞

Ce qui ressort de la propriété même de la traduction, est de créer la création, de capter à son avantage le temps bénévole.

—Radhouan Ben Amara

I completed my Italian translations of Cahan's *Yekl* and *The Imported Bridegroom* between 1984 and 1986, while I was working on a cultural history of the Lower East Side.[3]

To translate Abraham Cahan while I was working on my book provided me with a rare and peculiar experience. I could in fact enter the literary text, immerse myself in its fictional world, "créer la creation," and then, almost at the same time, emerge from it and put Cahan's narration (and my understanding/rendering of it) to the test by walking the very streets, by exploring the very buildings, and often by living in the very places, which he described. In a very peculiar way, I could "capter [. . .] le temps benévole" and, in doing this, become a "*récrivain*, ce qui est différent de l'auteur ou même de l'écrivain."[4]

Once more, this meant (and at the same time was made possible by) the vivid sense of a past which still impressively survived in the present, of a historical pattern which still held together the neighborhood's mental and physical places. Suffolk Street was there (remember? "Suffolk Street is in the very thick of the battle for breath. For it lies in the heart of that part of the East Side which has within the last two or three decades become the Ghetto of the American metropolis, and, indeed, the metropolis of the Ghettos of the world")[5] and so was Essex Street (remember? "the noisy scenes of Essex Street"),[6] and they were very much as they had appeared in Cahan's days, although in the

Fig. 13.1 The cover of Mario
Maffi's Italian translation of
Abraham Cahan's novella *Yekl*
(Milan: SugarCo, 1986).

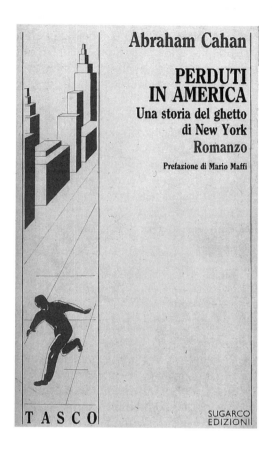

Abraham Cahan

**PERDUTI
IN AMERICA**
Una storia del ghetto
di New York
Romanzo

Prefazione di Mario Maffi

T A S C O

SUGARCO
EDIZIONI

meantime other patterns (both physical and cultural) had emerged,
and other languages had been added to the then-prevailing Yiddish
and to "all sorts of subdialects of the same jargon."[7]

In the sweatshops along Division Street and Catherine Street and
Ludlow Street, the cheap labor that now sweated came from Canton
and Hong Kong instead of Povodye and Pravly, but the rhythms and
the exploitation were very much the same as when Yekl Podkovnik or
Mr. Bernstein worked there. Meanwhile, Schapiro's *kosher wines* and
Streit's *matzos* on Rivington Street, Yona Schimmel's *knishes* and Katz's
pastrami on East Houston Street had been tasted by thousands of persons since Gitl and Mamie and Flora had lived, worked, and loved in
the area. One could even fancy that, through the windows on the sec-

ond floor of the building at 125 Rivington Street (where Eisl's Golden Rule Hall once stood with its famous dancing school), a voice could still be heard commanding, like Professor Peltner's, "Von, two, tree! Leeft you' feet! Don' so kvick—sloy, sloy! Von, two, tree, von, two, tree!"[8]

There were no more Roumanian restaurants and Yiddish theaters on the Bowery, but many of the buildings which had possibly hosted them were still standing—huge, sagging, blackish, with rusted fire escapes, as they probably had already been almost a century before. And if the roof of the place where you were staying did not necessarily provide you with a proper "housetop idyll" (to quote the title of chapter 8 of *Yekl*), the view from it surely gave you the feeling of a neighborhood which spread before your eyes as a city within a city.

Little by little, I realized that what I was drawing up was a sort of multi-layered map: a mental one, based upon Cahan's narration, and a material one, made up of my discoveries of the past and of the present. And this allowed me to project the present upon the past and vice versa, and thus to make the one still speak to and through the other, in a veritable Lower East Side fashion, so to speak: along the thread of time. In this way, it was not only *my* experience of the Lower East Side in the crucial 1980s and 1990s (years in which the neighborhood was undergoing some momentous transformations, as had always been the case with it) that took on new meanings. Cahan's words themselves grew even more revealing with regard to social and cultural dynamics, and to the ways in which individuals and groups related to each other and turned those relations into literature, into art, into creative expressions.

Of course, the very act of translating embraces other implications as well. By relating to different languages, cultures, and epochs, the process of translation helps lay bare the inner mechanisms of one society and culture as compared to another. For instance, Cahan's continuous shift from English to Yiddish (or, to be more precise, from a narration in English which contains dialogues in correct English when characters are supposed to speak Yiddish, and vivid, sonorous, colorful malapropisms when they try English) obliged me to think in terms of Bakhtinian dialogism and plurilinguism and "heteroglossy."[9] Also, it helped me retrace the subterranean flow of an immigrant fiction that was then, in the late nineteenth century, beginning to surface amidst difficulties of all kinds (the first literary text to come out of the Italian American experience, Luigi Donato Ventura's *Peppino*, 1884, was written in French!)[10] and was already leaving a peculiar seal upon American literature—as such refined *literati* as William Dean Howells and

Henry James were already perceiving, one with curiosity, the other with fastidiousness.[11]

But this implied not only the discovery of a different perspective. It also implied the very precise perception that, through Abraham Cahan's immigrant voice, accepted literary and cultural formulae were beginning to be recast and remolded. Take, for instance, Yekl's last chapter, titled "A Defeated Victor." In a way, what resounded there, but with a totally new (and implicitly transgressive) accent, was something which stood at the very heart of the Puritan experience—and thus, according to the univocal interpretation I recalled above, at the very heart of the American experience. Wasn't in fact Cahan proposing here a new model of Jeremiad, one which had to do with another kind of Atlantic Passage and with another kind of loss? It was—I began to understand—the Jeremiad of modern immigrants confronted, no more with a real or symbolic wilderness, but with metropolitan, technological America—that alienating sense of loss and defeat, which reformulated many delusions and received ideas about the "American dream."

Or take the famous discussions of American sport in Yekl's opening chapters, or the equally famous scenes in which immigrant couples literally toil through the new steps at Professor Peltner's dance academy. Wasn't Cahan reconsidering and redirecting here, ahead of his time, sociological conceptions of acculturation and Americanization which were already becoming ideologically rigid and passively accepted in the turn-of-the-century years? Wasn't he asking himself and his readers who is acculturizing whom and what kind of a social and cultural process Americanization really is?

Or take the chapter titled "Circumstances Alter Cases." The discovery that such a title came from a poem by black author Paul Laurence Dunbar bore witness to me of the kind of dialogue which, in the American 1890s, was already unfolding among different texts and authors and which invited me to read Cahan's work side by side with Mark Twain's *Pudd'nhead Wilson*, Kate Chopin's *The Awakening*, Charles W. Chesnutt's *The Wife of His Youth*, Stephen Crane's *Maggie: A Girl of the Streets*—all of them diverse but homologous and converging examples of a dark, ironic rethinking of *fin-de-siècle* America, all of them veritable pre-modernist texts.

Translating Cahan implied other experiences as well. It was, for instance, the necessary preparation to a better understanding of *the* great American novel on Americanization and the Lower East Side— Henry Roth's *Call It Sleep*. The theme of urban spaces, the initiation pattern, the role of language in enlarging the territory of experience, the tangible presence of a street culture, the generational issue, the city as novel and the novel as city, the Freudian and Joycean implications, the intricacies of the "city of words" of which wrote the late lamented Tony Tanner[12]—these were all elements that would evolve into the complexities of modern American fiction, that would make modernist literature both possible and inevitable in the early decades of the twentieth century, that would definitely open up the scope and range of Jewish American literature. The feeling was there (in the deep relationship which develops through translation) that what someone once said was true: Modernism was born on the lips of Polish American mothers. And that Cahan's work was the (still too little recognized) fount of what would come afterwards—and this not only, not purely, in terms of Jewish American literature.

But this was not all, obviously. The inevitable problems of translation (in James Clifford's words, "the vicissitudes of translation": how to transmit an experience, which is historical and cultural and material, from one context to another)[13] were enhanced by the fact that, in the Italian language, I could not always find terms which might approach those used by Cahan. The absence spoke of profound differences. For instance, how would I translate "greenhorn"? It was more than simply a matter of verbal choices, "greenhorn" meaning in fact a specific *condition*—that of the fresh immigrant not yet accustomed to the ways of the host country. Now, the very fact that the Italian language lacked the equivalent of such an expression betrayed an important historical gap. Italy had always been a country of emigrants, not of immigrants, and this reality was precisely recorded in the language. We did *not yet* have words designating a whole spectrum of relations to the host country, for the simple reason that, some fifteen years ago, we still did *not yet* have a large immigrant experience.

The Italian term I used ("acerbo," meaning "unripe") had to do with different semantic fields, and of course did not hold the same socio-cultural meaning as "greenhorn." Above all, mine was an "invented" term: a term which, while trying to convey part of the original meaning, was *not yet* familiar to the Italian reader. In this way, Gitl's self-addressed question in one of *Yekl's* key scenes ("What do they mean by it, anyhow?")[14] resounded with a deep-seated, ironic meaning for the Italian reader as well.

Thus, translating Cahan also provided me with the opportunity to think over a situation (that in which I, as a "cultural translator," was placed at the time), which was still on a kind of razor's edge. Italy was increasingly becoming a country of *in*-migration, and this new situation would surely bring with it the necessity of new words to describe the varied relationships of immigrants to a host country—such as, indeed, "greenhorn." From *his* past, and out of the Lower East Side of New York, Abraham Cahan was thus speaking to *my* present—another sign of his vitality and cultural importance.

∞

. . . to get at the whole through one or
more of its parts.

—James Clifford

Whenever I taught the Lower East Side at the university, or lectured on it on different occasions, I realized that the neighborhood contained a very peculiar and significant potential: it could function as a revealing observatory upon American culture and society, as a viable metaphor to help explain the processes of cultural creation.

As already mentioned, the real problem of teaching American culture in Italy lies in the fact that we are literally immersed in a sea of things American. Language, advertising, the media, the movie industry, music, mass culture, all contribute to weave a veritable mesh, in which it is often very difficult to move without being captured and ensnared, thus losing focus, perspective, and critical vision. American culture then risks becoming a shapeless, undifferentiated object, devoid of inner contradictions: a kind of purely reflecting image, a simple projection of myths and stereotypes.[15]

In order to rediscover its depth, in order to separate its various parts and components and to focus on them and their (often conflicting) relationships without losing sight of the rest (and, above all, in order to help students do this), a specific observatory thus becomes necessary, from which to view the territory at large—a kind of magnifier allowing one to see more in detail. Or, if you prefer, a synecdoche, which, by insisting upon a specific feature, could bring the whole to light.

The Lower East Side provided me exactly with that kind of observatory, magnifier, and synecdoche. Through it, I (and—I hope—my students) could better grasp what really is American culture in all its complexities and contradictions, how it developed and changed in those decisive turn-of-the-century years which remain to me crucial for an understanding of twentieth-century culture. The passage from an agricultural to an urban society, the closing of the frontier, the impact of technology, the emergence of monopolies and imperialism, the new rhythms and scenarios, the changing ways of working and living, the shift from Boston to New York, the new immigration, the spreading slums, the modern labor movement, the momentous changes in language, art and literature, the different manners of looking at and telling things and experiences—all these were themes of utmost importance for what would become the twentieth-century culture. And all of them were somewhat implicit in the Lower East Side experience: The microcosm irresistibly spoke of the macrocosm, the part of the whole.

For instance, to study and teach the Lower East Side really meant to deal with the socially and culturally important transformations of the Bowery, the crucial accomplishments of the Yiddish theatre, the vital innovations of the Italian "macchiette coloniali," and the evolution of such popular entertainment as vaudeville. It meant to analyze the linguistic and conceptual remolding implicit in the Jewish American and Italian American novels, the novelty brought about by the Ashcan School art scene, the realities of a multilingual and multicultural labor movement, and the break-up of gender roles within immigrant families. It meant to fully appreciate the importance of the street scene in the birth of the movies or the way in which the ruling culture tried to isolate, dismiss, and subjugate working-class experiences and memory.

And all this shed new light upon American culture, and, more at large, upon *contemporary* culture. In this way, the Lower East Side became—to me, to my students, to the audience of my lectures—something more than a purely American observatory and laboratory. It became a metaphor of modernity and contemporaneity, that very modernity which Marshall Berman summed up in his seminal work *All That Is Solid Melts into Air* and David Harvey further examined and put to a test in his likewise seminal *The Condition of Postmodernity*.[16]

In an Italian *academia* still very much characterized by idealistic and humanistic biases, where literature is still thought of as a separate realm, where American Studies departments are still so rare and American literature is still mainly referred to as "Anglo-American Literature," to teach the Lower East Side as a sociocultural laboratory, and to adopt it as a viable paradigm and metaphor for modernity, meant to convey a radically different perspective on literature, culture, and on the processes through which social groups create and grapple with them.

The idea of a laboratory implies, in fact, an idea of culture as the outcome of a complex dynamic, through which ways and mores bred by specific sociohistorical conditions come together along unfixed, nonhierarchical lines. They clash one against the other. They produce a kind of high voltage, which solidifies in cultural objects. And these, in turn, are not given objects, well-rounded and polished and complete products, but rather still contain the impurities, fluidity, and uncouthness of a work in progress. And such they remain, to be sure—a never-ending work in progress made up of parts and fragments, which interact and remold each other, as in an alchemic process.

It is my firm belief that this was always true of all the sociocultural products of the Lower East Side experience: from traditional folkways reinterpreted in the light of everyday life in America, to ethnic and class belonging and new dynamics of aggregation, struggle, and solidarity—from inherited cultural models to new, fluid forms—from descent to consent, to use Werner Sollors's categories.[17] And—as I keep studying the Lower East Side (this too—so it seems—is a kind of never-ending experience!)—I realize and am ever more convinced that this is the main legacy left by the neighborhood to modernity: something which we can detect everywhere in contemporary culture, after the "pollination," the "scattering of spores," which took place early this century, from within the Lower East Side to the whole American culture and beyond.

It is a reality, I would like to add, that still has to be fully appreciated. I am speaking here of the relationship of the Lower East Side to *modernism*—that is to say, the complex and dramatic tension and dialectics between traditional forms of discourse (such as storytelling and community theater, which imply a strong link between audience and author) and the immigrant urban condition of fragmentation and alienation and *anomie*. From this perspective, although of course the Jewish experience was largely dominant on the Lower East Side, in any discussion of modernism (or, even better, in any discussion of *twentieth-century culture*, to which I would *not* necessarily add the adjective "American"), one cannot stress enough the role played by such expressions as the Italian "macchiette coloniali" and puppet theater, the Harrigan & Hart Irish plays, the Chinese Opera theater (and the tremendous effects of the 1882 Chinese Exclusion Act); or, more generally, by the Bowery world with its mixture of Shakespeare and Buffalo Bill, Steve Brodie's monologues and Jacob Gordin's dramas. And one cannot stress too much the way in which all these experiences reacted upon each other, not only along ethnic lines, but also and often primarily along class and gender lines.

Since then, since those early decades of a century which has now drawn to a close amid clashes and rumbles as did the previous one, not only has the Lower East Side laboratory kept functioning, as everybody knows who is familiar with what is taking place below East 14th Street and east of Lafayette Street—something which is very much rooted in *that* tradition, whatever new forms it might be developing. But, also, new laboratories are springing up elsewhere, wherever groups of men

and women from different backgrounds are congregating together under the pressures of immigration, globalization, and worldwide reces-
sion—new crossroads of energy, creation, resistance, new neighborhoods in which "accents of the very ultimate future" (to use Henry
James's words, not devoid of fastidious anxiety)[18] can again be heard.
To study and to teach the Lower East Side today, to keep going
back to it and being involved in it, thus also implies a better understanding of what is happening around us. And this is—I believe—still
another important legacy which the neighborhood has left with us.

NOTES

1. An important, multifaceted analysis of the continual changes in the area is
Janet Abu-Lughod, ed., *From Urban Village to "East Village": The Struggle for the Lower
East Side* (London: Blackwell, 1994). An utterly negative example of the way in which
these changes continue to affect the neighborhood is the fact that Charas-El Bohio is
currently (1999) in danger of removal, the city having auctioned off the building. I
want to use the opportunity of this essay to express my full solidarity with Charas.

2. Most immigrant autobiographies from the early twentieth century stress this
contradictory feeling of living in a separate world and at the same time having the
whole city close at hand. See, for instance, Marcus Eli Ravage, *An American in the
Making: The Life Story of an Immigrant* (1917; New York: Dover Publications, 1971),
and Marie Ganz, *Rebels: Into Anarchy and Out* (New York: Dodd, Mead and Co.,
1919). The same feeling is conveyed by one of Jerome Myers's paintings, *Life in the
East Side*. In the foreground, the neighborhood looks like a self-contained shtetl, but
in the background Manhattan's huge towers hover over it.

3. See Abraham Cahan, *Perduti in America.Una storia del ghetto di New York*
(Milan: SugarCo, 1986); Abraham Cahan, *Lo sposo importato* (Milan: SugarCo, 1987);
Mario Maffi, *Nel mosaico della città. Differenze etniche e nuove culture in un quartiere di
New York* (Milan: Feltrinelli, 1992; English editions: *Gateway to the Promised Land:
Ethnic Cultures on New York's Lower East Side* [Amsterdam: Rodopi Editions, 1994;
New York: New York University Press, 1995]).

4. Radhouan Ben Amara, *Tradition, Traduction et Interprétation en Orient et en
Occident* (Cagliari: CUEC, 1996), p. 14.

5. Abraham Cahan, *Yekl and the Imported Bridegroom* (New York: Dover Publications, 1970), p. 13.

6. Ibid., p.24.

7. Ibid., p.14.

8. Ibid., p.15.

9. See Mikhail Bakhtin, "Discourse in the Novel," in M. Holquist, *The Dialogical
Imagination* (Austin: University of Texas Press, 1981).

10. On this, see my "The Strange Case of Luigi Donato Ventura's *Peppino*: Some
Speculations on the Beginnings of Italian-American Fiction," in Werner Sollors, ed.,
*Multilingual America: Transnationalism, Ethnicity, and the Languages of American Litera-
ture* (New York: New York University Press, 1998).

11. See my *Gateway to the Promised Land*, especially pp.187–188.

12. Tony Tanner, *City of Words: American Fiction, 1950–1970* (New York: Harper and Row, 1971).

13. James Clifford, *The Predicament of Culture: Twentieth-Century Ethnography, Literature, and Art* (1988; Cambridge, Mass.: Harvard University Press, 1994), p. 24.

14. Cahan, *Yekl*, p. 42.

15. One of the most common is indeed the "melting-pot myth," which receives from the media a kind of generalized and idealized ratification and becomes a sort of self-evident truth, empty of any kind of meaning: "America as the Great Melting-Pot Country."

16. Marshall Berman, *All That Is Solid Melts into Air* (New York: Simon and Schuster, 1982); David Harvey, *The Condition of Postmodernity* (Cambridge, Mass.: Blackwell, 1990).

17. Werner Sollors, *Beyond Ethnicity: Consent and Descent in American Culture* (New York: Oxford University Press, 1986).

18. Henry James, *The American Scene* (1907; London: Granville Publishing, 1987), p. 99.

Contributors

Stephan F. Brumberg

is Professor of Education at Brooklyn College, City University of New York, and the author of *Going to America, Going to School: The Jewish Immigrant Public School Encounter in Turn-of-the-Century New York City*. He has written extensively on the education of Jewish immigrants and on the education of Jewish girls in America.

Joseph Dorman

is an independent filmmaker living in New York City. In addition to *Arguing the World*, he has directed numerous other documentaries for public and commercial television. Mr. Dorman is also the author of *Arguing the World: The New York Intellectuals in Their Own Words*. He is currently producing a documentary on Sholem Aleichem and modern Yiddish culture.

Paula Hyman

is the Lucy Moses Professor of Modern Jewish History at Yale University, where she chairs the Program in Judaic Studies. She writes widely about modern European and American Jewish history. Her most recent books are *The Jews of Modern France; Jewish Women in America: An Historical Encyclopedia* (co-edited with Deborah Dash Moore); and *Gender and Assimilation in Modern Jewish History*.

Eve Jochnowitz

teaches Jewish culinary history at the New School University and is Foodways Researcher at New York's Center for Traditional Music and Dance. She is a graduate student in the Department of Performance Studies at New York University, where her current research is on culinary ethnography.

Seth Kamil,

the director and co-founder of Big Onion Walking Tours, Inc., is a doctoral candidate in American Urban and Ethnic History at Columbia University. His dissertation title is "The Management of Misery: Homelessness in New York City, 1857–1920." Kamil is the author of the forthcoming book *The Big Onion Guide to New York City*.

David Kaufman

is Assistant Professor of Contemporary American Jewish Studies at Hebrew Union College–Jewish Institute for Religion, Los Angeles. Author of *Shul with a Pool: The "Synagogue-Center" in American Jewish History*, he has also taught at Brown University, the University of Massachusetts, the City University of New York, and the Jewish Theological Seminary of America.

Jack Kugelmass

is Professor of Humanities and Director of the Jewish Studies Program at Arizona State University in Tempe. He is in his second term as editor of the journal *City and Society* and is the author of *The Miracle of Intervale Avenue: Aging with Dignity in the South Bronx*, the editor of *Going Home: How Jews Invent Their Old Countries*, and coeditor of *From a Ruined Garden: The Memorial Books of Polish Jewry*. The essay in this volume is drawn from his forthcoming book of essays on the public culture of American Jewry.

David Lobenstine

graduated in 1998 from Vassar College. In 1997 and 1998 he conducted photographic research for a forthcoming visual history of New York City. He is currently an editorial assistant for Harvard University Press.

Mario Maffi
is Associate Professor at the State University of Milan, Italy. He has published extensively on American culture and society, literature, and urban issues. He is the author of *Gateway to the Promised Land*, a study on the culture of the Lower East Side, and, most recently, *Sotto le torri di Manhattan*, a portrait of New York City.

Deborah Dash Moore
is Professor of Religion at Vassar College. An historian of American Jews, she specializes in twentieth-century urban Jewish history. Her books include *At Home in America: Second Generation New York Jews* and *To the Golden Cities: Pursuing the American Jewish Dream in Miami and L.A.* Her most recent publication is the award-winning *Jewish Women in America: An Historical Encyclopedia*, which she edited with Paula Hyman. Currently she is working with Howard Rock on a history of New York City in images. Her project on Jewish GIs during World War II involves extensive video interviews with veterans and will culminate in an exhibition at the Museum of Jewish Heritage, as well as a forthcoming book.

Riv-Ellen Prell,
an anthropologist, is Professor of American Studies at the University of Minnesota. She is the author of *Fighting to Become Americans: Jews, Gender and the Anxiety of Assimilation* and *Prayer and Community: The Havurah in American Judaism*. She writes about gender, community, and popular culture of twentieth-century American Jews and is currently studying Jewish youth culture in the post–World War II era.

Moses Rischin,
Professor of History at San Francisco State University, is completing a biography of Abraham Cahan. His publications include *The Promised City*, a landmark study of immigrant Jewish life in New York; *The American Gospel of Success: Individualism and Beyond; Immigration and the American Tradition; Grandma Never Lived in America: The New Journalism of Abraham Cahan; Like All the Nations? The Life and Legacy of Judah L. Magnes; Jews of the American West;* and *The Jewish Legacy and the German Conscience*.

Suzanne Wasserman

holds a Ph.D. in American history from New York University and teaches, lectures, and writes about New York City history. She is currently completing a documentary film about her cousin, Janet Rosenberg Jagan, who was the president of Guyana, South America, from 1997 to 1999.

Aviva Weintraub

is Director of Media and Public Programs at The Jewish Museum in New York. She writes and lectures on Yiddish and Jewish culture, film, and performance art.

Index

Page references in *italics* refer to illustrations.

BOOK AND JACKET DESIGNER: Sharon L. Sklar

COPY EDITOR: Joyce Rappaport

COMPOSITOR: Sharon L. Sklar with Tony Brewer

TYPEFACES: Goudy and Twang

BOOK PRINTER: Maple-Vail Book Manufacturing

JACKET PRINTER: John P. Pow Company